Bernard Moses, William Watrous Crane

Politics, an Introduction to the Study of Comparative Constitutional

Law

Bernard Moses, William Watrous Crane

Politics, an Introduction to the Study of Comparative Constitutional Law

ISBN/EAN: 9783337079376

Printed in Europe, USA, Canada, Australia, Japan

Cover: Foto ©Suzi / pixelio.de

More available books at **www.hansebooks.com**

An Introduction to the Study of Comparative

Constitutional Law

BY

WILLIAM W. CRANE

AND

BERNARD MOSES, Ph.D

PROFESSOR OF HISTORY AND POLITICAL ECONOMY IN THE
UNIVERSITY OF CALIFORNIA

G. P. PUTNAM'S SONS

NEW YORK: 27 AND 29 WEST 23D STREET
LONDON: 25 HENRIETTA STREET, COVENT GARDEN
1884

Press of
G. P. Putnam's Sons
New York

CONTENTS.

CHAPTER IX.

CHAPTER X.

CHAPTER XI.

CHAPTER XII.

CHAPTER XIII.

CHAPTER XIV.

CHAPTER XV.

CHAPTER XVI.

CHAPTER XVII.

CHAPTER XVIII.

CONTENTS.

CHAPTER XIX.

THE TENDENCY OF POWER IN SOME EUROPEAN FEDERA-

TIONS........ 253

CHAPTER XX.

POLITICAL PARTIES 265

CHAPTER XXI.

CONCLUSION.......... 287

POLITICS.

CHAPTER I.

INTRODUCTORY.

THE structure and development of the state, as an organism for the concentration and distribution of the political power of the nation, form the subject-matter of analytical politics, or of politics as a science ; while the determination of what the state should do falls within the sphere of practical politics, or of politics as an art. Analytical politics, or politics as a science, concerns itself with the construction of governments, with their instrumentalities for carrying out the will and using the force of communities or nations ; and with reference to a particular government at a particular period, it may point out in what person or department the preponderance of power lies, or how power is distributed. In short, it treats of the mechanism of government, illustrated by its development. It may be properly termed the science of government. Political motives and aims, on the other hand, represent merely the various states of mind and views of conduct actuating those, whether few or many, who aid in determining the will of the nation, and pertain properly to the art of government.*

To determine the structure of all political organisms,

* See Bluntschli, " Lehre vom modernen Stat," Stuttgart, 1876, III., pp. 1-3.

I

or of any given one, is one thing, but it is quite another thing to determine how this being or organism should express itself or act in any given case. The inquiry as to what should be the end or object of a government can find no place in the examination of what the government is. It is sometimes said that the state is an ethical being. It is, *per se*, morally neither good nor bad. Bad men may use it for bad purposes, or, on the contrary, virtuous men may make it a beneficent instrument. In either case, it is merely an instrument which, in consequence of its structure, lodges power in some particular part of the community. The Czar of Russia may use his autocratic power so as to promote the greatest good of the greatest number, and the people of the United States may so exercise their constitutional power as to produce general disaster and ruin. The one may be an immoral or irreligious use of the powers of the state, and the other the reverse, but neither cuts any figure in determining the structure of the two states. It must be borne in mind that the *quantum* of power in the two nations is the same; the fact of *how* it is used, or the character of the ends towards which this power is directed, do not properly come within the province of the science of politics.

It is not to be disputed, however, that the structure of a government may be, not only the result of particular social tendencies, but may be also promotive of certain of these tendencies, because government is not an abstraction, but is a specific agency of the sovereign part of the nation for doing certain acts, and maintaining certain relations between the members of that nation, and between the nation itself and other nations. In this view, it is not foreign to the scope of a science of politics to inquire what will be the probable political evolution of any given nation, and to reason deductively from known qualities of human nature to the probable outcome of any given political arrangements, as is sometimes done by the political economist with reference to economical affairs.

But we must be careful to draw the line between what the state *is*, or, under given circumstances, *must be*, and what the state *should be*, and *should do*. A very common fault in much of the current writing on politics, is the mixing up of the treatment of such subjects as the sphere and ends of the state, or personal rights, or national rights or law, or political ethics, or the limitations of the action of the state, with the consideration of the impulses which control men in the formation of political communities or with the consideration of the structure of the state, and the organs and instrumentalities through which the work of the state is accomplished. By clearly separating the two orders of topics, we are better able to comprehend each in its proper place. The direction of the will of the community or nation, and the use of the force of the community or the nation, will finally, among intelligent people, be guided by what experience teaches is the best code of private, as well as public, law. And the determination of what is the true sphere of the state, or what should be the maxims touching personal or national rights, or law, or ethics, would be the same without reference to the form of government, or even to its historical development. The consideration of these topics touches rather the daily movement of thought and action within the completed state, and while of the most vital interest to the members of a political community, yet furnishes merely rules of conduct, and should be eliminated from inquiries into the laws of the state's being. Even the theories as to the duties of the state which are so radically opposed to each other as those of the so-called Manchester, or free-trade, school of politicians, and the Socialists, may be applied, according to their advocates, under any form of government, from the most absolute monarchy, to the most democratic republic. The former would restrict the state to the narrowest limits, making a sort of policeman of it, whose only duty is to prevent men depredating upon one another. The extremists of this school would introduce absolute free-trade, and non-interference of the government in any business or pursuit. In their view, the state should not concern itself about the schools, or poor-laws, or religion, or morals; they assert that it fulfills its duty when it leaves every one entirely free to follow out his own ideas of happiness in his own way, provided, however, he does not, in so doing, encroach on the rights of his neighbor. The greatest degree of personal freedom is the cardinal point with this school. On the opposite side stand the Socialists, who claim that government should control all the instruments of labor, the soil, the mines, the machinery within the state, which should be used for the benefit of the workingmen; that wages should be abolished, and the state should see that the workingman is duly paid for his hours of labor, without reference to skill. Intermediate between these two extremes, are many who believe that the state should control the liberty of the citizen, at various points, for the good of the whole. Some would have all the land owned by the state, and leased for the common benefit; others think that the ways of communication, the railroads and telegraph lines, should be so controlled. Some are in favor of compulsory education; some believe in the prohibition of the sale of intoxicating liquors, and so on, through numerous applications of state power to the community. But all parties start from the same point; they all tacitly or argumentatively assume that in the sovereign political community there are no actual limitations of power, except those self imposed by the community. And further, their several views may be carried out without any essential alteration in the form of any government. So far as it concerns the political structure of the British government, the Socialistic scheme could be carried out without change. And the same scheme could be effected without change in Russia. So again, what are denominated personal political rights, as, for instance, those enumerated in our Federal Constitution, may exist and be protected under any form of government. An absolute king may consider it wise policy to concede them, and still be an absolute king, so long as he has power to abolish them. That they are fixed by a written constitution, as in the United States, simply indicates that the power to abolish them is deposited at another point in this organism than in the absolute state.

In states having popular governments, all these questions are more particularly addressed to political parties ; they pertain to the art of government. They should be taken account of by the person or body of persons who express the will of the nation and wield the force of the nation, but they occupy a field apart from scientific politics ; they hold with respect to this subject the position of an art in relation to its corresponding science.*

* For a brief statement of the views of various authors on the nature and ends of the state, see Kautz, " Theorie und Geschichte der National-Oekonomik," p. 261, note 11.

CHAPTER II.

THE nation is an organic social being, a growth, and not an artificial creation.

The human race is, and always has been, divided into social groups. These groups are of different sizes, varying between small bands of depredating savages and a great empire. Whenever we can outline a distinctive group, however insignificant it may appear, we shall find that it exhibits an internal tie of political coherence which, in a greater or less degree, individualizes that community. It is possible to contemplate these social groups apart from their governments, or the political forces at work in or between them. A prime essential of clear political discussion is to have at the outset a proper conception of the nature of the social group in question; if in national politics, then of the nation.

It may be thought that the term *state* suffices to convey an idea of what a nation is; but this term rather narrows the definition to the purely governmental part of the nation; there is something beyond. Again, the term state is now frequently applied to one of a federation, as in the United States and in the German Empire, and to dependent and unimportant political bodies, as the Slavonic states, Bulgaria, Servia, Herzegovina, and others.

In the use of the words nation, nationality, and people, there is still considerable confusion in political writings, especially in the ordinary periodical literature. German

writers on politics use the word nation in a sense opposite
to that usually given to it by Americans, Englishmen, and
Frenchmen. They mean by the word nation what we ordinarily understand by the word people. For instance, when
they speak of the German nation, they comprehend all
Germans living in German communities. As Bluntschli
expresses it, "the nation is an intellectual being (*Cultur-
wesen*), because its inner composition, as well as its separation from foreign nations, have principally arisen out
of intellectual development, and especially manifest their
effect in its intellectual conditions." * All Germans, in
Prussia, Bavaria, Austria, and elsewhere, compose, in this
view, the German nation. The word people (*Volk*), on
the other hand, imports a politically united body of persons, who need not necessarily be of the same race or
stock. In this sense, those subject to the German Empire are the German people, while those of the same stock
in Austria are part of the Austrian people, though belonging to the German nation. The Alsatian is considered
one of the German people, because the country now belongs to the German Empire, while he may, at the same
time, be styled one of the French nation, because he was
born a Frenchman, speaks French, and is socially and in
culture and sympathies assimilated to the French. German writers justify this use of the term nation upon ety-
mological grounds, because the word *natio* signifies a race,
a species. The more general use among French publicists, and those of England and this country, is of the
term nation as signifying a large political body. The
prominent mark is political sovereignty, though there may
also be the minor marks of community of race, language,
and possibly religion.

The term people, on the other hand, with the latter,

* "Lehre vom modernen Stat," Stuttgart, 1875, I., p. 95.

implies a common race origin. It is rather of social than political import. A nation may be an artificial creation, but a people is always a natural growth. We can properly, in this view, speak of the British nation, but not of the English or Scotch or Irish or Welsh nations, though, of course, it is correct to speak of the English or the Scotch or the Irish or Welsh peoples.

It is not out of place to call attention to these contradictory significations given to the same words, because the confusion of ideas alluded to is quite apt to mix together purely political with purely social conceptions.

Following the English signification, we may, in the most general way, define the nation to be a political being, consisting of the totality of persons who are subject to the same political sovereignty. But it is very much more. This bald definition only suffices to circumscribe our ideas to the body which we are to contemplate ; it merely points out the object distinctly. In truth, it is impossible to compress into a definition what a nation is. It is indispensable that there shall be a political tie. There must be sufficient political coherence to present to other nations the general characteristics of a distinctive state. Still, political bands alone do not suffice to stamp the real nation. It is a mere artificial jumble of individuals unless it has that inner cohesion, unity, and soul, which give it the character of an organic being.

The ripe, developed nation is an organic being. If it had so happened that the fifty millions of inhabitants within the boundaries of the United States had poured into this country from the different parts of the world during the past five years, and had already established an organized government which was being peacefully administered, and one were called upon to characterize this motley body, he could only say, that here were the beginnings of a nation, that it would take many generations to perfect that organic oneness which is the mark of the ripe nation. Out of these miscellaneous elements there might grow in time a complex fusion of dependent activities, of mutual sympathies, of common ideals, and finally of intense national consciousness.

We all know the mysterious tie which binds one to his native land, and to his nation—a tie which grows stronger as the years increase, and often becomes most intense in the decline of life. We cannot penetrate to the hidden springs of this universal feeling; we can only point to it as a great fact in human experience. It emphasizes, however, certain limitations and needs in the individual. We may imagine men, as at some almost incomprehensibly remote time, wandering alone in the depths of forests, and hiding in caves, each looking upon every other man "as an enemy to be slain, or spoiled, or hated," but it is only as an animal, as an "ape-like man," that we can thus think of him. As a human being, such as human beings have been since the beginning of historical times, we cannot conceive of him other than as having been in social and political relations with at least some of his fellows. By political relations we understand a condition where there is one, or more than one, who governs, and where there are others who are governed.

A cardinal fact in human history is, that all political evolution has been through groups of persons. The political unit is not one man but a group of men. It has always been thus, whether the unit was a family, the enlarged family or tribe, or lastly the nation. The nation is but an expansion of the original unit, or what is almost universally the case, the fusion of many units into one.

Go back as far as we please in the annals of the human race; and we shall always find a distinctive group or

1*

groups. There may have been, and very likely was, an era when there was promiscuous intercourse, but there arrives a period when out of the chaos the family emerges. The starting-point of all the progressive races has been the family. The first known tie binding men into groups was the blood tie. The characteristic of these primal social groups was their oneness. They contained within themselves every element of modern political government, the legislative or will power, the executive or administrative power, and the judicial power. These were mingled and confused, residing sometimes altogether in one person, and at others in parts, or in the whole of the community ; and growth, politically, has been the differentiating of these functions into departments of government. These original groups were organic social beings. The individuals composing them were subordinate parts of the organism. The ancient Greeks considered themselves as made up of distinct races, and we find in the great Amphictyonic assembly, which was held in the spring at Delphi and in the autumn at Thermopylæ, that there were twelve constituent members, or twelve races, represented. When Kleisthenes, 510 B.C., accomplished the great democratical revolution in Athens, he did not dare to break down and abolish, nor did he probably have any thought of breaking down and abolishing, the tribal organization. He wished to confer the suffrage upon that large body of persons who had gradually settled in Attica, but who were excluded from the primitive tribes, and in order to accomplish this purpose in conformity with the then existing conceptions of political unity, he abolished the four Ionic tribes and redistributed the population into ten new tribes.

In Greece, the city was the limit to which the unifying sentiment spread. The city was the Greek nation. It

was the central political power, to which territorial possessions might be attached, or from which colonies might
go forth. The initial point of the immense political power
of Rome was also in the clan. As in Greece, it expanded
into the city, which became the source of political power,
and also furnished the limit of nationality. The fiction of
the blood tie pervaded the tribal organizations of Greece
and Rome long after the memory of the facts upon which
it was founded had died out ; just as the English fiction,
that all titles to land find their source in the king, has
survived the feudal system. What may be called the unifying sentiment extended from the family into the tribe,
and, in Greece and Rome, into the city. In Greece,
however, time was not given, before its absorption by its
Italian conquerors, to develope a wider sentiment. This
grew up gradually in Rome, and had really assumed the
dimensions of nationality when, in the latter days of the
republic, the city was extended by fiction of law so as to
take in the whole of Italy.

The Roman state was circumscribed by the boundaries
of the city ; but it was an immense advance in the national
idea when it was so enormously enlarged by this fiction.
The family and communal social units that pervaded
India and Asia, in very early times, never developed genuine nationalities. There were, it is true, great aggregations of these units into empires, which, as has been justly
remarked, were no more than tax-collecting governments.
They lacked the necessary unity of nature, and consequently crumbled to pieces ; or rather, when the slight
political force which held them together was disturbed,
they passed into new forms or under new governors, without any change in their inner constitution. It was merely
a rearrangement of the same political units which were
inherently separate. The tribal or clan organizations of

middle and western Europe were gradually transformed into communities, whose political bands arose from the habitation of specific territories, instead of from the old blood tie, and the fictions which grew out of it. Hence it is that an essential mark of the nation is that it shall have exclusive occupation of a distinctive portion of the earth's surface.

Looking back over the troubled surface of history, we discover a leading fact, that human beings, always living in groups, have been pitted against each other in the incessant war which has been progressing since the infancy of the race, and that the natural selection, by which those best adapted to their environment have survived, has been of social groups rather than of individuals. And, other things being equal, that group will win the fight, and grow at the expense of others, which is most completely homogeneous and is the largest. The reasons for this are to be found in human nature itself. The individual human being has desires, physical and intellectual, which are capable of indefinite expansion ; but his ability to gratify them is so feeble that, if left alone, he could accomplish next to nothing.

Man has an insatiable desire to possess and use the forces of nature and to control his fellows, but alone he can barely maintain a precarious life. Hence, there is an incessant balancing between desires and the means of gratifying them. An uncontrollable instinct compels men to supplement themselves with the forces of others in social life, and the more civilized a community is, necessarily the more dependent are its members on one another. In truth, the individual civilized man, instead of being the most self-sufficing of animals, is the most one-sided and incomplete. One may say that the more self-sufficing he becomes, the nearer he approaches the ani-

mal condition. Pioneer life, therefore, is uncivilizing.
Men become self-dependent, but they take on a good
deal of the savage. Where this instinct, if such it may be
called, or disposition to fusion in a social group, is most
decided, there are the elements of the greatest progress.
It was this irresistible bias which undoubtedly pushed the
Greeks so rapidly along in their political development.
Of course, there were other inherent qualities, coupled
with advantages of geographical position, which must be
counted, but the social impulse was one of the most
potent civilizing factors. The wonderful political organization and stability of the Romans. is largely due to the
sinking of the individual in the tribe, and eventually in
the state.

Lieber * deprecates the view of the ancients, that man
appears in his highest and noblest character when considered as a member of the state or as a political being.
He esteems it to be on a much lower plane than the
modern sentiment which looks to individual rights, and
seeks the highest aim of civil liberty in the most efficient
perfection of individual action, endeavor, and rights. It
may be conceded that the modern conception is the
nobler; but judging ideas by what they accomplish in
lifting up the race, we must surely admit that the expansion and firm holding of the blood tie and tribal idea,
and its development into the state idea, together with the
sinking of the individual into the community, lent an
immense consolidating and invigorating force in developing ancient civilization. It produced what was then
necessary, and without which modern civilization would

* " Civil Liberty and Self-Government," chap. iv. See on this
point the introductory chapters to Stein, " Der Begriff der Gesell-
schaft und die sociale Geschichte der französischen Revolution."
Leipzig, 1855, especially at pp. 13 and 17.

not be what it is, a powerful, organized state, able to hold its own, and finally win, in the universal war of mankind.

Medieval ideas liberated the individual man from the clan, transferred him to a class, and, among the lower orders, attached him to the land. He became either a noble of greater or less degree, a burgher, if a resident within a city, or a peasant and villain, if living without the city gates. Social life was distributed in a series of circles. The corporate sentiment found expression in the several distinct classes ; and in the cities, in the guilds ; every man was fitted into some distinct class. The broad national sentiment which had grown in the latter days of the Roman republic and in the earlier days of the empire had been contracted into these narrow bounds. It was almost in abeyance. The great political transition which was going on was twofold—towards attaching political sovereignty to a particular territory and towards individuality, or, contrasted with the old idea, the separation of the individual from the great family in which, theoretically, he was supposed to be sunk.

The danger which threatened Europe for ten centuries was that classes would harden into castes, and thus prevent that fusion of all conditions of men which is necessary to progress. Fortunately, various causes operated to break down the noble classes, and to elevate the villains. Hallam ascribes the decay of the feudal system to the increasing power of the crown, the abolition of villanage, the increase of commerce, and especially the institution of free cities and boroughs, and, thirdly, to the decay of the feudal principle.

He says, however : " If we look at the feudal polity as a scheme of civil freedom, it bears a noble countenance. To the feudal law it is owing that the very names of right

and privilege were not swept away, as in Asia, by the
desolating hand of power." And further : " So far as
the sphere of feudality extended, it diffused the spirit of
liberty, and the notions of private right." The increasing
power of the crown carried with it the widening of the
spirit of nationality, from the petty bounds of the duke-
dom or margravate to the kingdom and empire, and the
elevation of the villain, and of the middle or burgher class,
sapped the strength of the nobility. The monarch and
the common people have been the upper and the nether
millstones between which the aristocracy has been
crushed.

The great political fact of the modern era is the formation of nations. Men are being liberated from classes
and fused into the nation. This readjustment is proceeding with varying degrees of activity and vigor in different
parts of the progressive world. At what time this new
political era can be said to have begun is often debated.

The question is apt to be answered by each individual
according to the point of view from which he surveys the
past. If from the standpoint of Protestantism, it will be
placed at the Reformation ; if the bias is towards philosophy or esthetics, it will be pushed back to the revival of
Greek learning and the new impulse in art, in the fifteenth
and sixteenth centuries ; while the political inquirer, if an
Englishman, will say at the deposition of James II. in
1688 ; if a Continental liberal, at the revolution of 1789.
Bluntschli dates it from 1740, because after that period
the Prussian kingdom arose, the liberal changes of Francis Joseph in Austria were attempted, the American union
was formed, the French revolution occurred, the Napole-
onic empire was established, constitutional monarchy was
transplanted from England to the Continent, representative democracy was introduced, national states were estab-

lished, Church and State were separated in administration, feudalism and class privileges were set aside, and the conception of national unity was developed.

We cannot, however, separate eras by absolute dates. The ideas and ideals which rule in one run over into the other, and their influence extends down with gradually fading power for generations, and with varying intensity in different classes of society, or on different temperaments in the several classes. There are large bodies of people even yet, and certainly many individuals, who are substantially of the medieval type in views and tendencies. We can only say that the set is in a different direction now from what it was two hundred years ago ; or perhaps, it is better to say, the point of view of the thinkers of this age, as to the relations of men to each other and to the world, as to man's place in nature and among his fellows, is essentially different from what it was at that time. The whole intellectual horizon has been vastly expanded and illumined with a clearer light than formerly.

The growth of the national sentiment has been very marked since the middle of the last century. It is not the result of one cause, but of all the causes which have been stimulating civilization ever since the decay of the feudal system. These influences have tended to increase the desires of men, and to enlarge, necessarily, the number of demands to satisfy them. It is a matter, it is true, which must rest almost wholly in assertion, because it is extremely difficult to prove, but it can hardly be doubted that the average man of to-day, in any of the progressive communities, has a larger susceptibility to pleasure and pain than his ancestor of, say, two centuries since. If this is so, then the man of to-day has greater self-consciousness, because it is in proportion to our points of contact with mind and matter exterior to ourselves that this mysterious attribute of our nature gains strength.

It is certainly true that the lower races have a less sensitive physical organization than the superior, and along with this they have less resisting power to disease. As a race develops, not only its physical, but also its mental structure, takes on a finer temper. A growing sensitiveness to pain is accompanied by an increasing indisposition to seeing it inflicted upon others. Most men become merciful, one may say, through their nervous organizations and their imaginations, so that the character and number of punishments inflicted by law furnish a very fair test of the susceptibility of a people in this respect. A hundred years ago it was no uncommon thing for a dozen men and women to be condemned to death at one sitting of a court, for ordinary robberies and felonies, and "hanging day" was a gala day for the multitude. Going back a hundred years earlier we find the thumb-screw and boot in common use. The "question," as it was called, was then applied in a variety of ways. There was the "preparatory question," which had come down from the Roman law of the time of the emperors. This was the torture applied to persons accused of crime ; it was not viewed as a punishment, but only as an energetic mode of procedure to obtain information, and was in general usage all over Europe from about the beginning of the fourteenth century, except in England, though in that country it was occasionally resorted to. Gradually it died out, and, when it had almost entirely ceased in practice, was formally abolished in France by Louis XVI. in 1780. The "definitive question" was torture applied to the condemned criminal in order to compel him to disclose his accomplices, and was continued later, until abolished by the National Assembly. It was justified by a leading French

jurist on the ground that "the accused has no motive to
conceal the truth, and besides there is not much care to
be taken of a body confiscated, and which is going to be
executed." Then, and later, the infliction of death was
not sufficient; it was necessary to accompany it with
quartering and other barbarities, in order to impress the
imaginations of a populace which required more than the
mere contemplation of the extinction of existence.

If the general physical tone of to-day is on a higher
pitch, so also is the mental. This pitch makes us more
susceptible to the harmonies, and alas ! also, to the dis-
cords of life. But, on the other hand, it gives to the
general life more fullness, more variety. As suggested, it
has increased self-consciousness, and, necessarily as the
outgrowth of this, a more intense longing for the satisfaction of desire. During this era the desires of men have
increased prodigiously, and what is often called the "un-
rest" of the age is merely the effort of the multitude to
balance these desires with the means for enjoyment. In
a progressive society this effort is constantly, in a greater
or less degree, producing fermentation. In such a society
a hundred years may decidedly change the *quality* of a
people, so that, though apparently the same, they are
really different.

Quality, in a people, comes from all the influences
which go to make up their civilization at any given period
of time, acting upon certain inherent race or stock traits.
The "strain" in the Indo-Germanic race is finer than it
was two centuries ago ; just as it is better to-day in the
winner of the Derby than it was in the Godolphin
Arabian. If this be true, then it is impossible to draw
exact parallels between the men of to-day and those of
this earlier period.

We may truly say that certain things in human nature

have always been the same. True, the instrument has the same number of strings, but, like an old Stradivarius violin, it is the same, but yet not the same, that it was when new ; the tones are richer, fuller, indescribably sweeter and more sympathetic.

It is this varying quality in the race which introduces an intangible quantity into the social problem, and warns us not to attempt its solution exclusively through a survey of the past. And further, it leads one to condemn that very common habit of multiplying instances, of customs, observances, of methods of government among existing savage tribes as indicating the past evolution of the progressive race ; a method which certainly is liable to mislead in investigating the present structure of society, because the probabilities are strong that the impulses of continuous change, which at some periods affect even the rudest tribes, may have carried them very far away from the common starting-point. Because we find that at the present time the Papuans or Zulus have certain customs, we are not justified in jumping to the conclusion that our remote ancestors had similar ones. Whenever there are distinct traces of similar institutions pervading the infancy of society, and surviving in communities which we know to have a history, and which are now, evidently, in a condition of arrested development, we are on safe ground, and may then profitably enter into a comparative study of customs and laws.

An instance in point is found in the universal existence at certain stages of social development of community property in land. This fact is so well attested that we can affirm without hesitation that it is a necessary incident in the advance to a higher civilization.

So, also, when we find that at all times the individuals of the human race have been fused into distinct groups of greater or less magnitude, we can, without hesitation, treat it as a fundamental fact, indicating a universal law or condition of social existence.

At this point, however, the variations commence, not only in manifestations of this great fact, but more especially in the direction and character of the changes within each group. Prince Schwarzenberg, the shrewd minister of the present Austrian emperor in the first years of his reign, was accustomed to say : "I can learn nothing from history." There was a grain of truth in this extravagant assertion. While we can, undoubtedly, learn much, we cannot learn everything from it. We can see from its records that the passions of men have always been substantially the same, but the infinite possibilities of development, and the tendency which a new modification may produce, are beyond its teachings. The first Napoleon remarked that "the passions form the great elements of calculation, at the same time they defy all human sagacity." These passions may be so tempered with physical, intellectual, and moral change, as to produce, as we see, in one direction, an Anglo-Saxon of the nineteenth century, and in another, his contemporary and antagonist, a degraded Ashantee ; or, what is more in poir.t, may at one time produce a certain average quality of man, and a couple of centuries later quite a different quality.

Hence it is that each age has what is called its "spirit ; " and the true vocation of history is to imbue us with the spirit, the temper, the quality of the age which it pictures. We can, unquestionably, gather this general assurance, that there is an "increasing purpose " running through all the ages, which, selecting certain people for progress, urges them on irresistibly to a higher development. These peoples move along in general harmony, so that we see among them a certain uniformity and likeness in social movements. The expansion of desire as the result of increased sensitiveness leads, necessarily, to enhanced mental activity, and by natural sequence to a greater longing for freedom of action ; for the expression of mental activity can be had only through mobility and variety in thought and deed. The increase of thought, the increase of desire, the increase of susceptibility, produce a great pressure upon the means and instrumentalities of satisfaction ; and as the individual becomes more self-conscious, he at the same time feels more acutely his inability to satisfy, by his own efforts, these growing demands, and thus he is unconsciously more and more impelled to supplement his own feeble powers with those of the members of the society in which he lives.

Hence, the tendency of civilization is to increase individual wants out of proportion to the capacity of the individual to satisfy them, unless aided by his fellows ; and the result of this growing inability is the division of labor and the specialization of pursuits, because a very little experience teaches a man that he can accomplish more in any field of activity, whether of thought or deed, by devoting himself to one special demand of very many, rather than to all the demands of one, even if that one be himself. Following this out, it needs but a moment's reflection to perceive that in the ratio of the specialization of pursuits do men become more interdependent. Separate a man from society and he would wither and die, because there would be subtracted from him the greater part of what he really is.

While these considerations, however, apply to social growth in general—to the whole of society—still they apply to the nation also, which is a part of the whole. Increase the desires of men in any way, either by stimu-

lating their intellectual powers, or by increasing their
wealth, or by improving their tastes, and they will be irresistibly impelled to set about enlarging the area from
which they can draw satisfaction for them. Or, to be
more precise, they will call into play new activities in
other men, and will be dependent upon a larger number
of them than before, in order to obtain the satisfaction
desired. We can readily understand how this would be
the result in the growth of physical desires, but it is
equally true as a concomitant of the increase of intellectual and emotional desires. These influences act
directly on social groups, and lead to their enlargement or
fusion.

War has been, heretofore, a potent agent in enlarging
or fusing social groups. A mountainous country will
afford retreats to small tribes and protect them in their
independence. This was the case for a long time in
Greece and Switzerland. But improve road-making, introduce railroads, and it is like leveling the mountains ;
not only armies, but new ideas and sympathies, can be
poured in. The enemy can come from a greater distance
in larger numbers, and there becomes an immediate need
of the union of detached communities into one, or an
alliance with a stronger power. Where the country is
open, and by means of railroads and steamships troops
can be rapidly concentrated by an enemy and marched
into the centre of the land, there will be need of a stronger
union of all the parts of the exposed country, and of an
increase in the standing army. We have a striking illustration of this impulse to union, in consequence of increased dangers arising from improved means of attack,
in the case of the new German Empire, though, perhaps,
it is putting it upon rather narrow ground to exclude intellectual and general economical causes.

Every nationality comes to have its own type. The American, the Englishman, the Frenchman, the German, the Italian, the Russian, has each his own national mark upon his face, and in his style and gait. Diversities of climate and soil will not explain it. Between the Atlantic Ocean and the Ural Mountains, on the same parallel, the varieties of these are not sufficiently numerous to produce the different types which the most careless traveler detects. And though, as between different sections of the same country, there may be marked diversities of soil and climate, yet there will still be exhibited the general national type, with minor variations. The distance between the northern and southern limits of the United States is as great as between Edinburgh and Gibraltar, or between Stockholm and Naples, and the line between Portland, Maine, and San Francisco is as long as from Paris to a point one hundred and fifty miles east of Moscow; and yet on the European side the area mentioned will present a dozen different well-marked national types, while in the United States there is really but one national type; yet, strange to say, cross the line into Canada, and you find a variation. Mere physical environment, or even what are accounted race differences, will not explain national expression. There is a subtle something which indicates the oneness of the national being.

It may be answered, as to the United States, that the settlement of the country west of the Alleghanies is too recent to admit of variation; but how is it that the first generation born on the soil, of European parents, exhibits marked American characteristics? And this is more prominently the case with the children born in the densely populated parts of the country than with those born in the remoter, sparsely settled sections. The truth is, the national soul or spirit or character, or whatever we may call it, instantly sets its stamp upon the new-comer, and incorporates him into the great national being.*

Herbert Spencer lays it down as a cardinal law, that social evolution is from the homogeneous to the hetero-geneous, but it would seem that there is a double process

* Walter Bagehot, in " Physics and Politics," especially in the chapter on " Nation-making," has called attention to this question. "Climate," he says, "is clearly not *the* force which makes nations, for it does not always make them, and they are often made with-out it. The problem of nation-making—that is, the explanation of the origin of nations such as we now see them, and such as in his-torical times they have always been—cannot, as it seems to me, be solved without separating it into two : one, the making of broadly marked races, such as the negro, or the red man, or the European ; and the second, that of making the minor distinctions, such as the distinction between Spartan and Athenian, or between Scotchmen and Englishmen. Nations, as we see them, are (if my arguments prove true) the produce of two great forces : one, the race-making force, which, whatever it was, acted in antiquity, and has now wholly, or almost, given over acting ; and the other, the nation-making force, properly so called, which is acting now as much as it ever acted, and creating as much as it ever created." And in dealing with the second problem he lays stress on " what," as he says, " every new observation of society brings more and more freshly to myself—that this unconscious imitation and encourage-ment of appreciated character, and this equally unconscious shrink-ing from and persecution of disliked character, is the main force which moulds and fashions men in society as we now see it." He would, moreover, " show that the more acknowledged causes, such as change of climate, alteration of political institutions, progress of science, act principally through this cause ; that they change the object of imitation and the object of avoidance, and so work their effect." In thus giving great weight to " the imitation of appreci-ated habit and the persecution of detested habit," he does not fail to recognize also the power of heredity, by which " the mind of the parent (as we speak) passes somehow to the body of the child," pp. 86–106.

going on ; that the tendency is to heterogeneity in social groups, but to homogeneity within each of them. It is true that up to a certain point a number of like groups will tend to flow together and separate sharply from the conglomerate group, but along with it there is developed a centripetal force, acting within the separate group, tending to fusion of all its elements. When the social group has been politically segregated, a cohering force immediately begins to work upon the old, repellent groups of which it is composed. The inherent repulsion of the minor groups to each other is the centrifugal force. Thus two opposing forces contest for supremacy in the new nation ; whether the one or the other will eventually gain the mastery depends, of course, upon such a variety of circumstances as to render the outcome, often for a long period, a matter of doubt. If, happily, the nation becomes a homogeneous unit, we see it stamped with its own intellectual and moral traits, and even with its own physical characteristics, as already suggested.

It may be asked, of what value is it to arrive at even the most exact conception of what a nation is ? and it may be added, that for living active men, it is more necessary to know what to do than to know what we are. But this is essentially a short view of things. We are only really prepared to know what to do when we have exact knowledge of what we are. Especially is this so in all governmental matters. If men understand their true relations to each other and to the whole body politic, they are better prepared to legislate on correct principles ; they then discover not only the scope of their duties, but also the limitations beyond which they cannot successfully act. The time has arrived when we should consider national rights as carefully as we have studied and protected individual rights. The effort for centuries has been, more especially in England and on this continent, to place individual political rights upon firm ground, where they can be clearly seen and defined. The "liberty of the subject" has been the chief object of solicitude. At first it was to protect him from the king ; now it is to save him from the tyrannical majority. We have established these rights firmly in Bills of Right, and written constitutions. We have, in truth, gone so far in this direction, that the corresponding obligations arising out of these "rights" are somewhat lost sight of. Indeed, the doctrines of personal freedom have been pushed to their remotest consequences. We see it in the accepted dogmas of the political economy of the English school, which preaches free competition as the true end of all economic legislation, and in the *laissez-faire* doctrine in politics. There is this to be said, however, that no government has ever acted up to the extreme limits of these doctrines, nor probably ever will. At bottom, there is in every nation a sub-consciousness that the general good must override, in many cases, what are deemed indefeasible personal rights. Politically, then, the nation is the prime fact in our consideration ; the individuals and communities forming it are secondary facts.*

* Prominent among American books in which this view of the nation is emphasized is Mulford's *The Nation*, New York, 1875. " The nation is an organism. It has an organic unity ; it is determined in an organic law, and constitutes an organic whole." It " is shaped by no external force, but by an inner law." It " has the characteristics of every organism—unity and growth and identity of structure " (p. 99). Savigny, looking at the nation as the source of positive law, considers that if in our contemplation of legal relations we abstract all that is peculiar in them, there still remains this broad fact of the living together of many persons whose relations are regulated in a fixed manner. We might, in

general, adhere to this abstract conception of a majority, and think of law as an invention of this majority, without which the external freedom of no single person could exist. But such an accidental assemblage of an indeterminate crowd is an arbitrary idea entirely lacking in truth. And if such a crowd should actually find itself assembled it would inevitably be wanting the capacity to create laws, since the power to satisfy the need of laws is not given at the same time with the need itself. In fact, however, we find everywhere where men live together, so far as history informs us, their relation to one another is that of a community of intellectual interests, which not only makes itself manifest, but also strengthens and perfects itself, through the use of a common language. Within this natural unity is the seat of creative law ; for in the common national spirit, penetrating the individuals, may be found the power of satisfying the above recognized need.

The limits of these individual nations are indefinite and fluctuating, and this uncertain condition manifests itself, moreover, in the oneness or diversity of the laws formed in them. Thus, it may appear doubtful, in the case of kindred tribes, whether they should be considered by us as one nation or several ; in like manner we also often find in their laws similarity, although not entire agreement.

But, moreover, wherever the oneness of a nation is undoubted, there are often found within its limits narrower circles, which, by the side of the general features of the national life, are united by a peculiar connection, as cities, villages, guilds, and corporations of all kinds, which together form popular divisions of the whole. Within these smaller circles, again, what is known as *particular* law may take its origin, by the side of the common national law, and, in many respects, may supplement and change this common law.

But if we consider the nation as a natural unit, and also as the bearer of the positive law, we should not thereby think merely of the individuals contained in it ; we should rather consider that this unity exists between the different families, and binds the present to the past and the future. The continued maintenance of law is effected by tradition, which is conditioned and founded throu.h the gradual succession of generations.

This view, which recognizes the individual nation as the creation and bearer of positive or actual law, may appear too limited to many who might be inclined to ascribe the creation of positive law rather to the general spirit of humanity than to the individual spirit of the nation. Upon a closer examination, however, the two views do not appear to be in opposition. That which operates in the individual nation is only the general spirit of humanity, manifesting itself in the nation in a special manner. But the creation of law is an act, and an act of the community. It is conceivable only of those among whom a community of thought and action is not only possible but really exists. Since now such a community is present only within the limits of the single nation, so only there can real law be evolved, although in the formation of the law the expression of a general human formative impulse is to be perceived.

There exists in the nation an irresistible impulse to manifest its invisible unity in an organic visible form. This bodily manifestation of the intellectual community of the nation is the state. If, then, we inquire as to the origin of the state, we shall be obliged to place it in a supreme necessity, in a force working from within, as already indicated, in general, in the case of law. And this obtains not merely with reference to the being of a state in general, but also with reference to the peculiar form which the state bears in each nation. For the creation of a state is a species of law-making; it is, indeed, the final step in the creation of law. See *System des heutigen römischen Rechts*, Berlin, 1840, I., 18–22, 28–32; also Stahl, *Die Philosophie des Rechts nach geschichtlicher Ansicht*, Heidelberg, 1833, II. 109–114.

In the *Fortnightly Review* for August, 1883, Frederick Pollock thus summarizes the views of Aristotle concerning the nature of the state: "A state is a community, and every community exists for the sake of some benefit to its members (for all human action is for the sake of obtaining some apparent good) : the state is that kind of community which has for its object the most comprehensive good. The state does not differ from a household, as some imagine, only in the number of its members. We shall see this by examining its elements. To begin at the beginning, man cannot exist in solitude ; the union of the two sexes is necessary for life being continued at all, and a system of command and obedience for its being led in safety. Thus the relations of husband and wife, master and servant, determine the household. Households coming together make a village or tribe. The rule of the eldest male of the household is the primitive type of monarchy.   Then we get the state as the community of a higher order in which the village or tribe is a unity.   It is formed to secure life, it continues in order to improve life.   Hence—and this is Aristotle's first great point—the state is not an affair of mere invention.   It is the natural and necessary completion of the process in which the family is a step.   The family and the village community are not independent or self-sufficient ; we look to the state for an assured social existence.   The state is a natural institution in a double sense : first, as imposed on man by the general and permanent conditions of his life ; then it is the only form of life in which he can do the most he is capable of. Man is born to be a citizen—Ἄνθρωπος φύσει πολιτικὸν ζῶον. There is hardly a saying in Greek literature so well worn as this : nor is there any which has worn better, or which better deserved to become a proverb.   It looks simple enough, but it is one of the truths in which we go on perceiving more significance the more our knowledge increases."

Waitz returns to this idea of the nation as a moral organism, in his *Grundzüge der Politik* :   " The origin of an individual state and the origin of states generally, are two distinct things ; one in no manner explains the other.   The beginning of a new constitution does not even make a new state.   The state grows organically as an organism ; but not according to decrees and for the ends of the national life ; it reposes upon the higher moral disposition of man, upon his ruling moral ideas.   It is not a natural, it is an ethical organism.   * * * * *   The idea of the state stands in close relation with that of the nation.   The nation is not an accidental fragment of humanity, not a capricious union of men, nor every collection of people bound together in a state ; it is an organic formation within the human family " (p. 1).   Bluntschli lays great stress upon the organic character of the nation.   1. *Lehre vom Modernen Stat.* I., p. 92.   Freeman says that the modern conception of the state is a nation.   *Comparative Politics*, 1873, p. 81.   See also Burke's *Reflections on the Revolution in France*, works, V., p. 79.

At a certain stage in the development of a nation, before it has realized the idea of territorial sovereignty, laws are addressed to the members of a tribe, or to persons possessing such common distinguishing marks as indicate a certain tie of union, irrespective of the place in which they may happen to be.   On this point see Holland, *The Elements of Jurisprudence*, Oxford, 1880, p. 280 ; also, Held, *System des Verfassungsrechts der monarchischen Staaten Deutschlands*, Würzburg, 1856, p. 171 ; Maine, *Ancient Law*, p. 99. " Territorial Sovereignty—the view which connects sovereignty with a limited portion of the earth's surface, was distinctly an off-shoot, though a tardy one, of feudalism. This might have been expected, *a priori*, for it was feudalism which for the first time linked personal duties, and by consequence personal rights, to the ownership of land " (Maine, *Ancient Law*, p. 102). " The history of political ideas begins, in fact, with the assumption that kinship in blood is the sole possible ground of community of political functions. Nor is there any of those subversions of feeling, which we term emphatically revolutions, so startling and so complete as the change which is accomplished when some other principle— such as that, for instance, of local contiguity—establishes itself for the first time as the basis of common political action " (p. 124). This identification of the nation with the territory which it occupies has naturally led to the modern idea that allegiance grows mainly out of the fact of birth within the limits of a particular country, though to this principle there are certain exceptions. In a recent work on international law, it is laid down, that while a state cannot enforce its laws within another state, yet that the personal relation which exists between the state and its citizens or subjects, travels with the latter into the new jurisdiction. They are not freed from allegiance by absence ; whether legitimate or illegitimate, the date at which they attain majority, the conditions of marriage and divorce, are determined by the state so far as their effects within its own dominions are concerned ; if they commit crimes they can be arraigned before the tribunals of their country notwithstanding that they may have been already punished elsewhere. On the other hand, there may be instances where the state will not de-mand the same duties from, or claim the same rights over, foreign-ers within its territory, as over its own citizens—but this is always *ex gratia*. It has power over them, but it does not choose to exer-cise it. Out of the rules which, by consent, govern these relations of the state to its citizens in other states, and its relations to for-eigners in its own dominions, has grown private international law (Hall, *International Law*, p. 43).

The doctrine of allegiance, more especially with reference to the United States, and also as affecting the question of citizenship of the State and of the United States, is discussed by Salem Dutcher, in an article on *The Right of Expatriation* in the *American Law Review* for April, 1877, p. 447. He shows that the distinction between a citizen of a State and a citizen of the United States was recognized in the Federal Constitution before the adoption of the fourteenth amendment (see Art. I., sec. 2 and 3 ; Art. I., sec. 1 ; Art. III., sec. 2 ; Art. IV., sec. 2, and Art. XI). The fourteenth amendment sets the question at rest, in providing that "All persons born or naturalized in the United States, and subject to the jurisdiction thereof, are citizens of the United States and of the State wherein they reside."

The duty of allegiance to the United States having become fixed, either by birth within its limits or by naturalization, cannot be abolished by the citizen without the consent of the United States, declared by law (Judge Story in *Spanks vs. Dupont*, Peters' Rep., III., 242 ; Kent's Commentaries, Il., 12, also Lecture XXV.). There may be a change of domicile for commercial purposes, but this does not necessarily include the right of expatriation. Of course when treaty stipulations so provide, as is the case between the United States and Austria, Sweden, Baden, Bavaria, Hesse, Wurtemburg, Prussia, Belgium, Denmark, Mexico, and Great Britain, the citizen may expatriate himself. By an Act of the Congress of the United States, July 27, 1868 (Statutes at Large xv., 224), it was enacted "That any declaration, instruction, opinion, order, or decision of any officer of this government, which denies, restricts, impairs, or questions the right of expatriation, is hereby declared inconsistent with the fundamental principles of the government." The executive branch of the government considered this act as merely a legislative expression of the opinion that the citizen ought to be allowed to expatriate himself. President Grant in his message of Dec. 7, 1875, treated it as such, and asked Congress to enact a law providing how expatriation might be accomplished. Our laws go even so far as to confer citizenship upon all children born out of the United States, whose fathers are citizens (United States Revised Statutes, sec. 1993).

The allegiance of the citizen of a State within the United States is, in many respects, different from the allegiance due by the citizen to the Federal Union. It must be borne in mind that while every citizen of a State is *ipso facto* a citizen of the United States, it is not necessarily the case that every citizen of the United States

is also a citizen of a State : he may be a citizen of a Territory or
of the District of Columbia. Again, a citizen of a State may
absolve himself from his allegiance by changing his residence
to another State, and the consent of the State of his former residence is not requisite.

CHAPTER III.

THE SOVEREIGN.

FROM the conception of the nation as a social organism, made up of a multitude of individuals bound together in a vast network of intimate relations, sympathies, and interests, we are led to the discussion of the nation as a power, as a society clothed with sovereignty.

The nation, viewed as a political society, is either independent or dependent. It is independent when the power, and the organs through which power is brought to bear upon the community, are contained within and proceed from the nation itself, or, as it may be otherwise expressed, when the nation governs itself. It is dependent when its governmental action is subordinate, in any essential particular, to the governmental authority of another political society. The independent political society is frequently termed a sovereign nation or state. The term "sovereign," when applied to the nation or state, is really synonymous with the term independent; it indicates that in the family of nations or states, the particular one about which the expression is used is the political equal of any of the other members of the family.

As applied to a state within a federation, as one of the United States, or a kingdom or duchy of the German Empire, it signifies that the community referred to is the political equal in the federation of each of the other members. Not that it may have in all respects the same weight as each of the others in the federal councils, but that its

2*

political tie with the others is alone through the federal government, and but for that tie the States would be independent of one another.

The term "sovereign," implies a superior and subjects, and hence it is not strictly correct to speak of an independent political society as a sovereign state, because such a society is not superior to any other state, nor subject to any other state. As Bentham and Austin have shown, there is no such thing as a limited sovereign, because the instant the sovereign is limited in his power he ceases to be sovereign. So that we cannot correctly speak of a state as "sovereign" which is subject to any external controlling power.

There has grown up in the United States, in the discussion of the many and important constitutional questions which arose out of the relations of the several States to each other and to the federal government, a nomenclature that discriminates between the supremacy of the United States and the positions of the several States with relation to that supremacy. The several States are spoken of as "sovereign" States. The abstract interpretation on which courts and statesmen are agreed is, that the State is supreme in the exercise of all those powers which it has not by the terms of the federal constitution surrendered to the United States, while the latter is supreme as to all powers granted by that instrument. The practical questions which have agitated courts, legislative bodies, and parties have mainly turned upon the definition of the limits of the powers granted and the powers reserved. As we shall see later (when we inquire, who is the sovereign in this great political body which we call the United States?) the individual State, accurately speaking, is not the sovereign, nor has it sovereignty.

This division of sovereignty between the United States

and the several States furnishes, it is true, a rough and
ready formula from which discussion can start when
measures are proposed or cases are to be decided, but it
cannot be denied, on the other hand, that it has introduced an element of confusion into the American mind
tending to cloud the perception of what is the real meaning of the terms sovereign and sovereignty in political
science.

Proceeding now to the consideration of the independent political society, the first inquiry should be, who is
the sovereign in such a society? Austin thus opens his
discussion of the subject:

"In order that a given society may form a society political, habitual obedience must be rendered, by the *generality* or *bulk* of its members to a determinate and *common*
superior. In other words, habitual obedience must be
rendered by the *generality* or *bulk* of its members to *one and
the same* determinate person or determinate body of persons." *

He then proceeds to enlarge upon this fundamental
proposition in its various aspects. Sir Henry Maine, in
commenting upon Austin's exposition of sovereignty, has
stated the ideas of the latter in a more satisfactory and less
cumbersome way than Austin himself, in this wise : †

"There is, in every independent political community
—that is, in every political community not in the habit
of obedience to a superior above itself—some single person or some combination of persons which has the power
of compelling the other members of the community to do
exactly as it pleases. This single person or group—this

---

* " The Province of Jurisprudence Determined," Lecture VI.,
Lond., 1879, I, p. 229.

† " Lectures on the Early History of Institutions." N. Y., 1875,
p. 349.

individual or this collegiate sovereign (to employ Austin's phrase)—may be found in every independent political community as certainly as the centre of gravity in a mass of matter. If the community be violently or voluntarily divided into a number of separate fragments, then, as soon as each fragment has settled down (perhaps after an interval of anarchy) into a state of equilibrium, the sovereign will exist and with proper care will be discoverable in each of the now independent portions. The sovereignty over the North American Colonies of Great Britain had its seat in one place before they became the United States, in another place afterwards; but in both cases there was a discoverable sovereign somewhere. This sovereign, this person or combination of persons, universally occurring in all independent political communities, has in all such communities one characteristic, common to all the shapes sovereignty may take, the possession of irresistible force, not necessarily exerted but capable of being exerted. * * * That which all the forms of sovereignty have in common is the power (the power but not necessarily the will) to put compulsion without limit on subjects or fellow subjects. It is sometimes extremely difficult to discover the sovereign in a given state, and, when he or it is discovered, he may fall under no recognized designation, but, where there is an independent political society not in a condition of anarchy, the sovereign is certainly there. The question of determining his character is, you will understand, always a question of fact. It is never a question of law or morals. He who, when a particular person or group is asserted to constitute the sovereign in a given community, denies the proposition on the ground that such sovereignty is an usurpation or a violation of constitutional principle, has completely missed Austin's point of view."

It will be observed that the following marks are associated with the idea of the sovereign :

1. A habit of obedience. The obedience must be sufficiently continuous to establish what may be properly deemed a habit. The obedience of the inhabitants of a country overrun by an army to the Commander in Chief does not create the relation of sovereign and subject, even though the occupation is of the capital of the country and it continues for a long period. The aim of the invading army is the destruction and subjection of its enemy. To accomplish these ends it may be necessary to overrun and occupy the enemy's territory and impose military law upon the inhabitants, and for this purpose to use whatever force may be necessary. Its aim is destruction, and is inconsistent with that condition of equilibrium upon which normal political government depends. When our forces invaded Mexico, finally dispersed its armies, captured the capital and remained in virtual occupation of the country for many months, the sovereignty of Mexico was not destroyed. Under similar conditions in France in 1870-71, there was not a transference of sovereignty to the Germans.

2. The obedience must be habitually given by the bulk of the members of the political society. Later, when we come to discuss the force embodied in a political society, we shall see that, from the nature of men, this must be the case ; that in order to constitute a state there must be a preponderance of the physical force of the community on the side of the sovereign, or what is the same, at his command.

3. The bulk of the society must obey a common superior. The requirement is that the major part of the people must be agreed as to the person, or the body of persons, who shall be supreme.

4. The possession of irresistible force within the society. This implies only that within the given society the sovereign cannot be legally, or continuously in fact, opposed by any countervailing force, when executing his commands or laws.

It will thus be seen that the idea of sovereignty involves the idea of freedom from all human control. From this it follows that the sovereign possesses absolute power over the persons, lives, and property of its subjects or citizens. We know that, as a matter of fact, there is some limitation placed on the sovereign by custom, law, or opinion in every state, no matter how despotic its ruler. As, however, the conception of sovereignty is somewhat of an abstraction, we must ideally, at least, recognize the presence of this irresistible power. Whatever moral or prudential considerations may operate to check or hedge the exercise of power, in no wise affect the fact of its possession. In this view, then, all sovereign political bodies are alike, in the last analysis, complete despotisms. The United States and Turkey do not differ in this regard.

We are now in a position to consider what is meant by the will of the nation. Every independent political society is an organic body and has a will. This will finds its expression in the organs and institutions of the government, and also in commands or laws. The use of the phrase "commands or laws" is in view of Austin's definition of law, which is more satisfactory than that of Blackstone. He says "Laws proper, or properly so called, are commands." * When a law is enacted in a political society it is the command of the sovereign or of the organ of the government invested by him with the power to utter it.

When we ascertain who, in any given sovereign state,

* "Province of Jurisprudence Determined," Lecture I, p. 81.

expresses and enforces its supreme will, then we have found the sovereign in that state. At this point, it is proper to consider more carefully what we mean by the supreme will of the nation.

The fact is, the great nation is made up of millions of human beings, each of whom has individual will power. But each one can only will as to what he shall do himself, or what another who is subject to his command shall do. In the latter case, the one who obeys the command surrenders his own will to the extent of the obedience given. When two come together to determine what shall be done in a given case and both proceed to exercise their wills on the given subject, the resultant is really one will as to that thing; and so with three, four, and any number. Where the wills are alike, the combination produces one will as to the matter in hand. Hence, if all the voters in a republic exercise a like will with reference to any matter affecting the state, their combined wills are fused into one will, which is the will of that state. If we could suppose the case, that all these voters should meet together, and all should agree upon and declare a law, then we should have an unmistakable expression of the will of that republic. While, however, there might be a million or more wills engaged in the conference, yet the resultant is one will and one expression of that will in the law which is declared. If, on the other hand, all the voters cannot agree, then the question immediately arises, which of the two or three or more wills, that result from an accord of the agreeing wills of fractions of the entire body, shall be accepted as the will of the single organism or the nation, for the nation cannot at one time and on one subject have more than one will. In the supposed case, the majority of votes would probably be taken as indicating the will of the nation. The reason of this will hereafter be examined when discussing the physical force of the nation.

This single will of the nation, instead of being the resultant of a *consensus* of all, or of a majority of the citizens, may be that of a large body, but less than the majority. We should then have a government by an aristocracy. If the numbers were small it would be an oligarchy, and if one person should be empowered to form and declare the national will, there would be the autocrat or despot. In every case, whether that of the democracy or the aristocracy, the oligarchy or the despotism, the decree or the law is the expression of the single will of the nation ; and further, the organ, or the government of the nation, which, for the time being, declares this will, exists with the consent of the people governed. In a broad sense, every sovereign government exists because of the consent of the governed, for if all the people so determine and so act, they can overthrow any form of government and establish any other. If they acquiesce in the rule of a despot they thereby consent to his government.

In every form of government which we examine it is always a question of fact who in the nation declares the will of the nation. When we have found this person, or these persons collectively, then we have discovered the sovereign in that nation ; assuming always that he or they who declare the national will have also the power to enforce it. It can therefore be asserted that in the modern state whoever makes the fundamental laws is the sovereign. When we come to examine this question more closely we shall find that in the representative government the law-making or sovereign power is what may be called a shifting power : at one time in one body, at another in another ; and that it is further complicated by a distribution of will power in many departments ; but, however intricate the disposition of it may be, we shall always be able to reach an ultimate body of persons who in the last analysis can declare the will of the nation, which must necessarily be sovereign and single. *

* This conception of sovereignty may be illustrated by reference to some points in the history of political thought. Jean Bodin (born 1530, died 1596), in *De la République*, was the first to emphasize the modern view of sovereignty. His work was published in Paris in 1576. Ten years later it was translated by himself into Latin. There is an English translation, made by Richard Knolles, and published in London in 1606 under the title of *The Six Books of a Commonweale*. A summary of Bodin's doctrines has been given by Bluntschli and also by Hallam, not to mention others. He defined the state—which he called republic, in order the better to indicate what is common to all states,—as the government, by law, of many families and their common property under the sovereign power. He censures the interpretation of the ancients, that the state is the union of many people with the intention to live happily and well, because it does not mention the three essential marks —family, common property, and the superior power,—and because it lays too much emphasis on happiness and welfare, forgetting that the state must preserve itself in misfortune and against the blows of fate and the enemy.

Bodin perceives the elements of the state not in individual men, but chiefly in the family. The family is to him an ordered community under the lead of the father, and therefore the type of the higher community of the state. Of greater force, however, was his reference to the third mark, sovereignty, in which he especially undertook to exhibit the quality of the state. He sees in sovereignty the unity and continuity of the power of the state, which is subject to no one but God. He styles only him sovereign to whom the continuous superior power belongs. The Roman dictator, notwithstanding his temporary power was without limits, is consequently not recognized by him as sovereign ; neither is the regent thus recognized, who wields the superior power in the place of the king while the king is unable to exercise it. The people, or the aristocracy, or the prince, can make over the superior power which appertains to him by procuration, but the agent has no claim to sovereignty, because, as Bodin observes, the true sovereign is the giver of authority, and the agent exercises the right only so long as the procuration is not withdrawn. The derivation of power is, however, not inconsistent with the conception of sovereignty, for elected princes may be sovereign, but their dependence and the revoking of their power is inconsistent with it.

Another characteristic which Bodin ascribes to sovereignty, and which he indicates as *absolute power*, is more important. Certainly not absolute in the sense that it may have been dissevered from the government of God, and consequently from the divine law and from the law of nature, but rather in the sense that it is not abridged by any other state power, nor by any state law. The sovereign power cannot be subordinated to any other power; the sovereign will is the highest, the final, deciding state-will. The law derives its strength from it. It is, therefore, not dependent upon the law, but the law is dependent upon it. As it creates the law, so it can disregard the law : it can make it ineffective. Even if the sovereign swears to maintain the law, he is not, unless there is something beyond, bound by it in law.

Bodin examined more carefully than any one before him, and laid more stress than most of those after him, on the truth previously propounded by Aristotle, that there is in every state a single superior power, in which the state finds its highest expression, and which, consequently, determines the fundamental character and form of the state. But in this he has, as was the case with very many before and after him, disregarded the distinction between the whole and its parts, between the body of the state and the superior organ in the state, and has fallen into the error of confounding the two and been thereby confused. He has so completely identified the power of the whole state, which, as the foundation, as the force at the base, is equal to the entire strength of the people, with the power of the highest organs of the state, which he styles sovereignty, that, before he is aware of it, the former disappears entirely and the latter alone remains. Because the total force of the nation is limited only by its own nature, he thinks the highest organs of the state can be limited only in like manner. He does not see that the second organized power is limited by the organism, in which it is itself only an organ, though the ruling, and thus is likewise only a part of the whole. He takes the sovereign power out of its connection with the remaining state arrangements, and places it as a thing by itself, as if it were an independent being and not merely an individual quality of another being, the state. This mistake forces him to the logical absurdity of ascribing to the part, which can exist only in and with the whole, an unlimited power over the whole.

The chief qualities of sovereignty, as indicated by Bodin, are : 1. The right to prescribe laws to the citizens, collectively and individually, without being obliged to obtain the agreement of a higher or of a lower power. The consent of a senate or of an assembly of the people, or of the classes in the state, may be useful, in a monarchy, but it is not necessary if the monarchial sovereignty is to remain untouched. 2. The right to declare war and to conclude peace. 3. The right to nominate the superior magistrates. 4. Final appellate jurisdiction : if a vassal is injured, that no approach and no appeal is possible from him to a lord paramount, because the vassal would then be on the way to wrest sovereignty from the lord, and even to become sovereign. 5. The right to pardon and restore fines. 6. The right to stamp coins. Thus far, in substance, the criticism of Bluntschli.

That Hobbes (born 1588, died 1679,) was influenced by the views of Bodin is probable, although there appears no positive evidence of the fact. He visited France as early as 1610, and again in 1629, and was several years on the Continent at different times later, and mingled freely with the scholars of the French capital. The *Leviathan* was published in 1651. In this work he postulates a condition of war between individual men as the primitive state, and affirms that in order to protect themselves from one another, and to obtain peace and security, political society was created. " The only way to erect such a common power," he says, " as may be able to defend them from the invasion of foreigners, and the injuries of one another, and thereby to secure them in such sort as that by their own industry and by the fruits of the earth they may nourish themselves and live contentedly, is to confer all their power and strength upon one man, or upon one assembly of men, that may reduce all their wills, by plurality of voices, unto one will ; which is as much as to say to appoint one man, or assembly of men, to bear their person " (" Leviathan," Lond. 1839, p. 157). And again : " A commonwealth is said to be instituted when a multitude of men do agree and covenant, every one with every one, that to whatsoever man, or assembly of men, shall be

given by the major part the right to present the person of them
all, that is to say, to be their representative ; every one, as well he
that voted for it as he that voted against it, shall authorize all the
actions and judgments of that man, or assembly of men, in the
same manner as if they were his own, to the end to live peaceably
amongst themselves and be protected against other men " (p. 159).
Here the idea of the sovereign is clearly presented, and it is declared that "there can happen no breach of covenant on the part
of the sovereign " (p. 161). The sovereignty is, moreover, indivisible. " Where there is already erected a sovereign power, there can
be no other representative of the same people, but only to certain
particular ends, by the sovereign limited. For that were to erect
two sovereigns ; and every man to have his person represented by
two actors, that by opposing one another must needs divide that
power which, if men live in peace, is indivisible " (p. 172). The
quality of the sovereign's power is not affected by the form of government. "The difference between these three kinds of commonwealth consisteth not in the difference of power, but in the difference of convenience or aptitude to produce the peace and security of
the people ; for which end they were instituted " (p. 173). " Elective kings are not sovereigns, but ministers of the sovereign ; nor
limited kings sovereigns, but ministers of them that have the sovereign power" (p. 178). " The sovereignty, therefore, was always
in that assembly which had the right to limit him " (p. 179). The
power to determine its own form of government was, moreover,
recognized as a mark of a politically independent and sovereign
state. " There is no perfect form of government where the dispos-
ing of the succession is not in the present sovereign " (p. 180).
Hobbes anticipated the later doctrine that what the sovereign permits it thereby wills. " For whatsoever custom a man may by a
word control, and does not, it is a natural sign that he would have
that custom stand" (p. 183).

More than a century later Jeremy Bentham, in *A Fragment on
Government* (published in 1776), propounds the view which his
disciple, John Austin, afterwards elaborated. He defines a political society thus : " When a number of persons (whom we may
style subjects) are supposed to be in the habit of paying obedience
to a person, or an assemblage of persons, of a known and certain
description (whom we may call governor or governors), such persons altogether (subjects and governors) are said to be in a state of

political society" ("Works" I. 263). In the sixth lecture of *The Province of Jurisprudence Determined*, Austin has elaborated and supplemented the views of Bentham on sovereignty.

Bluntschli has enumerated in *Lehre vom modernen Stat*, I. 563, the following attributes of sovereignty:

1. Independence of the political power of all superior political authority. But this independence is to be understood relatively, not absolutely. International law, which unites all states in an arrangement of common rights, is no more in opposition to the sovereignty of the state than is constitutional law, which limits the exercise of political power within the territory of the state. Whence it is possible that subordinate states may be regarded as remaining sovereign, although they may have become essentially dependent on the collective state, as, for example, in foreign political and military affairs.

2. Supreme political dignity, what the ancient Romans styled *Majestas*.

3. Plenitude of political power, as opposed to limited authority. Sovereignty is not a sum of separate individual rights, but a collective political right, a central conception of force similar to that of the conception of property in private law.

4. The sovereign power, moreover, is, from its very nature, the supreme power in the state. There can be, therefore, no other political power in the organism of the state superior to it. The French seigneurs of the middle ages ceased to be sovereign when they were obliged again to subordinate themselves to the king, their feudal lord, in all essential respects of independence and dominion. The German electors have been able to assert their sovereignty in their several territories, since the fourteenth century, for in fact they have possessed in their own right the supreme political power in these territories.

5. Since the state is an organic body, the unity of the sovereign power is a necessity of its welfare. The division of the sovereignty leads, in its consequences, to the paralysis or dissolution of the state, and is, therefore, not compatible with the health of the state.

The general excellence of Holland's *Elements of Jurisprudence* (Oxford, 1880) entitles the definition of sovereignty there given to our consideration. "Every state," he says, "is divisible into two parts, one of which is sovereign, the other subject." "The sovereignty of the ruling part has two aspects. It is 'external,' as independent of all control from without; 'internal,' as paramount over all action within." "External sovereignty, by possession of which a state is qualified for membership of the family of nations, is enjoyed in the fullest degree only by what is technically known as a 'Simple State,' *i. e.*, by one which is 'not bound in a permanent manner to any foreign body.' States which are not 'simple' are members of a 'System of States,' and collectively subject to a 'federal government'" (pp. 38, 39).

In his *Introduction to the Constitutional Law of the United States*, p. 28, Professor J. N. Pomeroy calls attention to the necessity of constantly preserving the distinction between "the nation and the government which that nation has actively created or passively permitted as the agent for the expression of its supreme will." He very properly charges a large part of the confusion of ideas, in this country, concerning the true import of the term "sovereignty" and "sovereign" to the long, and in a modified way still continued, discussion of "State rights" and "State sovereignty." It is more difficult to accept his criticism of Austin's famous sixth lecture, when he claims that in it nations and states are confounded with the ruling apparatus or organs of government within them. In reading this lecture it must always be borne in mind that Austin's primary object was to fix distinctly in the minds of his hearers the idea that a law, in the judicial sense, or, as he styles it, "a positive law," is a command "set by a sovereign, or a sovereign body of persons, to a member or members of the independent political society wherein that person or body is sovereign or supreme." His leading thought was to define positive law, and, consequently, he concerned himself mainly with making clear the conception of the sovereignty or characteristic marks of the independent political society, and, what was of more importance, with the definition and marks of the sovereign within the independent political body. In other words, he traces distinctly the two objects noted in the above quotation—the "sovereign" and the "independent political society."

CHAPTER IV.

THE nation must have organs to express its will in commands or laws, and to enforce the execution of its laws. These organs constitute the government, whose function it is to regulate the relations of the nation with other nations, and to regulate the actions and relations of individual citizens with reference to one another.

Having considered the nation as an organic social being, clothed with absolute power vested in that part of the nation which we call the sovereign, and endowed with a will, we turn now to inquire into the nature and general functions of those means through which the will of the nation is expressed and rendered effective.

The nation thus characterized, considered at any given time, appears composed of men, women and children inhabiting a certain territory. Let us take the United States as an example. Our last census report shows that within our territorial limits there were, in 1880, over fifty millions of persons. If we picture to ourselves this great multitude, we shall see at various points hundreds of thousands crowded into cities; then smaller cities and towns and villages, with the interspaces occupied by families living on farms in varying degrees of proximity. If we could embrace all these persons in a single glance, we should see all, or very nearly all, of the adults engaged in different avocations, and it would be particularly noted that each is, in a degree, only a specialist; that of all the things which contributed to the satisfaction of his own desires, each produced, ordinarily, but very little, and even in the country is largely engaged in furnishing what others consume. It would be further noted that these multitudes of individuals are constantly in contact and communication. Now, if we select one of these individuals from the fifty millions, we find that his nobler and better part is the resultant of the past efforts and contributions to the social stock of his predecessors, and also of the efforts of all his contemporary fellow-countrymen. The point is, that in this particular distinctive social division, comprehended within the United States, every individual is fitted in, and is so much a part of the general social organism, that, severed from it, or reduced to what is sometimes erroneously called a state of nature, he could not live. Such a distinct community, constituting a great unit of social existence, must have a government of some kind, otherwise it appears as a being with a will, but without organs through which this will may find expression.

It is true that, for the purposes of abstract consideration, we can separate the nation from its government, because a nation will exist though its government may be changed, or even if it be for a time actually dissolved; still we cannot conceive of a nation continuing any length of time without a government.

In a work which is used as a text-book in our schools, and which, besides, has a wide circulation,* it is laid down as a fundamental proposition, that "governments may be said to be necessary evils, their necessity arising out of the selfishness and stupidity of mankind." There could not be a greater error. Political government grows out of the nature of man, it is true, but it is as much a

* *Politics for Young Americans*, by Charles Nordhoff.

necessity of his being and growth as the vital forces of life themselves. Many centuries ago Aristotle profoundly remarked that "man is by nature a political being." It is an absolutely perverted conception that political government is a device which good men have invented to keep bad men in subjection.* On the contrary, it is a sign of the godlike attributes of humanity; of the supremacy of will and reason over mere instinct and animal desire. The assertion of such a view as that referred to is at this day a revival of the exploded fiction of an original state of nature antecedent to government. Political government is the expression of order in a community. It is the mark of collective reason. It is no more than the instrumentality by or through which the collective body makes and executes the commands which it imposes upon itself. In the earlier stages of growth, social groups have customs instead of written law; but both in their essentials are the same. Custom is a rule of action which has taken shape by degrees, and is finally universally acquiesced in. When thus accepted it becomes the law, and is enforced by the community. The written law is different only in that it was formulated at one time, and is more clearly defined.

The history of all primitive peoples shows that customary law is the first stage of progress from a condition of no law. At first, private wrongs can only be redressed by private vengeance; if a man is murdered, his relatives must pursue and punish the murderer. It is not long, however, before it happens that a man is murdered who

* "It is as a member of a state that man exists, that he is intended to exist, and unless as a member of a state, he is incapable of existing as a man. He can as little create a language as create a state; he is born to both, for both, and without both he cannot exist at all." Kemble, "The Saxons in England," i., 126.

3

has no relatives. Who shall avenge his death, for the general sentiment demands vengeance? It is undertaken by the ruler or chief who represents the whole body. This is actually what grew to be the rule in the early European world. Thus, then, the rude conception of a corporate injury, instead of a mere personal injury suffered, dawns upon the mind. So, also, originally, contract differences were settled by private contention, but were gradually taken in charge by the state.

The development of the state idea rests upon the growing apprehension of the great truth that the nation is not an accidental collection of human beings, who are so stupid and selfish that some superior power must step in and regulate them by laws, but that, on the contrary, it is a great corporate, organic being, whose individual members are intimately bound together, and must have government and rules of action, for it is impossible for a human being, single or corporate, to live without them. Every action in the nation, in a greater or less degree, affects all its members. There is a common interest which imposes, in return, a common duty to all.

Every form of government, no matter whether despotic or democratic, for the time being expresses the will of the state in which it exists. There is a vague way, quite common, of looking at a government as something apart and distinct from the citizens of the state. This view is more largely diffused in monarchical than in democratic states. But, of course, it is entirely erroneous. The forms of the government are merely the instrumentalities through which the whole given community expresses its will, and uses its force ; and this is just as certainly the case if one man is the autocrat as if every man is a voter. In the former case all permit this one autocrat to express the will and use the force of the state.

The general functions of a nation's government are, to determine the relations of the nation to other nations of the world-family, and to regulate the actions and relations of the individuals within the nation with reference to one another.

The nation in its relation to other nations is a single person. If sovereign, that is without any political superior, the government, or rather, as is usually the case, some particular person in, or department of, the government, negotiates and makes treaties with other powers, and represents the nation in other international relations. Out of this conception of the oneness of the nation, has in large part grown the whole circle of international rights and duties.

The second function of government, that of regulating the actions and relations of the individuals within the nation, with reference to one another, brings us immediately within the field of the present inquiry. But at the outset, when we speak of the individuals as fitted into a complex social organism, it is always with the limitation, that as a political body, this society is limited by the boundaries of the territory it occupies. Every political organism implies a distinct territory as well as a distinct body of people.

It follows, therefore, that a person may be temporarily or permanently severed from such an organism of which he has formed a constituent, by going out of the territory of his state. A citizen of the United States by crossing the line into Canada, though only to remain a day, enters into a new set of political relations, though he does not entirely depart from those of his own country. And so, in a less degree, a citizen of one State in the Union who goes into another, likewise changes his political relations. Within the territorial limits of the given political organism, it is manifest that the manifold relations growing out

of the daily contact of numerous persons, and in a complex society, of interests extending far beyond the person
who acts, cannot be left to the chance will, whim, or ca-
price of each individual, or of every voluntary combination of individuals, but must be regulated by uniform
rules of action, applicable to all relations of a like kind.
In truth, from the nature of things, fixed rules of conduct
must grow up.   In primitive, rude communities, customs
grow and furnish these rules of conduct, but as society
develops, written laws gradually take their place.

Hence, every distinct political community must have a
will, that is, it must be capable of *willing*.   If its members exclusively guide their conduct by customs, then the
society wills that this be done ; but if, as is the case with
the developed, civilized state, the rules of conduct are to
be promulgated through written laws, then each law is the
expression of the will of the state on the given subject.*
Austin expresses it : "Laws properly so-called are commands."   The nation has a will, and this will expresses
itself in commands.   Moreover, it must make its will

* It is not to be understood, however, that a nation in its legislation ever becomes entirely free from the directing force of custom
and usage.   Stahl (*Die Philosophie des Rechts*, II. 141) says :
"Every nation, indeed, in its later periods, is required to legislate,
but it is an erroneous view, that legislation in later times has to
accomplish just what was accomplished earlier by custom and
usage.   Custom arises at the same time with the relations which it
affects, and gives them a name and constitutes them legal relations.
But everywhere in the field of legislation are found norms, in ac-
cordance with which men direct their acts.   Whenever a case is
presented to the scrutiny of the legislator, it has already been, for
a long time, subject to that invisible, creative power of law, and
brought into a definite form.   In the latest and most enlightened
periods, just as in the earliest, all relations receive their primary
legal form from custom ; they can be altered and directed only by
legislation."

effective ; therefore it must be able to command the physical force of the nation, so that the nation, in order to accomplish these ends of its being, must have instrumentalities or agents through which to express its will, and
employ its force.   These constitute its government.

Every government consists of a certain framework of
what are sometimes styled institutions, but more generally,
in modern phrase, offices, together with the persons who
at any given time perform the functions assigned to these
offices.   In theory we may separate the offices from the
officers, but actually, in examining the government of a
country, the two must be considered together.   We may
discuss the office of President of the United States, or of
France, as something distinct from any one filling it, but
in the actual conduct of affairs there must be always a
living agent to perform the duties of the office.   It is
proper to speak of the government of the whole nation,
or of the government of a particular portion of its territory.   For instance, the expression "the government of
the United States" means all of the offices and all of the
incumbents of these offices pertaining to the federal branch
of our governmental system.   Or, if we speak of the government of the city of New York, we mean the offices
and their incumbents provided for that particular political territory.   The government is not the mass of the
people, nor, in our system, is it the constitution or
the separate States, but it is, as stated, the offices and
those filling them.   It is true that the term government
is frequently used in a more limited sense in current political literature, as, for instance, when it is said such or
such a scheme is a "government measure," or, "the
government is in favor of such and such a policy."   Here
is meant the small number of officials who have a controlling voice in the direction of governmental affairs ;

but when treating of the science of politics, we must confine our definition to the organs—meaning thereby the offices and officers—by means of which the nation or its subdivisions express the organic will or wield the force of the whole or the part, as the case may be. It is not necessary to particularize the very many ways in which at different times and among different peoples the will of the nation has been expressed and enforced through Emperors, Kings, Consuls, or Dictators, or through councils, or parliaments, or congresses, or to enumerate the host of inferior officials who have been subordinate to them. It is sufficient now to call attention to the underlying principles, which will be described more fully later in treating of the differentiation of functions, that whatever the system of government, it is made up of a body of persons who are each doing one of two things, either expressing the will of the particular community, or wielding its force in order to execute this will. Sometimes, it is true, the same person is performing both functions, but then he combines two distinct attributes of the political body.

CHAPTER V.

THE government of every nation rests on the total physical force of the nation. The function of a government, as already suggested, is both to express and to execute the will of the state. If the government cannot enforce the execution of its laws within the nation, then the nation ceases to be sovereign. And if a majority or plurality of voters, as the case may be, determines for the time being the will of any given state, it is primarily because such majority or plurality represents the preponderance of physical force.

When the will of the nation has been announced in the law, through the organs of the government empowered to make the declaration, the next question is, who shall enforce it? It will be seen at once that he who executes the law is subordinate to those who formulate and announce the law, because he does what a superior commands him to do ; consequently he is not the sovereign. In order to make the will or command of the nation effective, it must either be acquiesced in or enforced. In fact, in all nations there must exist the ability to carry out the law by the exercise of physical force, and if need be, of the entire physical force of the nation. It may be said that physical force is at the basis of every political community, whether independent or dependent. This force is either active or dormant ; generally the latter, lying as it were in the background, but ready to be aroused if any exigency demands. The whole political structure of every community rests, in a large sense, on physical force. If the body politic cannot bring the combined force of its members to bear upon any one of them in order to compel obedience to the commands of the sovereign of that body, then it cannot be said to be an independent political community, for it lacks one of its characteristic elements. Not only is an independent political community the embodiment of physical force, but, as regards its members or citizens, is, as has been suggested, an absolute despotism. If the sovereign in the nation makes a command, and any of the members of the state refuse to obey it, and the remaining members refuse to furnish the physical force to compel obedience, then the person or body of persons making such command ceases to be sovereign.

This has sometimes been styled the mere police theory of government, but in asserting that physical force is the basis on which all government rests, it must be understood in the sense that when any independent political community maintains a form of government—that is, provides an agency through which the sovereign in that community may express its commands—it necessarily, in order to make these commands effective, more than mere idle fulminations, places at the disposal of the sovereign whatever of physical force the community possesses for the purpose of compelling obedience to the commands. If such were not the case, the functions of every government would cease. It is not, of course, affirmed that every act is the exercise of propelling force. On the contrary, by far the larger part of government action is merely regulative. The reserve force may be compared to the banker's fund which is only to be drawn upon in cases of emergency; without this fund, however, he would be insolvent; and so a government unable to command its reserve is a mere form without vitality.

Laws are made by the legislature with penalties in case of disobedience. It is true that these are, in most instances, obeyed, not through fear of the penalties, but really because the law-making power has enacted them. It is certainly true that most people do not refrain from stealing because there are laws with penalties for the offence. The mass of people in civilized communities have the law-obeying habit. Still, it may be that, out of ten thousand, only one will violate a statute ; but unless all the physical force of the state can be brought to bear, if necessary, to enforce the sanctions of the violated law on this one, the state has not, in fact, a government.

It is certainly not to be overlooked that very much of the mechanism of every government is provided for by laws without penalties, or, apparently, very inadequate ones. The postal system, for instance, consists of elaborate arrangements for the reception and distribution of letters. It is designed and administered entirely as a convenience to the citizen. No one is compelled to avail himself of its instrumentalities. If one does not comply with its rules, as in not prepaying the postage on a letter, he merely loses the advantages of its expeditious service. Yet at proper points this service is guarded by adequate penalties. Severe punishment is inflicted upon robbers of the mail, or for the opening of letters by unauthorized persons, or for carrying letters not stamped, on mail routes. The whole service moves, as it were, from its own volition ; but, in fact, is held up, one may say, by the passive force of the community.

So with the complex body of rules regulating procedure in courts of justice. A person whose legal rights have been invaded may quietly submit to the wrong, or he may seek redress by a civil remedy in the courts. His action or non-action is entirely voluntary. If he chooses
3*

to ask reparation he does so in a certain formal way, and the whole procedure to the decree is by methods established by statutes, or by rules adopted by the practice of courts.   Up to the last moment he may abandon the pursuit of his remedy.   It is only when the decree is executed by the sheriff or other officers of the court that there is any appearance of physical force.

The rules and regulations which control the interior workings of the several great departments of state are in large part provided for by voluminous statutes without penalties.   The sovereign authority simply says, in substance, there shall be a Department of State, a Treasury Department, a War Department, and an Interior Department, and they shall be conducted by such and such officers, and in such and such a manner.   Apparently these several functions of government do not require a basis of physical force, but if we follow out to the last degree their manifest relations to the nation, we shall see that none of them could be an active agent without the basis of that force.   They live and act because they are held up and sustained by a latent force which at any moment may manifest itself.

But why is it, that in a republic the majority, or sometimes merely a plurality of voters, is permitted to form and express the will of the community?   Because the majority, as between two parties, and a plurality, as between three or more, represents the preponderance of physical force, which by supposition, may be used to make the majority or plurality will effective.   A thousand men may cast their votes in favor of a certain measure, but fifteen hundred may vote against it.   Now, each side deeming itself in the right, there is no inherent reason why the minority should acquiesce, there is no immutable standard of policy by which to gauge the measure in question.

Why, then, should the less number of voters submit to the greater? It is, at bottom, because the majority in numbers possess the preponderance of force. Long experience teaches self-governing peoples that, instead of fighting every political controversy out to the bitter end at the point of the sword, it is wiser, it is safer, to acknowledge one's weakness. After awhile we conclude it is every way more reasonable to draw up our forces in battle array, and then, instead of opening fire, calmly count each other's rank and file, in order that the weaker may leave the stronger in possession of the field. It is the growth of this practical good sense which constantly suggests the advantage, in the long run, of counting the enemy's forces, and retiring from the contest when they are too strong for us, that distinguishes the self-governing nation from other nations.

At the root of all civil institutions is conflict, incessant conflict. Out of the continuous struggles of man with man, has gradually grown the complex political structures of ancient and modern times. The theory that political relations are based on contract, which prevailed for so long a period, is, however, only an incomplete truth. It is true, that in civilized communities, men, in a sense tacitly agree, each to recognize the rights of the others, and to perform the obligations corresponding to those rights, but, really, behind or above this agreement stands the will and the force of the political group to which the parties belong. One may cheerfully, actively, and, to all appearances, voluntarily recognize the rights of another, and perform all the obligations due to him; and he may act in the same way to all others in the state, but it is not because he feels that he has so agreed, but because he *must* do so; the obligation is based on force, of some character. He may consider it a moral obligation, or even a religious one ; but either, or both, are no doubt the outward expression of the subconsciousness of a commanding physical power.

What we know of social evolution leads to the same conclusion. The strong influence of the blood tie in early society grew out of the family, which may be called the primitive political cell. Originally, in the family, the wife or wives, children and dependants had no separate rights ; the individual man was socially and politically nobody. He had no recognized existence outside the family. He had no rights, nor was he subject to any obligations, apart from the family. He could not own property or make contracts, except through the family. All transactions were family affairs, and family dealt or warred with family, and not with its individual members. Sir Henry Maine says : "There was no brotherhood recognized by our savage forefathers, except actual consanguinity regarded as a fact. If a man was not of kin to another there was nothing between them."

In the original family group the father was a despot. His power extended to life and death ; he was the one who gave commands, who judged when they were violated, and who inflicted punishment. All the essential attributes of political government as now developed, executive, judicial and legislative, were there enfolded in the germ.

As the family grew, it became what in India is known as the Joint-Undivided Family ; that is, the numerous descendants of a common ancestor constitute a family association, in which, as in the simple family, the individual is merged. In these larger families, the places of honor are reserved for those of the purest blood, who are those most directly allied to the founder.

In the earlier stages of society members were taken into the family by the fiction of adoption ; enemies were captured and made slaves, or whole tribes were conquered, which, frequently for purposes of protection, were also adopted. Always, however, there was first the fact and then the theory of the blood tie. Tribes were aggregated and grew into small nations or states, and thence into larger ones. When the little primitive community expanded into the village, paternal despotism in the family still continued. Sir Henry Maine further recounts, that in the Teutonic village communities "each family in the township was governed by its own free head, or *pater-familias*. The precinct of the family dwelling house could be entered by nobody but himself and those under his *patria potestas*, not even by officers of the law, *for he himself made laws within and enforced laws made without.*" Here is the sovereign state in embryo.

It is true that, in the earlier stages of society, the popular imagination invested the ruler with divine attributes and authority, and we know that much of the obedience to kingly authority arose out of this superstition. This was the motive only ; the fact remains unaffected by it, that then there was one man who was recognized by all as expressing the national will, and who could wield the national force. The motives which at this day induce free, civilized men cheerfully to contribute their forces to carry out the will of the nation may be more intelligent, but after all, as in primitive days, they are only influences which may, more or less, control the formation and expression of the national will and use of the national force, but are not themselves either of those factors in the life of the state.

There is this to be noted with reference both to the will and the force of the group, that in the simpler communities they act more directly than in highly civilized states. In the primitive family, the father called up the offender, tried, condemned, and punished him immediately. In the tribe the common assemblage, with almost equal swiftness, adjudicated and inflicted the penalty, and we know that in the semi-civilized despotisms of Asia and Africa, the action of the central power on offenders seems to us startlingly direct and sudden. Our more indirect way of using the general force to accomplish political and social ends is the consequence of that specialization which inevitably follows upon advancing civilization. On the economical side of life, we see every day that very few persons expend their forces directly upon the object which is the ultimate aim of their efforts. The mechanic, whose desire is to obtain a coat, will have to work a certain length of time, perhaps at laying a brick wall, in order to get sufficient money to buy the needed article. An analysis will show that his individual force has distributed itself through many channels before it produces the object of his desire. So in the political relations, there is a division of labor, and in the highly developed nation, the general force is usually set in motion, and reaches its object only by a series of indirect methods. In a simple democracy, the people would assemble, adopt the needed law instantly, and perhaps execute it with equal celerity ; but in a representative republic, many instrumentalities have to be used before the law can be enacted, and before the force of the nation can be brought to bear to compel its execution.

CHAPTER VI.

LOCAL POWERS.

THE nation is in structure a fusion and expansion of a series of units, which were originally little sovereignties, and which in their new relations as departments, or counties, or municipalities, retain portions of their old sovereign powers. Thus the nation consists, as it were, of a series of political circles through which its power is distributed. Local institutions find their beginnings in these units. National institutions are the instrumentalities which come into existence because of the aggregation of the units.

Thus far the nation has been considered as the synonym of the sovereign state, and as a homogeneous organic being ; as one body with one will, and a common force. In such a state, theoretically, the central national will would be expressed by the authorized person or body of persons directly on all the relations existing between the individuals of the state with reference to which the national will had power to express itself. There would be one central administration which would act directly upon everybody, as we might suppose would .be the case in a pure despotism where there are no laws except the will of the despot for the time being.

In fact, however, very few sovereign states have ever existed which were not, historically considered, an accretion of what may be called political units. Every nation is socially a growth, and politically, in part, a welding together of units of various sizes, and in part an expansion of these original units. It must, however, always be borne in mind that the unit is not the man, but a group of men. Speaking of the politics of the Greeks in the earliest stages of authentic Hellenic history, Grote says that, "in respect to political sovereignty complete disunion was among their most cherished principles. The only source of supreme authority to which a Greek felt respect and attachment was to be sought within the walls of his own city." "Political disunion—sovereign authority within the city walls—thus formed a settled maxim in the Greek mind. The relation between one city and another was an international relation, not a relation subsisting between members of a common political aggregate." * Moreover, "the Roman territory was divided in the earliest times into a number of clan districts. * * * Every Italian, and doubtless, also, every Hellenic canton, must, like that of Rome, have been divided into a number of groups associated at once by locality, and by clanship. Such a clan settlement is the 'house' of the Greeks. The corresponding Italian terms 'house' or 'building' indicate, in like manner, the joint settlements of the members of a clan, and these come by easily understood transition to signify, in common use, hamlet or village." "These customs accordingly having their rendezvous in some stronghold, and including a certain number of clanships, form the primitive political unities with which Italian history begins." † And, according to Sir Henry Maine, "the true view of India, is that, as a whole, it is divided into a vast number of independent, self-acting, organized social groups—trading, manufacturing, cultivating." ‡ In England, says Stubbs, "the

* "History of Greece," ii., 257.
† "Mommsen, History of Rome," i., pp. 63, 65.
‡ "Village Communities," New York, 1876, p. 57.

unit of the constitutional machinery, the simplest form of social organization, is the township, the *villata* or *vicus.*" *

The political unit of every nation was, originally, a little nation usually possessing all political powers, legislative, executive, administrative, and judicial, in a confused mixture ; and in expanding into the great state, or becoming fused with other similar units, there has not ordinarily been a surrender of all power by the smaller unit. Actually, much of the old local authority has been retained in these smaller units which afterwards become the subordinate departments, counties, communes, or municipalities of the larger state. The sovereign ruling over this congeries of units which has become the nation has power to interpose his superior will to change the old-time constitution of the original political unit, but more frequently he does not ; he retains its form, and perhaps enlarges and more clearly defines its powers. Sometimes this unit is in the nature of a root from which a system of districts, county, city, and state, or department governments grow ; a series of expanding branches. Through such processes the institutions of a country grow up. What are these ? They are the instrumentalities through which the general will expresses itself, and the general force acts.

It is always to be remembered that, "what the sovereign permits, he commands," because the act of permission implies its antithesis, the power to prohibit. Hence, if a township has now certain political powers, and the county certain others, and the city still different ones, and these are exclusive within their several spheres, it by no means follows that these are subtractions from the central national will, and reduce it *pro tanto.* The central will permits them, therefore it wills them. These town-

* "Constitutional History of England," i., 82.

ships and political subdivisions are not sovereign powers; they are strictly subordinate, because there is a power at some other point of the political fabric which can change and modify them. The difficulty of clearly perceiving the unity of the sovereign nation is largely because we see that all political action takes place in groups or circles, generally of no great magnitude. The nation at large, the national will and force, are more or less vague abstractions. The political movement which we see about us, is in wards of cities, or in election precincts, or townships, or counties, or, in the United States, in the state. Every subdivision has a certain jurisdiction.

The will and power of the nation distribute themselves through these, by means of political institutions. The growth of these is to be studied in the history of the expansion or the aggregation of the original units to the nation.

The political institutions of a country constitute the framework of the nation. They are the bones, heart and lungs of the commonwealth, but they are not the life-blood which momently courses through the arteries and veins. Institutions always tend to become permanent in form, though, among progressive people, the spirit which animates them may change every half century. They may be divided into two classes, local and national. In the states which are the product of long growth, as those of Europe, the various circles or districts of administration, as a rule, represent the different points where sovereignty has resided before a further growth or fusion. The towns, counties, or departments, as the case may be, retain the substance of the original administrative powers, though, of course, modified, or more or less supervised by the superior power from time to time. When several of these smaller sovereignties are united, then the necessity for national institutions arises. The peculiarity of Asiatic political growth is that of arrested development. In the Orient, small communities have petrified, and are held together by a central despotism, without, however, arteries throughout the whole system for the free circulation of power. In Western Europe, the local institutions have been more flexible, and have expanded by degrees into those of the nation. We thus see that even in the perfectly developed nation the national will is single only in the sense that there is, and must be, the ability in some person or persons within the organism to form and express it in the last resort, and to use the national force to effectuate its mandates. It is through all the institutions of the state, both national and local, that this sovereign will expresses itself, and is thus apparently shared by many departments, but it will be found in every state that every district or department of administration traces its title through a superior power, and that they really all exist because of the permission of this higher power—the sovereign.

CHAPTER VII.

AN error in much political writing is the overestimation of intelligence and the underestimation of instinct. This appears with prominence in the writings of the seventeenth and eighteenth centuries; in those of Grotius, Hobbes, Spinoza, Puffendorf, Locke, Rousseau, in all, in fact, where the origin of government is explained by the hypothesis of a social contract; for this hypothesis involves the idea of intelligent beings, in the earliest stages of history, consciously and deliberately setting about the construction of a government. The influence of this contract theory on political thought lingers even to this day, though in a constantly diminishing degree. At present it may be considered as having generally given place to the view first advanced by Aristotle, which is, in brief, that man is by nature a political being, and that government is a result of social growth, and is, moreover, a necessary condition of human existence. Accepting this position, we have to consider the method and forces of this growth. Among the purely human forces we find intelligence and instinct. It is with the latter that we have here mainly to do, and especially to point out the nature and extent of its operation in the field of politics.

Instinct has been defined in a general way as "a generic term, comprising all those faculties of mind which lead to the conscious performance of actions that are adaptive in character, but pursued without necessary knowledge of the relation between the means employed and the ends attained." It may, therefore, be well illustrated by contrasting it with intelligence. " Intelligence," says Prof. Joseph Le Conte, in substance, "works by experience, and is wholly dependent on individual experience for the wisdom of its actions ; while instinct, on the other hand, is wholly independent of individual experience. If we regard instinct in the light of intelligence, then it is not individual intelligence but cosmic intelligence, or the laws of nature working through inherited brain structure to produce wise results. Intelligence belongs to the individual, and is therefore variable, that is, different in different individuals, and also improvable in the life of the individual by experience. Instinct belongs to the species, and is therefore the same in all individuals, and unimprovable with age and experience. Whatever difference in the skill of individuals or improvement with age is observed, must be accredited to the intelligence of the individual, not to the inherited element. In a word, intelligent conduct is self-determined and becomes wise by individual experience. Instinctive conduct is predetermined in wisdom by brain structure. The former is free; the latter is, to a large extent, automatic." *

As to the origin of instinct, it can hardly be said that any theory has as yet gained universal assent, but no hypothesis appears more worthy of acceptance than that which regards it as habit grown to be hereditary. An act frequently performed in the consciousness of a specific purpose may continue to be performed, through the determinative force of structure, after the consciousness of the purpose of the act has been lost. When this peculiarity of structure, or the mental bias caused by the frequent and continued exercise of the mind in a given

* *Popular Science Monthly* for October, 1875.

direction, has become hereditary, the habit has grown into an instinct.

As we descend in the scale of animal life, we find that the ratio of the instinctive to the intelligent acts of the several individuals continually increases,—that is, the actions of animals of any lower order are more nearly exclusively instinctive than those of animals of any higher order; but it does not follow from this that there are absolutely more and higher manifestations of instinct in mollusks than in man; only that relatively to the whole of the actions of the mollusks the instinctive form a larger part than is the case in man. " Intelligence and instinct are not mutually exclusive, as some seem to suppose; the one is not simply a characteristic of man and the other of animals, but they coexist in varying relative proportions throughout the animal kingdom."* In the sum of *human* actions, therefore, we may expect to find a large number that are purely instinctive in character. Important among the acts of this class are those which bear on the political organization of society.

The long continuance of a people under any given political order engenders a habit of political thought and action which ripens into a political instinct, and becomes powerful in determining the form of institutions and the direction of political progress. In the early stages of political life changes are less frequent than in the later stages; and opportunity is thereby offered for the ideas of social organization peculiar to primitive times to impress themselves upon the mind, and in the course of centuries of political monotony, to ripen into a firmly fixed instinct. Thus the political instincts of a race have their origin in a pre-historic age, in an age when generation after genera-

* Prof. Joseph Le Conte in *Popular Science Monthly*, October, 1875.

tion passes away, leaving no record of change in social forms, or of the acquisition of new ideas. And it is this political instinct that must be taken account of if we would fully understand later political progress; it is in its force and persistence that we discern the main cause of that tendency displayed in kindred nations to preserve in their governments the essential features of the primitive political institutions of the race to which they belong.

One of the most striking results of the influence of a political instinct common to the Western nations is to be found in the analogies which may be observed between the political institutions of the different states, taken in connection with the fact that their common features are at the same time the characteristic features of the primitive Aryan government. In speaking of the early institutions of the Aryans, Freeman says: "The first glimpse which we can get of the forms of government in the early days of kindred nations shows them to have been wonderfully like one another. Alike among the old Greeks, the old Italians, and the old Germans, there was a *king* or chief with limited power, there was a smaller *council* of nobles or of old men, and a general *assembly* of the whole people. Such was the old constitution of England, out of which its present constitution has grown step by step. But there is no reason to think that this was at all peculiar to England, or even peculiar to those nations who are most nearly akin to the English. There is every reason to believe that this form of government, in which every man had a place, though some had a greater place than others, was really one of the possessions which we have in common with the whole Aryan family." * This appears, then, as the type of the Aryan government. The existence of a strong political instinct would lead us to

* "General Sketch of History," p. 6.

expect to find this type perpetuated in the later history of
the race, and, in fact, we find that its essential features
have been maintained in many governments. Wherever
variations from the type have occurred, they have been
either the result of a more complete development, and
carrying out of the hereditary scheme, or due to influences, like, for example, that of the church, foreign to
the hereditary traditions of the nation in question. One
of the prominent characteristic features of this typical or
primitive government is the co-existence of three elements: 1, the national chief with limited authority;
2, the council, comprising men of distinguished birth, or
of extraordinary experience and wisdom ; 3, the assembly
of the people, in which the several individuals comprising
the people act either immediately or through their representatives.

With a very few exceptions, every sovereign and subordinate state of the Aryan race is marked by the prominent characteristics of the primitive Aryan government.
This fact, taken by itself, does not appear of great significance. When, however, it is remembered that this peculiar organization of the central government is almost
exclusively confined to Aryan states, and to states in
which the Aryan influence predominates, and that among
these states it is virtually universal, there appears to be
something more than a mere coincidence. This view is
further confirmed by the essential similarity between the
modern governments of the Aryan race and that which
has been pointed out as the primitive and typical government; and this indicates, in the race, an inborn force leading it to resist foreign influences, and seek the realization
of its primitive ideals.

The fact of a striking similarity between the governments at present existing and the old Aryan government

is by no means the strongest indication of an instinctive force operating to determine political forms ; for we have only to assume a standpoint a few centuries back in order to discover that then, apparently, no such similarity existed. Of vastly more importance is the persistence of a tendency, everywhere manifest in the political development of Western nations, to overcome the result of foreign influences, and reëstablish original forms. The commonwealth's men set aside the king and lords, and proposed to establish a new order of things. In thus reorganizing the government they ran counter to the political instinct of the nation, and the ultimate failure of their scheme was, therefore, a foregone conclusion. The king, lords, and commons stood for the primitive king, council, and assembly. Any other form of government failed to meet the instinctive demands of the nation, and insure political stability. Cromwell at last appreciated that there was no hope for the commonwealth except in a return to the ancient threefold division of power, which was effected through the institution of the "other house," and the office of Lord Protector. The republicans, in their attempts to carry out their original plans, had, therefore, to contend not merely with an opposing party called the royalists, but they also carried on a hopeless struggle against a political tendency deriving its force from a strong national instinct.

The antagonism between the national or race instinct and the existing organization in any given case is brought about either through the conscious efforts of powerful political leaders to carry out their own ideas regardless of the early history of the nation, or through the growth of a great institution or of great institutions standing on a basis independent of the national life, but determining certain features of the national organization. The first

4

case is illustrated by the English commonwealth in its
early years, and by the first attempts of the French to
found a republic ; the second by the growth of the church.
What specially distinguishes the form of the national
government in the middle ages from that of earliest and
latest times is the existence of the estate of the clergy by
the side of the third estate, and of the estate of the nobles.
Eliminate the estate of the clergy from the mediæval governments, and they assume essentially the same form as
the primitive Aryan government ; and to accomplish this
has been one of the aims of political progress since the
beginning of the political power of the church. The
retention of political power by the clergy as a separate
branch of the legislature was a standing protest against an
instinctive tendency that has finally culminated in our
day in the overthrow of the church as a separate and distinct factor in legislation.

The force of instinct in political development is fur-
thermore illustrated by the parallel constitutional growth
of kindred nations, which in their progress have been
largely independent of one another and independent of
common foreign influences. The English and the Swedes
are such nations. In England the essential features of
the primitive Aryan constitution not only mark the existing government, but also characterize that form of
government which the English people have struggled to
maintain throughout their history. The king, the
witenagemote, and the folkmote shared the supreme power
probably in all the earliest kingdoms.* But as the
primitive kingdoms coalesced, the folkmote was either
neglected or continued as a local institution, while the
witenagemote remained the supreme council of the new
government of enlarged dominion. Thus in those states,

* Stubbs' "Constitutional History of England," I., 119.

as Wessex and Mercia, which were aggregations of smaller states, there is no evidence of the existence of the folkmote. So also, after the consolidation of the Anglo-Saxon kingdoms into the kingdom of England, we hear only of the witenagemote. The folkmotes of the old kingdoms became the popular assemblies of the shires ; and in the larger kingdom formed by their union it was impossible for the whole body of freemen to participate directly in the affairs of the government, and as yet no means had been discovered through which their authority could be expressed indirectly. After the establishment of a general government for England, and the relegation of the folkmote to the subordinate position of a local assembly, the nation entered upon a political struggle which resulted, after the introduction of a system of representation, in setting up a popular assembly constituted through the medium of representation, and in restoring to the government its ancient and hereditary form.

In England, as throughout Christendom, the clergy, under their peculiar and independent organization, did not hesitate to demand separate recognition ; and the lords, the knights of the shires, and the representatives of the cities had separate origins and separate interests, in which each class might have found ample reason for the formation of a distinct assembly. But such was not to be the order. The clergy were merged in the lords, while the representatives of the counties and the representatives of the cities were joined to form a lower house, in sympathy with the people, and answering to the folkmote of the primitive kingdom.

The history of the Scandinavian nations shows the same general political tendency ; yet the various stages of development were attained here later than in England. In the earliest period over which historical research has thrown any clear light, these nations appear in a state of political transition. The tendency which had led to separation and to the establishment of small independent kingdoms had been superseded by a new phase of progress towards unity. The petty kingdoms had lost somewhat of their independence, and appear as provinces in a confederation, at the head of which stood the king. The political status of the Swedes at this time corresponded to that of the English subsequent to the union of the Anglo-Saxon kingdoms and prior to the accession of the commons to power. The political drift of the two kingdoms, England and Sweden, which had been formed by the aggregation of the preëxisting smaller kingdoms, was toward the realization of the primitive form of government; yet in Sweden, powerful influences arose through which the attainment of this end was for a long time delayed. Prominent among these influences was the growth of independent and strongly-marked social classes—the nobles, the clergy, the burghers, and the peasants.

These several classes, whose individuality was becoming continually more marked, furnished the basis of a system of class representation, yet at the end of the fifteenth century no such system, in any degree of perfection, had come into existence. The general affairs of the kingdom were deliberated in meetings of the council; for as in England the witenagemote remained an institution of the general government after the folkmote had been relegated to the position of a local assembly, so in Sweden the king was surrounded by his council and acted under their advice, before the general popular assembly had come into existence, and while the ancient popular assemblies remained as the assemblies of the provinces.

In the course of time, representatives of the towns and of districts in the country were invited to meetings of the

council, and in this way there was developed a system of
representation, and the meetings of the council grew into
the parliament, just as the meetings of the witenagemote,
through the addition of the representatives of the shires
and of the towns, grew into the parliament of England.
At first, as in England, all met in a single assembly. The
next step appears to have been a division into two bodies,
the temporal and the spiritual magnates constituting one,
representatives of the cities and of the peasants forming
the other. Here Sweden was following a parallel to the
line of English political history, but the forces which had
produced the strong distinction of classes changed the tendency later, and led to the organization of four houses,
through the influence of which the fusion of class interests
was hindered and the spirit of the middle ages continued
into the present century. But ultimately the instinctive
force that had been checked by the rise of classes asserted
itself, and Sweden attained a form of government bearing
an essential likeness to that of the early Aryans, and also
to the existing government of England and of the United
States.

In England and Sweden, two nations of a common stock,
but of widely different circumstances, there is revealed
the same inherent impulse which has given to both, in
spite of the different circumstances, essentially the same
course of political progress. The primitive Anglo-Saxon
kingdoms correspond with the petty kingdoms of ancient
Scandinavia. These, in both cases, gave way to a central
government in the ninth century. With this change, the
direct participation of the great mass of the freemen in the
affairs of the central government ceased ; and in the thirteenth century, in both England and Sweden, power fell
largely into the hands of the magnates, who constituted
the councils and limited the authority of the kings. In

1265, representatives of the towns and of the counties were added to the English council ; and in 1435, representatives of the burghers and of the common people were first called to unite with the Swedish council in the formation of a national assembly. The national assemblies of the two nations thus embraced the same elements, and a common principle of division, carried out in both cases, would have resulted in a common parliamentary organization. But through purely external circumstances the individuality of classes became more marked in Sweden than in England, thus preventing that union of the nobles and the clergy, and of the burghers and the peasants, through which the English parliament early attained its present form.

This comparison is adequate to illustrate the point to be emphasized, namely, that different nations branching from the same stock carry with them into their different circumstances a common political instinct which gives them an impulse toward a common end, and that the resultant of this instinctive impelling force will vary in different nations according to the environment, or according to the different external circumstances, of the nations.

In directing attention to similarity of organization and similarity of political development as the result of an instinctive impulse common to different nations of the same stock, it is not intended thereby to overlook the efficiency of subordinate forces operating to the same end, as, for instance, the force of imitation. But when we have accorded all possible importance to the act of conscious imitation, there still remains the fact that imitation of political institutions takes place mainly between nations belonging to the same race, and only to a very limited extent between nations of different races. The Roman may copy certain institutions from the Greek, the Ger-

man may copy from the Roman, or any one of the
modern nations of the West may copy from any other,
but we do not expect to find nations of different races
copying from one another. The presupposition of imitation in political matters is a certain inherited propensity,
an instinctive adaptation to certain forms of thought and
to certain lines of action ; whence it would appear that
the influence which imitation exerts in determining political institutions rests on an instinctive faculty. Between
nations having no common inheritance, we look in vain
for any lasting similarity of institutions, except in cases
where members of one nation dominate the governmental
affairs of another of a different race. One nation may
borrow of another, although the two share in no common
inheritance, yet the borrowed institution finds no soil
adapted to its normal growth, and it either passes away
or becomes unrecognizably distorted. On the other
hand, history has ample record of institutions transplanted
from one kindred nation to another that have taken root
and developed a strong and natural growth.

No idea has contributed so much to put linguistic
science on a firm basis and to insure its future progress
as that which explains the existence of features common
to the several languages of kindred nations on the ground
of inheritance from a common source. The same idea
applied to the early literature and mythology of Aryan
nations has thrown a flood of light over subjects that
before were in darkness and confusion. In like manner
the science of politics may embody a similar idea in its
foundation ; it may start with the notion that every nation
enters upon its career of independent existence with a
certain hereditary endowment, an instinct which gives to
its political development an impulse toward a pre-deter-
mined end ; and, moreover, that this instinct is common

only to those nations which belong to a common race. Through its failure to recognize this fact, Herbert Spencer's elaborate system of philosophy grows weak when it reaches the realm of political discussion. He collects his data promiscuously from the most varied sources—from the civilized peoples of the progressive West, and from the most degraded savages of the Pacific islands—and on the basis of this information makes his inductions, apparently forgetting that inductions made on the basis of facts gathered from the declining or petrified peoples of Central Africa, Further Asia, or the islands of the Pacific, have no immediate and necessary application to the Aryan nations. The condition of these peoples is not that of the civilized European nations minus some centuries of progress; they belong to another great branch, or to other great branches, of the human family, and have part in another inheritance.

Although two nations may belong to the same race and be endowed with essentially the same political instinct, yet it does not necessarily follow that it operates with the same force in both cases. The uninterrupted continuity of political growth in one nation may have helped to strengthen the instinctive tendency, while in the other this tendency may have been frequently interrupted by recurring revolutions, and consequently weakened. England and France are cases in point. It requires no very profound knowledge of English and French history to perceive that in the determination of their political affairs the forces of intelligence and of instinct have not operated in the same ratio in the two nations. The political conduct of the French nation has been determined by purely intellectual conceptions to a much greater extent than that of the English. It has become almost proverbial that in effecting political changes the French follow theories, while the English are directed by their common sense, which is simply another way of stating the dominance of intelligence in French politics as contrasted with the dominance of instinct in English politics. The French revolutions of this and the previous century have been a practical outgrowth of French political philosophy, and appear as attempts to carry out certain conceptions of political organization which this philosophy had impressed upon the mind of the nation. In most English revolutions, on the contrary, always excepting the Puritan revolution, the dominant factor has been the conservative force of the nation—political instinct. This superior strength of instinct in the English furnishes ground for an explanation of important facts in the social history of this people, such as : 1. The almost unerring wisdom with which any colony of Anglo-Saxon blood, however unlettered its members, proceeds in the organization of a government ; 2. The wonderful assimilative power in which this people has shown a superiority over all others with which it has come in contact in its course of worldwide colonization.

The political intelligence of our race may vary, but the instinct remains stable. The intelligence is fickle, and turns with every breath of argument ; the instinct is beyond the reach of argument, and bears ever steadily towards its predetermined goal.

4*

CHAPTER VIII.

THE political development of colonies planted in new
countries is through forms analogous to those which have
marked the constitutional growth of the parent stock, and
illustrates, not merely the influences of imitation, but
also the force of an hereditary political sense or instinct.
This tendency is clearly manifest in the history of the
movement toward national unity in the British colonies
of America. As the colonial settlements proceeded from
a completed nation, so they manifested an irresistible
tendency toward unification in the form of a fully organized nation. The town, or the plantation, or the parish
as the successor of the plantation, which became the
political unit in the colonies, corresponded to their pro-
totype, the parish, the political unit in England.

In the history of the United States we have a striking
example of the rapid growth of a nation up through the
rudimentary stages ; and we have here more clearly
shown than in other instances of such growth the working of the centralizing and disrupting tendencies which
have been, in a greater or less degree, the accompani-
ments of all natural development throughout the world.
With us these opposing tendencies were especially active
during the period of seventy-seven years, between 1778,
when the Articles of Confederation were framed, and the
close of the Civil War in 1865. During that period, especially after 1800, all party strife hinged, more or less, on

this antithesis. Looking further back we can see that
the seeds of political discord were planted among the
colonists almost at the beginning.

The nationalizing influences are to be found in the
fact that the colonists, with few exceptions, belonged to
a common stock, and proceeded from a single nation,
taking with them common political instincts and the
traditions of common institutions.

The settlement of Virginia dates from 1607. Thirteen
years afterward, in December, 1620, the Pilgrims landed
from the *Mayflower*. Within three years, in 1623, the
Dutch settled in New York, and very soon spread in
small numbers into the present territory of New Jersey
and Delaware. An interval of thirteen years elapsed
before the next colony, that of Lord Baltimore, in 1634,
planted itself on the Atlantic coast. Shortly afterward a
small settlement of Swedes was made within the limits of ·
Delaware. Then thirty-two years passed by before South
Carolina was colonized. This long interval was followed
by another of twelve years before Penn brought his
Quaker co-religionists over to the banks of the Delaware ;
and finally it was as late as 1732 when the Oglethorpe
colony came to Georgia.

Thus there were seven germs of European civilization
planted at intervals along the Atlantic seaboard during
this period of one hundred and twenty-five years. Six of
these were from England, and one from Holland. It is
hardly worth while to consider the Swedish immigrants,
as their distinctive character very soon disappeared. ·
Even the Dutch settlement in New York lost its special
characteristics after its capture by the English in 1664,
and counts for very little in the future political development.

The men and women who laid the foundations of the

social and political structure on this continent were mostly of the Anglo-Norman stock. Their language was one, their customs were largely similar, and their social life was marked by the same general peculiarities. Moreover, their ideas of present and future happiness grew from, and were shaped by, their common circumstances.

The fact that the colonists possessed a common nationality is an important consideration. We are not always ready to appreciate the profound impression which a fully developed nationality makes upon the mental and moral structure of its individual citizens, nor, especially, how much it consciously and unconsciously shapes all their political actions and ideals. A fully developed nationality brings about a certain sameness in these particulars. There grows to be an hereditary habit of thought and of action in dealing with political institutions. There is a political sense which can be cultivated, and becomes a native quality, going from father to son. Our colonial history and the annals of the settlement of new states are replete with instances of rude, unlettered men, possessed with a fine political sagacity, laying the foundations of new communities. State-making aptness, and a proclivity to build up the state in a certain way, become fixed in a whole people, so that it is just as much an hereditary necessity for them to construct a new state upon certain transmitted principles, as it is for bees to build their honeycombs as their remote ancestors did. It is true, the state-making faculty is common to all the Germanic peoples, but as they successively developed into nations, each has taken on special political characteristics, which fasten themselves on any new communities that may spring from the parent stock. If the parent stock is fully developed into a nation, the emigrants who go out from it as colonists have a strong impulse to form a new nation ; they are taken out from a nation, and their tendency is, as soon as they can, to get back to the parent form.   New communities grow in the likeness of the ancestral nation, as children grow in the likeness of their parents.   The many colonies that went from Greece over to the coast of Asia Minor, rapidly reached the city form, which was the limit of Greek political development, but they were unable to enlarge by fusion into a common nation, though a favorable geographical position, and more, a constantly menacing danger of conquest, would almost seem to have compelled it.

Now, when the English began to colonize America in the early part of the seventeenth century, the mother country had been a nation for more than four hundred years.   Within a century and a half after the landing of William the Conqueror in 1066, at the close of the reign of Henry II. and his sons, there had come about a fusion of Norman and Anglo-Saxon blood, and with it a developed national feeling, which became very strong during the succeeding four centuries.   The breaking away of Henry VIII. from the Roman hierarchy intensified this feeling, because he transferred the allegiance of the strong religious feeling of the age to himself, as the head of the nation.   Before that, there was a double sovereignty in England, as there is in every country where the Roman Catholic is the state religion ; a religious sovereign outside the country, and a civil sovereign within.   The national homogeneousness became more complete during the long reign of Elizabeth, so that, when James came to the throne, English nationality was fully developed.   The Englishmen of that day had a certain stock of ideas and ideals in common. Their religious views were in substance the same.   There was a common agreement upon governmental methods.

They accepted without question a government in which there was :

1. A monarch.

2. A legislative body consisting of an Upper House, representing, or, rather consisting of the aristocracy, and a Lower House representing the middle class, and through them the lower orders.

3. A distinctive judiciary.

4. Local self-government in counties and parishes. Further, they were agreed upon certain general principles, such as the co-relation of taxation and representation, trial by jury, etc. The king represented the unity of the nation, and the two houses of parliament its common judgment. The English nation, then, constituted an organic political being. It might have been expected, therefore, that those colonies which were sent off from the parent stock, and which attached themselves to the soil and grew, would have an inherent tendency to develop into like national organic beings, provided, of course, there should be no exterior hindrances. It might also have been expected that several such colonies, planted near one another, would be drawn together at last into a single nation.

The political units, or the primary political organizations existing in the English nation at the time of the establishment of these colonies, were, as we have already seen, the townships.

In Anglo-Saxon times the tithing was the rudimentary district. Each tithing had its court, which was an assembly of the freemen of the district. These tithings, or townships, were subsequently aggregated into the hundreds, and these last into the shires or counties. These three parts were not well defined ; the boundaries of authority were somewhat confused. In the tithings, the freemen

had the right of meeting, and exercised some sort of a
jurisdiction ; they seem to have had the power of adopting local regulations, or by-laws, and also of electing
their own officers. The assemblies provided for the representation of their interests in the courts of the hundred and the shire, and performed certain duties imposed upon them by these higher courts as to taxation
and other matters. When we reach the Norman period,
we find the county the chief district of the kingdom,
with a ruler who was a revocable appointee of the king.
We find also, the hundred courts and the tithing courts.
Anglo-Saxon institutions continued in full force, and in
some respects became more sharply defined. The changes
were in the upper administrative frame-work, not in the
lower, which remained, with reference to local powers,
very much as before the conquest.

After the time of Magna Charta, about 1377, there appears a house of commons, with a speaker, yet the
county, hundred and township administrations were but
little changed. This was a period when the church had
become a great power, and was insinuating itself into all
the branches of political administration

Now appears the parish, which is the ecclesiastical
form of the old township and tithing, with boundaries
coincident with these. For nearly five hundred years,
the parish, which is the old township transformed, has
been the constitutional unit of England, and we shall
find that the parish is also the constitutional unit of the
United States, though in some of the colonies, especially
in New England, re-transformed into the township.

The first care of the old English parish was to keep the
church in repair, and attend to its ordinary business interests. It required money or labor and officers to
supervise the repairs and business. Here, then, was an

occasion furnished for the exercise of two very important functions of local self-government, the levying of taxes, and the election of officers. To do these things, and for the discussion of parish affairs, there were assemblies of all the householders of the parish at stated intervals. The beginnings of the representative system appear here, when, from among the householders the vestry was chosen. These assemblies also elected wardens, or general overseers. Then arose a system of parish taxation through a committee of the church, in part voted for, and in part nominated by superior authority. The notable fact in this connection is, that all Christian householders as such, without distinction as to freehold or copyhold, or long or short terms of land tenure, or without reference to property possession, were active members of the parish assemblies, and had a voice in discussion, and could vote. There was essential democracy.

In the course of time, the jurisdiction of the parish was enlarged, so as to include the making and repairing of roads and bridges, and the arresting and punishing of vagrants. In very early days, the sheriff of the county had appointed constables in the townships. Gradually many of the duties of this officer were transferred to the church wardens. At first the clergymen had only certain disciplinary powers in connection with the church, but little by little these were extended to offences like drunkenness, infractions of weights and measures in retail trade, and certain offences against the game laws. They became also the overseers of the poor, and had certain police functions, such as registering servants' certificates, and ordering the whipping of vagabonds. In consequence of the great increase of vagabondage, a poor-law was passed in the twenty-eighth year of the reign of Henry VIII., which was afterwards enlarged into the elaborate statute of 43d Elizabeth, which, as is well known, is the basis of the present extensive poor-law system of England.

The parish, as already suggested, became also the territorial district for the maintenance of roads. In the reign of Bloody Mary, the office of road overseer was created. For the purposes of tax assessment and local administration, standing committees were formed, and, as was the case in the old township, the parish made by-laws, or local regulations. The court of the Justices of the Peace became the parish court.

The Tudors extended the parishes to the cities, from which arose the double system of government found in England to-day, as, for instance, in London, where the "city" proper has a municipal organization, with a Mayor and Board of Aldermen, while without this small central area, but within the widely extended limits of the metropolis, there is a series of parishes, which have local administrative bodies.

There were in the time of James I., three principal parish taxes, or, as they are called in England, rates :

1. The church rate, which was granted by the community assembly for the maintenance of the church building, and the needs of the church service.

2. The poor rate, levied according to statute of Elizabeth, by the church wardens, and overseers of the poor. At this time two church wardens were appointed by the church community in conjunction with the clergyman, and in case they failed to agree in a choice, then one was appointed by each. The nomination of the overseers of the poor was made by the two Justices of the county, who were the nominees of the king, so that the direct voice of the parish householder in the levying of this tax, was, it is true, limited to the choice of one warden. Nevertheless, it is reasonable to suppose that the discussions of the

general parish assembly must have indirectly exercised a powerful influence on the other officers, appointed from rate payers, in the levying of these taxes.

3. The highway rate, which was also levied by the church wardens and overseers of the poor in the same way as the poor rate. In the time of the Tudors, there were other local taxes levied by Justices of the Peace, for repairs of bridges, for the building of county prisons, for the transport of vagrants, for the house of correction, for jail money, and for the support of poor debtors. In the time of James I. there were larger territorial administrations of a local nature; there were aggregations of parishes and boroughs and hundreds, and of these last into counties. Some of the counties, or shires, were originally kingdoms, as Kent, and Sussex.

The unit or cell, however, upon which the English system is built, is the old township, and its successor, the parish. It was here that the mass of the people were educated in local self-government. It was here that those affairs of a governmental nature which most concerned their daily lives were considered before their eyes, and in which they had more or less a part. Even those who were not householders, and had no direct voice in the discussions of the parish assemblies, could learn, more or less, of the methods of carrying on the local administration; and what was not of less import for the future, there was here, practical, political equality.

In its earlier days, the house of commons represented more particularly the aristocracy; the democracy found its expression in the parishes.

Through the force of the political instinct and the power of political tradition, small colonies sent out from a ripe nation, such as England had already become in the early part of the seventeenth century, will naturally, if allowed freedom, model their early political institutions on those prevailing in the political unit of the mother country.

The growth of new political communities from the materials of an old one may be likened to that of the human being. The new social body goes successively through all the earlier stages of social and political development, in the order in which the parent has been evolved. There is the family, the community of lands, local self-government, and, finally, the growth into the mature nationality.

This growth, however, very seldom follows the normal order ; very few colonies are left to themselves entirely. There is from the beginning constant interference on the part of the parent country, as happened to the original charter colonies which came to America during the seventeenth century. They were, more or less, hampered at the outset, with conditions imposed by the authorities at home ; but, fortunately, the internal dissensions which arose in England very soon left them largely to themselves, and we find them all falling back into a local system based upon that to which they had been accustomed at home.

The little band which sailed from England in December, 1606, and landed on the 13th of May, 1607, at the point in Virginia where Jamestown was built, consisted of one hundred and five persons. Of the first company, the greater part very soon died, victims of the hardships of pioneer life. Within a little time after the sailing of the first expedition, a second started with one hundred and twenty persons, and from time to time fresh emigrants were sent to the new settlement under the auspices of the Virginia Company. The three charters to this company of 1606, 1609, and 1611, proceed from the royal bounty of James I., and are framed upon the theory that the king is the owner of the fee in all the lands in the new country, and that whatever of political government its future inhabitants should have, would proceed from him.

These charters, which are substantially alike, are grants to a commercial or speculative corporation, composed of noblemen, knights, and also of fifty-six companies, or guilds, of traders and workmen. There was to be a council appointed by the company, which was to remain in England, and this central body named all the officers and made all the laws for the settlers. The organizers of the enterprise pretended that one of its objects was—as an address issued by them says—"to advance the kingdom of God, by reducing savage people from their blind superstition to the light of religion;" but cupidity, no doubt, led most of the shareholders to invest their money. They expected great gains from the cultivation of the new lands, but more from the anticipated discovery of mines of gold and silver. The scheme was to carry on the colony as a joint commercial and speculative adventure for a certain period, during which time it was to be substantially a single plantation under the supervision of the home company, the shareholders of which were to receive and divide the whole product.

The charter in force when the first band of emigrants sailed, provided that the king should nominate a council of thirteen to remain in England, and this body should appoint a sub-council of thirteen to reside in the colony. Both the home and the colonial councils should govern according to such laws and instructions as should be given by the king; and it was further provided that the lands were granted to the settlers in free tenure, and should be inherited and held as like estates were in England. It was further provided that jury trial should be preserved. The monarch was very careful to enact that all trade must be with the mother country, and that all goods imported into the colony must be stored in magazines belonging to the colony, and thence distributed under the direction of its officers. This original charter was modified in 1609, and again in 1611. The king gave up legislative power over the colony, transferring it to the council of the corporation in England, which was authorized to choose the governor, and in fact had unlimited control over the inhabitants. The grantees in the charter consisted of two classes : adventurers and planters. Those who invested money in the enterprise but did not go in person were the adventurers, while the planters were those whose names were mentioned in the patent, and who came in person to settle. A single share was twelve pounds ten shillings sterling. Every ordinary man and woman who came over and dwelt in the colony was allowed a share. The ingrained belief of the time in classes was shown in the provision made for what were called "extraordinary men "; that is, divines, governors, ministers of state, justices, knights, gentlemen, physicians, who were to be maintained at the common expense, and to receive their dividends at the end of seven years.

Everything was to be in common for seven years, and all products were to be returned for the common benefit, and at the end of seven years there was to be a division according to shares made by commissioners appointed by the king. It was estimated that every share would be equal to five hundred acres of land. The project of the colony contemplated three distinct ranks of persons. The extraordinary men, the planters, and the ordinary men. It was expected that the latter class would be gathered from the dregs of society. A writer of the time, speaking of the early emigrants to Virginia, describes them as

"loose, vagrant people, vicious and destitute of means to
live at home ; " and further that they "were gathered up
about the streets of London, and transported to be employed upon the plantations." Smith, in his history of
Virginia, published in 1753, finds fault with "that early
custom which arose of transporting loose and dissolute
persons to Virginia, as a place of punishment and dis-
grace."

The original colonists of Virginia were not, certainly,
promising materials with which to found a state. A very
small proportion of them were mechanics or laboring
men ; the greater part were impoverished gentlemen,
bankrupt tradesmen, and dissolute youths, who rapidly
died off. Indolence and vice had reduced the number in
1610 to only sixty persons, who were upon the point of
abandoning the colony when relieved by the arrival of
Lord Delaware, with aid and recruits. He restored a
certain degree of order among the dispirited, disorderly
settlers. After his arrival, the attempt to work in common and to support the colonists out of the common
stock was abandoned as impracticable. Then, for the
first time, individual property was allowed ; to each man
were assigned a few acres. Nevertheless the colonists continued to be treated as servants of the home corporation.
They were not allowed to return to England without
passes, and even their letters homeward were examined.

This second stage of modified servitude continued until
the arrival of Sir George Yeardley, in 1619, who published
a proclamation that every person should be freed from
the public services and labors. Then, for the first time,
the Virginia colonists began to act under free conditions.
The attempt to make laws for them in England was given
up and they assumed that function themselves, subject to
the supervisory power of the directors at home to reject

the laws framed. The connection of the colonists with the home company, however, continued only a few years longer, as James I., in 1624, procured a vacation of the charter in the courts, and from that time the relation of the colony was directly to the king.

A comparatively free political life began in 1619 upon the arrival of Sir George Yeardley. At that time there were not above six to seven hundred persons in the colony who were distributed among eleven different plantations.

It will be remembered that the original charter provided for a class of colonists known as planters who were share-holders in the company and were to come over in person. These persons distributed themselves at various points along the water courses in the neighborhood of Jamestown, and thus formed points of settlement which were called plantations. These little settlements consisted of the proprietor and his immediate family. Perhaps a few small landholders, also, who were either indented servants, who had served their time and were assigned land, or those who wished the advantages of protection and convenience found in a settlement. The larger part of the people, however, at a plantation were indented white servants, who had no voice in public affairs. These servants consisted of those who came out under contracts from England, for terms of years, or of the vagabond class transported for petty crimes and sold to planters for a certain number of years. At the suppression of Monmouth's rebellion in 1685, a large number of his followers, small farmers and farm laborers, were sold into servitude in Virginia and the Barbadoes for terms of ten years.

One is struck in looking over the colonial legislation of Virginia and the other Southern States, with the large portion of it devoted in the earlier days to the relations of masters and indented servants, and later, of master and slave. From the first, a comparatively small number possessed the power and wealth of the country, and class lines were distinctly marked.

The year after Sir George Yeardley's arrival, over twelve hundred persons, mostly indented white servants, came to the colony. Only freemen could vote, but as the white servants acquired their freedom, they were incorporated among the free citizens, and if they became householders or freeholders had a voice in public business.

The tendency of the population of Virginia, from the first, was to disperse into small communities, and even into single plantations more or less remote from one another. These plantations were the seats of single families, each, at the outset, with its complement of white servants, and later, of negro slaves. By an ordinance of the home company, which was continued in force by the king, every person removing to Virginia to settle was entitled to fifty acres of land. A husband received besides, fifty acres apiece for his wife, for each child, and for each person in addition brought to the colony at his own cost. The rights thus established were assignable, and patents were issued after survey. There was thus a constant inducement for settlers to bring as many servants with them as possible. The cultivation of tobacco was almost the sole industry from the outset, and this constantly demanded fresh land.

An estimate of the size of the farms at this early day may be gathered from the schedule of grants made in 1626, numbering one hundred and eighty-three. One was for 2,200 acres, one for 1,700, one for 1,300, one for 1,150, and two for 1,000 acres each. Of the remainder, one was for 650, and two for 600 acres; the greater number, however, were of the average size of 200 acres. These land grants were scattered at first along the York River, and afterwards, along the James, and their tributaries ; and for the purposes of protection, the early settlers held together in close neighborhood. But the village formation was unknown at the beginning ; the only pursuit, tobacco culture, forbade it. After 1611 the settlers were allowed separate ownership of land, and then they, in great part, broke loose from the leading strings of the home company. Whatever of government there was, was based upon the local institutions of the mother country. When Sir George Yeardley, in the summer of 1619, concluded to convene a general assembly, he sent a summons to his council, and as the early record states, "also for the election of burgesses." The summons was sent to eleven plantations, from each of which two delegates appeared. This assembly, the first legislative body that convened on this continent, was in session at Jamestown, only five days, "being constrained," as the record concludes, "by the intemperature of the weather, and the falling sick of diverse of the burgesses, to break up so abruptly."

It was convened in pursuance of the charter, and confined its business, first to drawing up a petition to the council of the company in England, praying the enactment of certain regulations desired by the people, and secondly, to passing upon such laws as had already been adopted by the council. They were all of a very simple nature. It is evident that the colony had already been, in some way marked off into political districts, because, in order to convert the Indians, it was enacted that "each town, city, burrough, and particular plantation, should educate a certain number of Indian children." This first legislative body established two or three very important points in Virginia. It initiated the election of the local

5

legislature by the general suffrage of all the property
holders ; it introduced representative government at a time
when it was about to enter upon a deadly struggle for its
existence in England, and it gave the right to individual
members to initiate laws, a right which is the great lever,
when controlled by the representative of the people, in
lifting their political power to the highest point.

It appears that in 1620, a certain quantity of public
land was set apart in each borough for the clergymen,
and as early as 1623-4, parishes were in existence ; for
it is provided that there shall be in every parish, a public
granary, to which shall be contributed corn, equal to one
bushel for each planter, to be disposed of for the public
use of the parish, "by the major part of the freemen."
It was further provided that three suitable men in each
parish should be sworn to see that every man planted
and tended sufficient corn for his family, whose duty it
was to present for censure to the governor and council,
those who neglected to do so. The evident object of this
regulation was to avoid the danger of famine, arising out
of an exclusive cultivation of tobacco. The church wardens were directed to present to commanders of plantations, for punishment, all persons guilty of swearing or
drunkenness. The commanders of plantations had more
of a civil than military character. About 1628-9 commissioners were appointed to hold monthly courts in some
of the more remote plantations for the trial of small cases.
The proceedings of the legislative assembly of 1619 show
that the House of Burgesses also acted as a general court
for the colony. In addition, the governor and council
had judicial powers. In 1631, an order was enacted,
that the clergyman, and at least one church warden of
every parish, were to present to the midsummer quarter
court, yearly, a register of christenings, marriages and

burials, together with an account of all disbursements in church affairs; and clergymen were directed to keep a parish register. The clergymen were to receive tithes in tobacco, corn, and domestic animals. In the assembly of 1632 there were six burgesses returned from the upper and lower parishes of Elizabeth City; three from each, showing that at that early day, these districts had a political as well as religious character. There was likewise a relation between the church wardens and the monthly courts, as the former were obliged at stated intervals to present to the latter the names of offenders violating the regulations which the wardens specially supervised. In the assembly of 1642–3, there was a sort of codification of all the old laws. These indicate that each parish had a vestry with power to make assessments and levies for repairing the church, and for other needs of the sacred society; that two or more wardens should be chosen, who, with other selectmen chosen, should form the vestry. It was provided that the commanders, who were the military chiefs, and the commissioners or judges of the county courts, which, in 1642, were the substitutes for the monthly courts, should constitute a board of visitation in parish affairs.

The democratizing tendency was early shown by the law, according to which the appointment of the clergyman was given to the vestry with the approval of the commander and of the judges of the county court, if they resided within the parish, or with the approval of the commander alone, if the judges were non-residents.

In 1634, the colony was divided into counties, which generally coincided with the parishes, though afterwards, they were, from time to time, divided into two or more parishes.

It appears that at the beginning, the little settlements known as plantations were without boundaries for political purposes. They were centres of organization in the Church of England, so that they were political and ecclesiastical units. The representatives to earlier assemblies, came, as we have seen, sometimes from the plantations, and sometimes from the parishes. The two were more or less confused.

As new counties were created, they were divided into parishes by the assembly, and even as early as 1655–7, county courts were permitted to carve out parishes in counties.

The fundamental political conditions of Virginia were fixed between 1607 and its division into counties in 1634. As already stated, the population in 1619, when the first legislature met, was less than one thousand. Immigration then began to increase rapidly. In 1622, the population of Virginia was twenty-five hundred, and in 1634, several thousands. During the progress of the civil war, and while the Puritan party was dominant in the mother country, between 1642 and 1660, there were large accessions of Royalists, and it appears that in 1648, there were fifteen thousand whites and three hundred imported negroes. Large numbers of the whites were indented servants, bound for various terms of years, but in course of time, these emerged into a condition of freedom, and many became landowners and voters.

We thus see that the unit of political organization was the plantation, which was the form assumed by the old Saxon township, and its successor, the parish, under the new conditions of emigrant life. The plantation was the township and parish rolled into one. From this point grew the county governments and parish administrations, and the plantation formed the initial elective district or borough, from which representatives were sent up to the little Parliament, the Houses of Burgesses.

Let us now turn and examine the political germs planted by the next band of Englishmen who broke away from the parent nation. The Puritans who fled to New England had, also, the hereditary political aptitudes, the acquired nature of the body of the nation from which they sprung ; they were imbued with the same political ideas as their countrymen who had crossed the ocean to Virginia, thirteen years before. In looking into the history of political institutions in New England, one is struck with the similarity in their fundamental ideas ; their substantial likeness in form, and development with those of the more southern colony.

The Puritans became voluntary exiles, in order to escape ecclesiastical tyranny at home ; they were animated solely by ardor for religious independence. Political aims were secondary, and an after-thought. They had no governmental theories to carry out, and so it is not strange that when they found themselves alone, a little band of enthusiasts on the borders of a vast wilderness, dependent upon themselves, they spontaneously fell into those ways of securing civil order which had become part of their mental constitution.

The first emigrant body was a Church congregation, which, in consequence of the persecutions set on foot by Archbishop Bancroft, escaped from England, and settled at Amsterdam, under the leadership of John Robinson, and William Brewster. Here they found two English congregations of non-conformists already settled ; one from London, the other from Gainsborough. It turned out that these three societies could not live together in harmony, and in consequence the body under Robinson and Brewster removed to Leyden, and after twelve years residence there, a large portion of it determined to go to America. They arranged with the Virginia company to occupy a portion of the lands granted to it by the king, and formed themselves, with some people in London, into a joint stock company; the latter sharing the expenses of the voyage, expecting in return a share of the anticipated profits of the adventure. This partnership was to continue seven years; all profits obtained from traffic, work, fishing or other means, were to remain in common; the colonists were to be divided into parties for various kinds of work; at the end of seven years, the capital and profits were to be divided among the stockholders, and until the division, all the colonists were to be provided with food, clothing, and other necessaries, from the common stock.

In these respects the Plymouth colony was like that in Virginia, a commercial adventure. There was, however, one essential and important difference; the Pilgrims did not have a charter directly from the king. They expected to settle within the charter limits of Virginia. It so happened that their settlement was made without those limits, and consequently they escaped the annoying control of a home corporation.

The written covenant entered into by the voyagers of the Mayflower, when they came to anchor in the roadstead near the site of Plymouth, is often referred to as a remarkable exhibition of capacity for self-government. It may not be out of place to transcribe the document.

"In the name of God, amen; we, whose names are underwritten, the loyal subjects of our dread sovereign King James, having undertaken, for the glory of God, and advancement of the Christian faith, and honor of our king and country, a voyage to plant the first colony in the northern parts of Virginia, do, by these presents, solemnly and mutually, in the presence of God and one of another, covenant and combine ourselves together into a civil

body politic, for our better ordering and preservation and
furtherance of the ends aforesaid ; and, by virtue thereof,
to enact, constitute, and frame such just and equal laws,
ordinances, acts, constitutions, and offices, from time to
time, as shall be thought most convenient for the general good of the colony.   Unto which we promise all due
submission and obedience."

All the men, forty-one in number, signed this agreement.   Bancroft in his history of the United States speaks
of it as " the birth of popular constitutional liberty."   But
this is exaggerating its significance.   When we consider
the circumstances, it can justly be regarded as merely
such a precaution as might be expected from earnest men.
It illustrates clearly, moreover, how men instinctively, as
it were, when called upon to provide for civil order, fall
back upon the common basis of physical force.   The tie,
which up to this time had held the body together, was
merely the voluntary one of a self-constituted church, the
allegiance due to common deeply cherished religious beliefs ; and the submission of its members in the interior
conduct of the church affairs to the ecclesiastical officers
chosen from themselves was merely moral and spiritual.
As long as they remained on the Mayflower they were
theoretically on the soil of England ; in fact, within its
jurisdiction, and the ship's captain represented the national
force.   At first it was intended to settle within the limits
of the Virginia Company.   When, therefore, it was re-
solved to land at a point outside of the old colony, entirely new considerations presented themselves.   The
question was, how shall the civil relations of the colonists
to each other be maintained, how shall civil order be
enforced ?   Until this moment the society had been a
voluntary collection of co-religionists ; it was now impera-
tively necessary to construct the form of the state.   Hence,

nothing more natural than that they should "covenant
and combine themselves together into a civil body politic."
The only noticeable peculiarity in their procedure is, that
they should in advance have written out the obligation
which later they would have been compelled for self-pres-
ervation to act out.   The members of the little church,
which was about to establish itself on the shores of the
new world, were, probably, as powerfully and constantly
influenced in their daily conduct by intense conviction as
those of any religious body had ever been ; their religious
and moral code was most clearly defined, but the penalties for transgression acted upon the mind and conscience
alone.   However effectual those penalties had therefore
been, it became instantly apparent to the Pilgrims when
placed face to face with the startling fact that they were
now without the pale of civil society, that they must use
the means which men in all ages have used to maintain
civil order.   Perhaps comment upon this elementary fact
would be unnecessary, were there not a constant tendency
to confuse the general or even particular motives which
actuate men with their methods of accomplishing their
ends through the agency of the state.

   Now, the motives which carried the Pilgrims to New
England were of a much higher order than those which
influenced the adventurers who hoped to better their for-
tunes in Virginia ; but all alike, when they set about
building up a state started from the same political unit,
worked in the same general way, and all advanced towards
the common end of reconstructing a nation.

   The Plymouth Colony was a trading partnership as
well as a church congregation.   Whatever of government
there was, was exercised by one of its members, aided by
another called an assistant.   Both were chosen by a majority of voices.   The colony grew but slowly.   At the

end of four years there were only one hundred and eighty
persons, with a village of thirty-two cabins. It maintained
its separate existence for seventy years, at the end of which
time it is estimated to have contained not above eight
thousand persons. The land was treated as partnership
property, and was distributed proportionately to the contributions made by the several members to the payment
of the debt which had been incurred in sending out the
colony. At the end of the seven years the partnership
with the English company was dissolved, and the debt
due the latter was assumed by some of the prominent
men among the colonists. A new partnership was then
formed among the latter, in which every freeman had a
share. A division of the stock and land then took place.
The colonists were now in an emancipated condition
similar to that of the Virginia settlers when they gave up
working in common, except that they had not, as already
remarked, a charter from the king.

In sixteen years the population materially increased,
and little settlements, offshoots from the parent stem,
were planted in the immediate neighborhood. During
this period the few necessary laws had been adopted in
mass meeting by a majority of voices of the freeman. In
1636, a committee of eight from three of the towns,
Plymouth, Scituate, and Duxbury, was appointed to
codify the laws, and upon its report the form of government was somewhat modified. There were to be a governor, seven assistants, a treasurer, a coroner, a clerk, a
constable, and other inferior officers annually elected. It
was further provided that the town of Plymouth could
elect four, and the other towns two deputies each to the
general court, with power to make laws. At the same
time the power of legislating was preserved to the whole
body of freemen when assembled. In 1664 there were

5*

seven towns besides Plymouth, which then received the
title to their common lands. The governor and any two
of his assistants had a power, remarkable in a democratic
community, of expelling any person from the colony
whom they did not like.

The desire for religious freedom, was, no doubt, the
principal motive influencing the Puritan Church at Leyden
to remove to America, but it is also evident that the
longing to become again a part of the British nation was
also a strong impulse, acting upon men who felt themselves out of place in a strange land, and who feared that
their descendants would be absorbed into a foreign nation.

Nine years after the settlement at Plymouth, a new
project of Puritan colonization ripened into the corporation known as the Governor and Company of the Massachusetts Bay in New England.   It received a charter
from Charles I., which continued in force fifty-five years.
This charter authorized the freemen of the corporation
to elect annually from their own number a governor,
deputy governor, and eighteen assistants; and also to
make laws and ordinances not repugnant to the laws of
England.   It was a charter intended, more especially,
for the government of the corporation in England.

A little while after the grant to the company, a very
important step was determined upon by its members.
This was the transfer and settlement of the corporation in
New England.   It was a means of preserving the new
community from undue interference from the crown,
until many years after the restoration of Charles II., and
thus allowed time for local self-government to become
firmly established.   In the summer of 1630, a company
of about one thousand persons, under the leadership of
that noble, if somewhat narrow man, John Winthrop,

came over and laid the foundations of the colony of Massachusetts. The design of its projectors in England was, to furnish a place of refuge for persecuted non-conformists, where they could worship as their consciences dictated. All Englishmen could become members of the Massachusetts Company, but no one could vote, or take a share in the government of the colony, or the election of governor, until he had been elected a freeman by those already free-men. The congregational system of church government was adopted before the emigrants left England, and when they were fairly seated in their new home it was ordered at the first general court in 1631, that no man should be eligible to be a freeman unless he was a member of some one of the churches within its limits. No churches were permitted to be established, unless in harmony with the parent church, and as a great number of persons settled in the colony who were not members of the church, the result was that the voting power was, in not a very long time, in the hands of a minority. In 1634, four years after the arrival of the colony, it was estimated that there were between three and four thousand English persons in the several settlements, but the freemen, the voters, numbered only three hundred and fifty. In the first year a change was made in the distribution of power, by the delegation of important attributes to the assistants. These were to be in the future the only officers chosen by the company at large and they were empowered to elect the governor and deputy governor. The making of laws and appointing officers to execute them was entrusted to the assistants, and their appointees, the governor and deputy. This created a sort of oligarchy, which continued but a short time, as in 1632, its power was curtailed somewhat, by the direct election of the governor and deputy by the freemen, though from among the assistants.

The new immigration had distributed itself into eight
"plantations." At first it was the practice for all the
freemen of these neighboring little settlements to go up
to Boston, to hold the general court, twice in the year.
At the outset, the assembled freemen must have been
merely an approving or listening body, a sort of conference for discussion. The substantial power, however,
of proposing, or at least of passing laws, was in the
governor, deputy governor, and assistants. At this early
day the assistants had exercised the power of levying
taxes, though even then it was opposed and was finally
abandoned.

In 1632 the germ of a lower house in legislation made
its appearance in consequence of an order of the general
court that each plantation should choose two persons to
confer with the court about raising "a public stock," that
is, taxes. Two years afterwards, the number of settlements
or plantations had increased to sixteen, containing three to
four thousand inhabitants. The most distant, Ipswich, was
thirty miles, and it was unsafe and inconvenient for all
the freemen to leave at one time in order to go to the
general court, so, naturally, the system of representation
was adopted, and each plantation sent two delegates to
the court. At this time, also, the oligarchical cast of the
government was modified. Winthrop told the deputies
that the supposition had been when the patent was
granted, that the number of freemen would be limited so
as not to be too great to be conveniently assembled for
the transaction of public business, but as the numbers had
greatly increased they could now better act through representatives; but he added, "for the present they were not
furnished with a sufficient number of men qualified for
such a business ; neither could the commonwealth bear
the loss of time of so many as must attend it." He would,

therefore, only consent to the appointment of a committee each year to revise the laws but not to make any new ones, reserving however to the representative body a decisive voice in levying taxes. The democratic spirit of the people rebelled against this assumption of power, and Winthrop was not re-elected governor, and the freemen proceeded to affirm by a resolve of the general court that that was the only body which had power to choose and admit freemen, to make laws, to elect officers, to raise money by taxation, and to dispose of lands. They went further and abridged the judicial power of the assistants, ordering that capital cases, and those involving banishment should only be tried before a jury ordered by the freemen of the plantations. It was now directed that there should be four general courts in the year. This revolution in affairs introduced a government representing the freemen, and lodged the law-making power in a representative legislature.

During the next fifty years, and until the abrogation of the charter, the administration remained substantially the same. The magistrates, that is the governor, deputy governor, and assistants, were chosen by a joint vote of the freemen. The settlements, which were originally known as *plantations*, but which about 1632–4 began to be known as *towns*, elected, through their freemen, deputies or representatives to the general court, which held two annual sessions instead of four.

The legislative body or general court, consisted of the governor, deputy governor, and assistants, in conjunction with the representatives of the towns. During this half century the legislature was divided into two bodies, sitting apart, and each having a negative on the other. The upper house consisted of the governor, deputy governor, and assistants ; the lower, of the representatives of the towns. At first the ousiness of the towns was transacted at meetings of its freemen, but very soon, within three or four years, a custom arose of designating a committee to supervise affairs during the intervals between these general meetings, whose members were finally known as selectmen. The custom was, to continue these in office only one year. It is worthy of note that as early as 1634 election by ballot came into vogue.

The judicial system was, at the same time, made more perfect. The general court was still the highest tribunal, but to facilitate business quarterly courts were established to be held four times a year in Boston and in three other towns.

At the outset, as is always the case in communities in process of formation, powers were confused, but by degrees these were separated and defined. Especially was this the case as to towns. The powers of the town were derived from the general body of the community, but what these powers were was not at first clearly outlined. In 1634, the general court, in order to define them, provided that the freemen of every town had authority to dispose of lands and woods, grant lots, make orders respecting the welfare of their towns not repugnant to the laws and orders established by the general court, impose fines not exceeding twenty shillings, and choose constables and surveyors for highways. An attempt was made two years later to regulate the right of representation on the basis of population, but finally in 1639 each town was allowed two representatives in the general court.

In 1643 there was a further development in administration ; the towns then thirty in number were distributed into four counties. Already four quarterly courts existed, which corresponded to the new divisions, and there was also a military organization by which the militia were

locally divided into four regiments, the militia of each
county being placed under command of a lieutenant corresponding to the lord-lieutenant of the English shire.
In this year the division of the legislature into two bodies
was accomplished ; the magistrates in one, the popular
delegates in the other.

Religious intolerance drove Roger Williams in 1636
from the Massachusetts Bay Colony. The little settlement which he founded at Providence at first consisted of
a single township based upon a written contract, which affirmed that : " We, whose names are here under, desirous
to inhabit in the town of Providence, do promise to subject ourselves, in active or passive obedience, to all such
orders or agreements as shall be made for public good of
the body in an orderly way, by the major assent of the
present inhabitants, masters of families, incorporated
together into a township, and such others whom they shall
admit unto them, only in civil things." This was the
first instance of the separation of church and state.

New settlements were formed in the neighborhood of
the first, and for three or four years each was independent
of the others. In 1640 a general court was held, which
appears to have consisted of all the heads of families who
had been admitted as members of the different townships.
It was a pure democracy, which, far in advance of the
bigotry of the age, permitted freedom of opinion in
religion.

Connecticut was also an offshoot of the Massachusetts
Bay Colony, and owes its settlement to those who were
opposed to the decision of the general court in 1636,
which restricted the voting franchise to those only, who
were members of churches recognized and admitted by
the magistrates and a majority of the elders. The new

colony broadened the basis of the suffrage by not limiting the franchise to church members. Beyond political reasons for the migration, no doubt the inducement with many was the exceeding fertility of the valley of the Connecticut. The first immigration settled in four plantations. On the theory that they were all within the jurisdiction of Massachusetts, the earliest administration of the common affairs of the four plantations was through a commission of eight appointed by the general court of that colony. Local affairs were attended to in township meetings. In the second year the commission was abolished and a general court of the colony convened. The New Haven Colony was established through the consolidation of several small settlements in the southern part of the new territory. This new colony was not as liberal with the voting franchise as its neighbor, prohibiting those from voting for magistrates or delegates to the general court, who were not church members.

In 1639 a settlement was commenced at Exeter, within the present limits of New Hampshire, a church established, and a political organization formed ; a democracy, in which the whole body enacted laws. Other small settlements of a similar character, and taking on the plantation or township form of political administration were made as far east as the Piscataqua River, and even into the present limits of Maine.

During the period of twenty-two years succeeding the landing of the Pilgrims at Plymouth, English Puritan settlements had scattered themselves at various points, more or less isolated, over a wide expanse of territory, extending from the borders of Maine to Long Island Sound. There were five separate political bodies, four of which, Plymouth, Massachusetts Bay, Connecticut, and

New Haven, were formed, in 1643, into the confederacy, known as the United Colonies of New England, the remaining one, Rhode Island, standing aloof.

This confederacy then embraced a population of about twenty-four thousand persons, fifteen thousand being in Massachusetts, three thousand each in Plymouth and Connecticut, and twenty-five hundred in New Haven.

This was at the period when in the mother country the Roundheads and Cavaliers had come to blows, and the colonies were left largely to themselves.

The political and social foundations of the New England colonies were now laid ; subsequent changes were only developments from forms at this time established. Emigration almost entirely ceased after the commencement of the civil war, and the growth was thenceforth the natural increase of the population.

The political unit of New England was the "plantation," which grew around a church congregation, as in Virginia it had grown around the farms of the "planters," mentioned in the charter of King James. In New England, as we have seen, the plantation, which was in fact the congregation, became the town, with territorial boundaries, and a corporate character. The town was the analogue of the parish in England and Virginia. If all the inhabitants of an English Parish had been bodily transferred to New England, in 1630, and thrown upon their own resources, they would, naturally, have fallen into the methods of conducting local affairs through meetings at intervals, of all householders who were church members, and they would have appointed a vestry, or church wardens, or selectmen, to supervise affairs during the intervals, or for stated periods. The English parish was in those days a local democracy of householders, with, it is true, a limited range of powers, because of the development above it of a complicated system of national administration ; but its characteristics were such that, if taken out of the nation, and transferred to a wilderness, it could instantly adapt itself to the new conditions, by simply extending the range of its powers ; because the changes that would have been necessary would have been only such as the new circumstances made imperative.

As stated, the basis of each plantation in New England was a church congregation. The one which came over in the Mayflower, was Brownist or Separatist, and had been formed at the time of the withdrawal of this sect from the Church of England. The Separatists subsequently became, in the old country, the powerful sect of Independents. They deemed that a national church was not justified by the word of God, and claimed the right to elect their own pastors, and to manage their own internal church affairs. It was a democratic movement in the Church of England, connected with the greater democratic upheaval of the Reformation, and more particularly with the religious movements in Germany, even antedating Calvin. As early as 1523-4, twelve years before the appearance of the Institutes of the great Genevese, the Landgrave Philip of Hesse, in conjunction with the spiritual estate of his realm, held a synod, at which a scheme of independent church government was framed. The churches could admit any citizen of irreproachable life, and competent instruction. Each parish or congregation was obliged to set apart a certain number of its members for military service, and to have a common fund, to which all should contribute, and out of which the poor and persecuted should receive assistance. There was entire independence of the several church communities. Every year, the churches, represented by their elected bishops and deputies, were to assemble in general synod to hear complaints and resolve doubts. This scheme, it is probable, furnished the model upon which Calvin framed his laws, and upon which the French Protestants, and the Scotch and Puritan Churches were founded.

Calvin's plan of church government was not so democratic. The clergy predominated in the two courts which managed church affairs, but there were two democratic features. All nominations of pastors had to be approved by the members of the church, and there was a lay representation in the consistorial court of discipline. The self-governing quality of these new churches was an attractive feature to the Separatists in England, who were mostly composed of poor and radical people. At first the non-conformists did not go as far as the Separatists. Their effort was to reform the parent church, but they very soon found themselves subjected to the Acts of Supremacy, and of Uniformity, passed in the reign of Elizabeth, and were finally driven to deny the supremacy of the crown in religious matters. The original settlers of Massachusetts Bay Colony, and their offshoots in Connecticut, were non-conformists, though when they came over in 1630 they stood toward the government in much the same attitude as the Separatists. They had no common church government of their own, but were split up into separate congregations, each managing its own spiritual and temporal affairs.

Yet, while the church tie and organization were so powerful, and the colonists of Plymouth and Massachusetts Bay were so careful to confine the voting power to church members, it is still clearly evident that their local political institutions were modeled upon the parish system to which they had been accustomed at home.

The town being the unit, the county was an aggregation of towns; and, subsequently, the counties and
the towns were the political divisions of the state.

In the Massachusetts colony, at the period of the New
England Confederacy of 1643, the freemen of each town
could choose not to exceed nine selectmen, who could
exercise certain restricted powers. At stated intervals the
freemen could assemble in town meeting, and pass laws
concerning the general welfare, provided they were of a
"prudential nature," not repugnant to the general laws
of the colony, and the penalties of which should not
exceed twenty shillings. Although it is not clear what
powers the freemen of the "plantations" and parishes
of Virginia exercised prior to 1640, yet there is little
doubt that they took upon themselves the local authority,
in temporal matters, of an English parish, and extended
this authority to meet the new exigencies of pioneer life.
It is certain that, in 1662, the house of burgesses passed
an act which in terms provided that counties and parishes
should be allowed by a majority vote to make laws for
cases where there was no general law. This was probably a legislative recognition of an existing practice, as
was undoubtedly the case when the Massachusetts general court in 1641, defined the powers of towns.

There was this marked difference, however, between
the New England colonies and Virginia, that the freemen
of the former elected their executive officers annually,
while in the latter the greater part of them were appointed by the governor, who was, at first, the appointee of
the home corporation, and subsequently of the king.
Some, it is true, were appointed by the governor in conjunction with his councilors. This early assumption by
the New Englanders of control of the executive branch
of the government marks a distinct step in the direction

of democracy beyond the Virginians. It was in this manner that the democratic structure of the Puritan churches was distinctly reflected. They had cut loose from the king as head of the church, and they had transferred to their new home the seat of the corporation which held the royal charter. Under these circumstances, they did what the corporation, if it had remained in old England, would have done, elected their own officers by the body of freemen.

Turning now to New York, we find that it owed its first settlement, like many other colonies, to a speculative corporation. The Dutch West India Company, under its charter from the government of the Netherlands, undertook to colonize the new territory in the neighborhood of the Hudson River. It is not necessary to our purpose to examine very closely the history of this commercial venture, because the Dutch régime made little or no impression politically, however great its impression socially, upon the future State. As early as 1630, a feudal element was introduced, which afterwards was the occasion of considerable agitation about land tenures, even late in this century. This was in consequence of the large grants of land made to the patroons, under conditions of colonization, and with certain governmental prerogatives attached to them. The elements of local self-government then existing in Holland were not transplanted. It is from the capture by the English in 1664 that the political life of New York dates.

The first body of laws was, in part, borrowed from New England. These laws, it is true, were only made, at first, applicable to Long Island, which was largely settled by people from the eastern colonies. In each town, eight men were to be chosen as overseers by the freeholders for

one year. A constable was also annually chosen by the
freeholders ; and the overseers and constables had power
to make local ordinances for the town. This is a variation from the New England town meeting system, and
furnishes the model for the local arrangement prevailing
in most of the middle and western states, where it is
customary for the voters to elect supervisors or overseers,
who enact the laws of the county or township. The
sheriff and justices of the peace were appointed by the
governor, taxes were assessed annually in each town.
There were parishes also, with church wardens elected
annually by the overseers and constables. The clergyman
was elected by the major part of the householders. No
person could be disturbed on account of religious belief.
When, later, the English were securely in possession of
the country, the government was very rapidly shaped in
conformity with the parent system.

The eastern part of New Jersey was, at first, under
the influence of the Dutch West India Company, and,
like New York, did not have local self-government until it
also came into the possession of the English.

As early as 1677, western New Jersey was purchased
by the Quakers, and they immediately adopted, in the
settled portions, a system which recognized democratic
political equality and religious freedom. They even
went to the extent of requiring the elected deputies to
the general assembly to promise in a sealed agreement to
obey the instructions of their constituents.

The Maryland charter to Lord Baltimore was issued
in 1632. It conferred legislative power upon the Lord
Proprietor, together with a majority of the colonists, or
their deputies. Every freeman could participate in
making the laws, in person or by proxy, and, at the out-

set, all the colonists were privileged to meet in general assembly. As the colony grew, the local government was carried on in hundreds; each of which
elected the burgesses to the legislative body. For a long
time, the Lord Proprietor was vested with a singular
power, that of summoning by special writ any person
whose presence he particularly desired, to participate in
legislation. By this means, he could at any time obtain
control of the lower house through his friends. At first
there was but one house, but finally two, an upper and
lower. The governmental unit was the hundred. In
course of time counties were formed. In 1671, there
were seven, containing a total population of about 20,000.
Local self-government appears to have been more restricted than in Virginia, as most of the officers were
appointed by the Proprietor. His power was hereditary,
and, naturally, tended constantly to become despotic.
The disposition for freedom and equality which seemed to
spring up spontaneously on American soil, excited the
people to struggle for the privileges of self-government.

Religious tolerance prevailed until 1692, when the
Church of England was established, and the colony was
divided into parishes, each of which was subject to taxation for the support of a clergyman.

The religious tolerance which prevailed in colonial
Maryland, so much vaunted, and so often contrasted with
the narrow intolerance common in New England, was
evidently dictated by worldly prudence, rather than
prompted by an advanced charity. It must be remembered, that at that time, the feeling in England was bitterly hostile to the Papists, and that the grant of lands to
Lord Baltimore was from a Protestant monarch, of a
portion of the territory claimed by Virginia, a Protestant
colony. Considerations of prudence, also, forbade exciting

the animosity of the Puritan colonies of New England.
Obviously, therefore, Lord Baltimore, whatever might
have been his disposition, could not, with safety, have
founded his new settlement upon the basis of intolerance.
Evidently the prosperity of his dominions was linked
with liberality in religion, because a contrary policy
would have· brought upon him not only the especial
enmity of Virginia, but also the decided ill-will, and
possible active hostility, of the mother country and New
England. Besides, he was sufficiently worldly-minded to
hope to make his colony profitable, and by leaving the
door wide open to all, it would become so, and at the
same time afford an asylum to his persecuted co-
religionists.

We have another illustration of the formation of democratic self-government in the early settlements along the
borders of Albemarle Sound in the present State of
North Carolina. A small body of emigrants from New
England, with others who subsequently joined them from
other quarters, immediately adopted a simple form of
government. There was a council of twelve, six of
whom were nominated by the proprietors, and six by the
assembly, which body was elected by the freeholders of
the settlement. A little later, in 1670, a new body of
emigrants from England landed in what is now South
Carolina. The Carolinas had been granted to eight proprietors, who projected an elaborate, impracticable system of government, which, when the attempt was made
to apply it to the infant settlement of scattered planters,
was so ludicrously out of proportion, and so unsuitable
to the new conditions, as to fall immediately into substantial desuetude.

The "Fundamental Constitutions of Carolina" sought

to establish a government on monarchical principles, in order, as expressed in them, to "avoid erecting a numerous democracy." A kind of feudal system was ordained, in which there should be a palatine, also admirals, chamberlains, chancellors, constables, chief justices, high stewards, and treasurers chosen from among the proprietors. The province was to be divided into counties, these into seignories, baronies, and precincts, to be owned by an hereditary nobility which should consist of landgraves and caciques. The power of alienating their domains was denied to the nobility. The common people were to be known as leetmen, and were to be under the jurisdiction of the respective lords of the seignories. Nor would any leetman or leetwoman have liberty to remove from the land of his or her particular lord without his license in writing ; and all the children of leetmen were to be leetmen from generation to generation.

An elaborate system of courts was provided for, among others a chamberlain's court with jurisdiction to regulate all fashions, habits, badges, games, and sports. A parliament was contemplated with a house of nobility, and a lower house composed of one freeholder from each precinct, who owned at least five hundred acres of land, and who was to be elected by freeholders, possessed of fifty acres each. It seems almost impossible that so absurd a scheme of polity could have been suggested for a body of Anglo-Saxon immigrants in a wilderness, by men, some of whom, like Shaftesbury, were practical statesmen, and that it should be acquiesced in by so clear-headed a thinker as Locke. A recent biographer of Locke* remarks that the plan was initiated by Shaftesbury, and modified by his fellow proprietors, but that Locke had a large share

* H. R. Bourne.

6

in the work, though some of its features were distinctly
at variance with views previously expressed by him.

These constitutions are, however, worthy of study as
indications of the ideals of the ruling class and leaders of
opinion in England on government and society. Their
framers saw in the virgin fields of the Carolinas an opportunity to build up a prosperous state on what they believed to be true social principles. Their plan shows
what a strong hold feudal ideas still had on the ruling
classes. It is a striking confirmation of the truth that
political freedom finds its nourishment and growth among
the mass of the common people and not among social and
intellectual leaders. The redeeming feature in the scheme
was the broad tolerance in religion, which, no doubt was
the result in part of the actual indifference, if not positive
skepticism of some of the proprietors, but, more probably,
because the enterprise was at bottom like most of the colonial undertakings of that day, a huge land jobbing
scheme, and the object was to draw settlers from the
dissenters. In point of fact, many Puritans did go to the
colony.

The colonists never tolerated these absurd constitutions.
The attempt to enforce them, together with the constant
interference of the proprietors, obstructed for a long
time the natural effort to frame local democratic institutions. Even the people would accept only such regulations of the proprietors, made from time to time, as they
thought useful.

In the earlier years there were three governments in the
two Carolinas ; one at Albemarle, one at Cape Fear, and
one at Charleston. These were really no more than single
counties each presided over by a governor. In the first
years of the settlement the people, disregarding the constitutions, met at Charleston, and elected representatives

for the purpose of making laws. As already stated, many Puritans had been attracted to the new colony, and they, with other dissenters, constituted the most numerous party in the country. A number of Cavaliers having received grants, brought over their families and very soon secured most of the appointments within the gift of the proprietors. Before long there were two distinct parties, the Cavalier or aristocratic, and the democratic or Puritan. Between 1700 and 1719, the hostility between them became virulent, and at last in the latter year the people disavowed the proprietary government, and transferred their allegiance directly to the king. The general framework of the government under which they now continued until the revolutionary war, consisted of a governor and council appointed by the king. The governor being invested, as far as compatible, with the executive and judicial powers of the English monarch. The council was the upper legislative branch ; the assembly consisted of representatives elected by the freeholders.

Prior to 1704, there appear to have been parishes. In that year, a carefully drawn statute was adopted, regulating church affairs. The boundaries of parishes were designated. The clergyman was to be elected by the major part of the inhabitants of the parish, who were of the Church of England, and were freeholders or taxpayers. In each parish nine vestrymen were to be elected annually, also two church-wardens. All church-rates were to be levied by the vestrymen. It appears also that the delegates to the assembly were elected from the parishes. In 1740, the government, when the new system had been in force twenty years, consisted of the governor, twelve councilors appointed by the king, and an assembly of forty-four members, elected every third year by the freeholders of sixteen parishes. Some of the executive officers were appointed by the crown, and some by the assembly. The administration was so arranged that the power to initiate laws, and to regulate the amount of taxes, their custody and disbursement, were in the hands of the landholders, while the executive and administrative branches charged with the details of public affairs were in the hands of the representatives of the crown.

As was the case in all the colonies, so in the Carolinas, the king had a veto power over all legislation. At the period last spoken of, 1740, there were in South Carolina about twenty-five thousand whites, and thirty-nine thousand negro slaves.

North Carolina, in 1729, was separated from South Carolina, and thenceforth, as a royal province, was governed in substantially the same form as the latter. Its primary division was into three counties. There were also parishes. At that time the whole of the scattered population did not exceed ten thousand.

It is not necessary to linger long over the governmental foundations of Pennsylvania. They were from the beginning very nearly as democratic as those of Massachusetts. There was a council consisting of an upper house, whose members were elected for three years, one-third being annually renewed ; there was also an assembly chosen annually. At first a strange custom prevailed, by which the laws were proposed by the governor and council, and then submitted to the people in their local meetings ; if these proposed laws were approved, the assembly reported the decision to the people. This peculiar system was, however, very soon modified, so that the assembly proposed such laws as it desired, and a veto power was left in the governor. The people elected most of the executive officers, except the governor. The government developed rapidly into democracy, for as early as 1696,

the governor had became no more than the chairman of
the council, the tenure of the judiciary depended upon
the legislature, and rotation in office was insisted upon by
the people.

Georgia was founded more for benevolent objects than
for gain ; it was intended as a place of refuge for poor
debtors. The charter was designed for a close corporation,
as all power was given for twenty-one years to the trustees.
When the first band of one hundred and sixteen settlers
arrived, the new territory was laid off into eleven townships, lying along the river. Each township was to form
a parish, and when it had one hundred families was to
have the right to send two members to an assembly. The
attempt of the home trustees of the corporation to carry
on the government of their distant possession in the
parental way proved in this, as in all instances where
similiar attempts were made, an utter failure. The
colonists, and the servants who were sent over, deserted,
when they could, to the neighboring colonies. Those
who remained, complained bitterly of the restrictions upon
the tenure and leasing of lands. They complained also
of the method of cultivation, because negro slavery was
denied ; and moreover that they were not given a sufficient voice in the government. At last, after twenty years'
experiment, the proprietors surrendered the charter, and in
1752, the king made Georgia a royal government, to be
under the control of the Board of Trade and Plantations.

A government was, thereupon, framed similar to those
prevailing in the neighboring colonies.

CHAPTER IX.

In beginning with a system of local self-government
analogous to the parish system of England and developing through counties into states, the British colonies
within the present limits of the United States were moved
to a very great extent by the inherent force of a political
instinct. The impulses to a closer union of these separate
colonies and to their fusion into a nation can be traced,
in part also, to external causes, which accelerated a growth
that might otherwise have required a long period of time
to develop a nation.

The especially noticeable feature of the progress of the
British colonies is, that whenever the first colonists were
left to themselves to arrange their own political relations,
they fell spontaneously into a local self-government analogous to the parish system they had been accustomed to
at home ; and as soon as it became necessary they naturally adopted a parliamentary system of government to the
extent at least of having representatives elected by the
householders, and of having two houses of legislation.

The passengers who landed from the Mayflower constituted, at first, a little sovereignty ; and while in the
isolated and self-dependent condition of the first two
decades of the settlement, they adopted methods of administration which in large part remained structurally the
same when the community was merged into the larger
province. There was at first the church congregation,

the members of which alone had the privilege of voting. In England every householder was obliged by law to contribute to the support of the parish church, whether technically a member or not, and in return he was allowed a voice in parish affairs. In New England the funda-mental idea was the same. The pivot around which the political life of the new settlement revolved at first, was also the church. The church congregation was turned into the town, as in earlier days the town was turned into the parish in England. In the other colonies, a parish system, more or less modified, appears as the basis of local self-government. These parishes, or plantations, or towns, have local officers, like selectmen, or overseers, and the power through local assemblies to make local laws. The further process of growth was through the union of these several primitive communities, into coun-ties, with special officers and jurisdictions, and the union of the counties into the province or the State.

It is true the political development of the colonies did not go on in this orderly manner. In most of them there appeared a simultaneous evolution of the different parts ; but this was only because there was a rapid repro-duction of the national growth of the parent, which had been centuries in reaching the national unity it had acquired in the early part of the seventeenth century.

A great variety of circumstances, external as well as internal, controlled and shaped the aggregation of the primal units into larger political bodies. It is only in the history of each nation that the physical and intellectual conditions can be discerned which moulded it into its present shape. England is as much indebted to the span of water which separates her from the Continent, as to the sturdy qualities of her people, for her parliament-ary government ; and certainly the United States may

ascribe the free political institutions it now enjoys, in part
to its geographical position, as well as to the genius of
the pioneers.

Reverting to the colonial life of our country, we see
that there were also external forces operating in the direction of nationality.

The settlements during the first century and a half
kept very close to the Atlantic seaboard, and the principal
bays and rivers connecting with the ocean.   These settlements had very rapidly formed themselves into distinctive
political communities ; that is, distinctive in many particulars as to each other, but all bound by a common tie
to Great Britain.   By 1760, each colony had a government in essence, though not in all its forms, like that of
the mother country.   There was a single executive head ;
an upper chamber of legislation, in some elected, in some
appointed ; a lower legislative branch directly elected by
the people, and a judiciary to pass upon disputes between
members.   Moreover, each colony was divided into territorial subdivisions, such as counties or towns, in which,
subject to the superior legislative power of the general
assembly, the people could make local laws, and in
many, though not in all, elect the officers to execute the
general as well as local statutes.   These structural forms
had grown almost spontaneously and very rapidly, and in
their growth they follow the natural development of the
already matured institutions of the mother country.   The
variation from the parent form was in the enlargement
and elaboration of local self-government, and, in the New
England States and Pennsylvania, in the frequent elections
of executive officers.

The territorial sovereignty was British.   Each colony
was only a subordinate local government ; all were part
of the greater kingdom.   The influences which impelled

the colonies to a closer union arose from external dangers. As early as 1643 there was, as already mentioned, a confederation of the four principal New England colonies : Massachusetts, Plymouth, Connecticut, and New Haven. The written compact which they entered into gives as a reason for their action, that they "live encompassed with people of several nations, and strange languages, which may hereafter prove injurious to us or our posterity ;" and in addition, referring to the distractions in England, in consequence of which they were thrown entirely upon their own resources, concludes that it is : "Our bounden duty without delay to enter into a present convocation amongst ourselves for mutual help and strength."

The proposed confederation was based upon three ideas : 1. The practical severance of the colonies from the sovereign power in consequence of the civil war in England ; 2. A danger from foreigners directed against them as Englishmen, and a danger from savages directed against them in common ; 3. Because they were one in nation and religion and should therefore in other respects be one.   These ideas rested upon the anterior sentiment of a common nationality.

This confederation continued with, one may say, diminishing force for nearly half a century. It was in many respects in the nature of a sovereignty, but it contained the inherent defect common to federations between independent states, where the delegated central power can deal only with the states and not directly with the individuals in the states.

In three or four years after the formation of the confederacy a serious dispute arose between the three smaller colonies on one side and Massachusetts on the other. Again, in a few years new dissensions arose, and threats

6*

of dissolving the confederacy were loudly expressed. Its greatest vigor was naturally prior to 1660, when the attention of the home authorities was almost entirely withdrawn from the colonies in consequence of their domestic troubles ; but when Charles II. was restored to the throne renewed attention was given to the American dependencies, and the confederacy rapidly lost importance.

Again, prior to 1688, a series of French missions and trading posts had been established along the St. Lawrence from its mouth to the waters connecting it with Lake Champlain and down through western New York and Pennsylvania, taking in the valley of the Mississippi, and extending to the mouth of that river. The base from which these were projected was a growing French colony in lower Canada.

After William III., the implacable enemy of Louis XIV., ascended the throne of England in 1688, the effort of France during the succeeding seventy-four years was to establish itself in North America and to harass the English colonies settled there. The French were constantly intriguing with the Indians with the result of almost continuous warfare between the savages and colonists in which the French were more or less implicated, so that, with the French colonies in Canada and the cruisers of the enemy on the ocean, the weak communities scattered at intervals over a narrow strip of territory, about twelve hundred miles long and not much above an average of one hundred miles in depth from the shore line, were constantly menaced in front on the coast and in the rear and flanks in the wilderness.

This continual pressure naturally brought the colonies into increasingly closer relations. As early as 1690, a congress of delegates from Massachusetts, Connecticut, and New York met at Manhattan and planned an expedition against Canada. Subsequently, from time to time, there were congresses or joint conferences of governors of the colonies to consult as to defence against Indians, or to arrange for quotas of men and money for attacks on the French in the North. Sometimes these conferences were by governors alone, but often they were accompanied by deputies from their colonies who were usually called commissioners. Before the close of the French war, writers and politicians had advocated the idea of uniting all the colonies under one royal government. At the congress of commissioners from the colonies north of the Potomac, which met at Albany in 1754 to consider questions concerning the common defence and to treat with the Six Nations of Indians, and other tribes, Franklin presented his plan of a union of all the colonies. This proposal was favorably received by the assembled commissioners, and directed to be laid before each of the colonies. It, however, excited opposition on both sides of the Atlantic. In England it was thought too democratic ; in America that it inclined too much to prerogative. The most noticeable feature in the matter is the evident existence of a body of public opinion of imposing weight in its favor ; and that the feeling and conception of community of interests and ideas was quite general in the colonies. We see in this the beginnings of a national consciousness.

The growth of nationality was also aided by the early literature of the colonies. Moses Coit Tyler in his " History of American Literature," traces its gradual expansion. At first isolated, provincial, feeble, and timid, it became broader in its tone and sympathies, and by 1763, had in a degree drawn the leaders of opinion into intellectual relations with one another. Already each section had its mental tone. Naturally the grim analytical qualities of Calvinism prevailed in New England, while

in Virginia and the south the gay, sensuous side of the
English mind was represented, though everywhere the
conditions of pioneer life inclined the people to practical,
rather than imaginative writings.   Burke, before the revolutionary war, remarked the aptness and fondness of the
Americans for legal studies.

The newspaper press also strengthened the bonds of
union.   In 1765 there were as many as forty-two journals
in the different provinces.   It is true original discussion
did not occupy much of their space ; nevertheless, even with
its comparatively feeble limitations, the newspaper press
was a subtle and powerful force in the direction of nationality, because, even through its scanty scraps of news, it
accustomed the people to interest themselves in affairs
beyond the narrow bounds of their own colony.   The colleges were also potent in cultivating largeness of view and
breadth of sympathy.   Harvard, Yale, William and Mary,
Princeton, and Columbia were already firmly established
in 1763.   The cultivation of the physical sciences had
also made some progress and brought its votaries more or
less into fellowship.

In 1763 the pressure of the war with France and her
Indian allies was lifted from the colonies by the treaty of
peace between England, France, and Spain, by which
England obtained Canada, Florida, Louisiana to the
Mississippi, and Acadia.   This event is justly considered
a turning point in our history.   The colonies had now
become self-dependent ; their populations largely homogeneous, and when the assistance of the mother country
ceased to be necessary, the tie which held them to her
was thenceforth merely a traditional one.   The young
nation began then to feel its own individuality.

At this time a broad statesmanship would have fostered
the autonomy of the colonies.   England has been wise

enough since our Revolutionary war to pursue this liberal policy with her dependencies. It is certainly a fact that the obstinacy, the folly, and the malice of English monarchs have been the cause of the acquisition of the most valuable treasures of civil liberty in both hemispheres, and as Americans, we owe it largely to the narrow stupidity of George III. that the occasion was given for the rapid growth of a nationalizing and free spirit.

It is not necessary to repeat the familiar story of the enroachments of the home administration and the resistance of the colonies, commencing with the passage of the Grenville Stamp Act in 1765, followed by its repeal in the next year ; succeeded by the Townshend Bill in 1767, "granting" duties in America on tea, glass, and other articles, and its repeal in 1770 as to all duties except tea. The preamble of the Act of 1767 said that "it is expedient that a revenue should be raised in your majesty's dominions in America." Lord North speaking for the King asserted that it must be retained as a mark of the supremacy of parliament ; and it finally came to be true that the controversy raged over an abstract principle rather than a practical oppression. Burke significantly said to the House of Commons : "It is the weight of the preamble of which you are so fond, and not the weight of the duty, that the Americans are unable and unwilling to bear."

The seemingly spontaneous turning of the people of the colonies to joint counsel and resistance through congresses of delegates, and the sensitiveness of their sympathy for each other in all attacks on their rights, which manifests itself so peculiarly after 1761, show that already the latent forces of nationality were present, and only needed a sufficiently potent cause to be excited to vigorous action.

As to the cause, the more one considers the events which so rapidly led to hostilities the more one is impressed with the belief that it lay in ideas entirely. The actual specific oppressions were trival, but the general mind had grown to the consciousness of independence and was ripe and ready to fall away from the parent stem. The variation of the American stock from its English progenitors began almost from the beginning of colonization.

After the treaty of 1763 there was, regarding separation from the mother country, only a question of time and occasion.

The foregoing brief sketch of the early political life of the colonies is not intended to furnish an exhaustive study of the subject, but rather to illustrate the general proposition already stated, that nation-making is the fusion and expansion of small social groups, and that the political structure of a nation consists of what may be termed progressive circles of power, which represent usually the original unit and the various stages of progress between the independence of this unit and the fully organized nation.

The history of the political institutions of all the great modern states will, if traced with sufficient minuteness, show that, nothwithstanding the very many influences, external and internal, which have shaped the development of each one, the general outlines of growth are as stated above. It is only because in the case of the United States the phenomena of growth are comparatively so fresh, and the records of our colonial life are in many respects so copious that we can trace the various forms of institutional growth more readily and certainly than in the case of probably any other nation.

CHAPTER X.

MEN are moved by inherent impulses to dominate over their fellows and to be themselves free ; and when associated in organized societies, as superior and subordinate instrumentalities of government, these impulses of the individual manifest themselves in giving to the societies in question the tendency to enlarge their jurisdictions and to absorb power. Hence, between minor jurisdictions in the state, political attraction and repulsion are always acting, so that every state contains within itself disintegrating forces, as well as nationalizing tendencies

The people of a nation or state may be looked at from at least two points of view, the social and the political. Viewed socially, there seems to be general intercommunication ; the currents of business and pleasure flow unchecked through the body politic. All the various relations of life act and re-act among the individuals over all the land.

Yet we know that all these relations are marked round with jural guards. These guards, these commands express the will of the state. In order, therefore, to know how this will is ascertained and expressed, we must also view the people from the political standpoint. This view discloses to us the fact that the general and the local will express themselves through a series of administrative organs, and that the people are divided off into groups, each of which manifests its particular will in a prescribed way. The great fundamental fact remains, however, that the state consists of human beings, each of whom is by nature a political as well as a moral and intellectual being.

In considering the political manifestations of men we may, provisionally at least, exclude from contemplation all the secondary motives which actuate them during such manifestations and fix our attention solely upon the master motives which come into play in their political relations. What are these motives? An impulse deeply imbedded in human nature is the desire of each individual when brought into contact with his fellows, to overcome and subject them to his will. Emerson has expressed this idea in his felicitous way in his essay on Power, when speaking of the new comer into any circle of men, he compares him to a strange ox driven into the pasture of other cattle : "'There is at once a trial of strength between the best pair of horns and the new comer, and it is settled thencefore which is the leader." The innate propensity to destroy or subjugate is only turned in new directions by civilization. It does not always manifest itself as among rude people in common slaughter. On the contrary, there is a growing disposition to mitigate physical suffering. We read with horror of the wholesale murder and rapine of ancient war, of the sacking of cities, and the selling of men, women, and children into slavery ; but the Englishman of to-day learns with ill-disguised complacency from the *Times* that his fields of coal and his machinery have paralyzed the iron industries of France, or Germany ; and the American is rejoiced to think that competition with our acres and enterprise is undermining the agriculture of Great Britain, although misery is brought to the doors of thousands ;·and yet both think themselves peaceful, merciful men.

The truth is, warfare is still the normal condition of humanity, and in the general scheme of things no doubt, necessarily so. Measureably, however, the theatre of contention is now in the domain of opinions. War is only an ultimatum. The civilized man has come to feel that the gratification derived from subjecting to one's will another's sensations and thoughts is greater than that which arises from holding his body in slavery. The poorest use to which one can put a man is to kill or enslave him ; there is a keener satisfaction in subjugating his rebellious mind. This disposition to dominate over others is not always self-conscious. More often it is an unconscious activity. It is a force which, when diverted from the attempt to appropriate the bodies or services of others, attacks their wills, opinions, imaginations, desires, and seeks to enthrall them with impalpable chains. The destructive and fighting qualities are as strong now as at the beginning, but they have been supplemented by a brain growth which deflects and distributes them over a greater number of objects and employs more intangible and more indirect methods. Let men be united in bodies for any purpose, social, religious, political, even benevolent, and this passion for domination becomes so active that it inevitably develops into leadership and often into despotism. Moreover, there is a common human feeling closely akin to the desire for domination and constantly in collision with it—the desire for free action. It is the action and reaction of these two impulses which maintain the constant current of political activities. In a community where the forces arising from these two desires are nearly equally balanced, there are present the conditions of a stable, vigorous, free state ; where, however, these desires are strong in a few and indifferently developed in the bulk of the people, power will tend to settle in the hands of the few, and the many will be in danger of governmental oppression.

The disposition of the individual to grasp and wield power is transferred to the political body of which he may be a member. Associate men together in corporate bodies, whether of a private nature for gain or other purposes, or in departments of government, local or general, and the individual disposition to control, to aggregate power, is merged in the body, so that there is the same constant tendency in the body as in the individual to extend the scope of its powers. Out of this perpetual conflict of grasping and resisting there arises in the course of time a certain practical balancing of rights and duties, which settles into maxims of action and becomes the positive morality of the community.

In this way in England were worked out the great maxims of personal and political freedom. Every valuable right which has been secured and fixed in constitutions, or in the public conscience, has had to be fought for and won by hard blows : freedom in the exercise of religion ; freedom of the press and of speech ; the right to assemble and petition for redress of grievances ; the right of security of persons and papers against unreasonable search, and others. There is reached also by gradual steps a specialization of the functions of government. The more distinct tracing of the lines of power is imposed, as occasions arise, by the action of the superior will in the state, upon the conflicting individuals and departments.

Unless there is this superior will at some point in the political organism, the result will surely be either disintegration or the violent subjugation of the weaker parts by the stronger. It follows naturally from the structural formation of every state,—because it is really a congress of units, of departments, of lesser administrative circles,— that there is this latent tendency to disintegration. In certain stages of state growth the external or even internal circumstances may be such that the disintegrating influence becomes predominant. This is prominently illustrated in the histories of Italy and Germany. Many circumstances, geographical and other, may, on the other hand, give full play to the inherent disposition of cognate peoples to fuse into nations with a common political organization. This we have seen in France, Spain, England, and the United States.

Whenever a political organism has become sovereign, that is, has reached a point of development where there is one will which has no superior, no matter how many subordinate developments there may be within the organism, then, if it joins itself to another sovereign state or to several others in order to effect a common political object, a conflict is sure to begin; the dominating and counter resisting forces begin to act, and it is merely a question of time when the league will break to pieces or become a consolidated state.*

It is not strange that confederacies have been failures. Human nature is arrayed against them. In the long run two wills acting in conjunction cannot remain entirely independent. It almost goes without saying that the confederation of the British Colonies, entered into in July, 1778, could, in the nature of things, survive but a very short time. It is a mark of the sacrificing patriotism of the people that it lasted through the war. The especially interesting feature of our history at that period, from

---

* It is significant that the league was the last phase of the governmental history of independent Greece. The Greeks appear to have taken the first step from the city or tribal government toward a national government. At the point of transition, when there appeared to be wanting only time to bring about political consolidation, the course of their independent political life was interrupted by the conquest of the Romans.

a political point of view, is, the actual and theoretical attitude of the colonies to one another.

Up to the outbreak of hostilities with the mother
country, the different colonies had not certainly been
sovereign states. Great Britain was the sovereign and
the colonies were subordinate parts of the kingdom ; yet
they were in a degree independent parts. They were
dependencies, not parts, as a county or shire is a part of
the kingdom. When, therefore, they cut the tie which
bound them to the common superior, they were sovereign
as to one another. The articles of confederation were an
agreement between States ; the action of the central congress was upon the States and not directly upon the individuals within the States. Here, as has often been
pointed out and as the framers of the subsequent constitution clearly understood, was the fatal defect.

When afterwards this confederacy broke down, the
problem which the constitutional convention attempted to
solve was to establish a working frame of government involving two leading ideas, State sovereignty and at the
same time United States sovereignty. Theoretically, the
several States were sovereign ; they passed directly from
the dependent, colonial condition into the condition of the
independent state. The social fact, however, was that the
whole people constituted a nation. They were not, it is
true, really conscious of their nationality ; this consciousness came by degrees later. We may call them an
embryo nation ; at least all the elements of a nation
were there. Politically they were parcelled off into States.
There was still a large fund of colonial pride which
merged into State pride, but no doubt the apprehension
which turned the greater number from the national idea
was the belief that a strong central government would
crush out State autonomy, and especially that there was

serious danger that the executive might gradually grow into something akin to a monarchy. We must remember that although at that period parliamentary government was firmly established in England, yet that personal government was also strong ; and there was no adequate surety to the general mind that kingly usages might not gradually drift back towards the old pretensions of divine right. Then again, the small States were jealous of and feared the large ones. The preponderating influences were in favor of an alliance of the States, rather than their immediate' fusion.

It is said that the fathers of the Republic invented a new kind of government, a federal state, founded upon a written constitution. However true this may be, we are now able to assert that in so far as they violated fundamental principles in government their work has not been interpreted in all respects as they supposed it would be. The intent of the constitution did certainly violate the fundamental principle that two wills cannot at the same time be sovereign in the same state. The conflict introduced at the very beginning was between the two wills ; the one of the State and the other of the nation. The key to our whole national political history since 1789 is here.

CHAPTER XI

WHEN we have determined with reference to any given nation where sovereignty is lodged, we should next inquire how does the sovereign express his will ? We shall find that it is usually in two ways, one is in the establishment of a form of government and organs of state power, and also frequently of fixed rules of state action ; this may be styled the permanent will of the nation. The other is manifested in the statutes and ordinances enacted from time to time by the law-making organs of the government. This may be styled the occasional will of the nation. If there is a written constitution which can be modified only in a specified way, it constitutes this permanent will. Such an instrument furnishes a written enumeration of those features of the political system which it is desired shall remain unchanged except by a formal act of the ultimate sovereign in the way pointed out in the instrument itself. There is no difficulty under these circumstances in ascertaining what is this permanent will. But in those instances where, what is called the constitution is unwritten, there is more or less vagueness in its definition. We can only say there are certain features in the governmental system which the bulk of the people consider ought to be permanent, and a change in which they would look upon as revolutionary.

Such a constitution consists of provisions for the national government, as, for instance, the king or executive head, the houses of the legislature, whether two or more, including their internal structure and relation to each other, and the courts of justice.   It provides also for the fixed institutions pertaining to the local jurisdictions, as those of provinces, shires, counties, towns, or townships.   It may likewise include certain established laws and even maxims concerning personal rights, as that there shall not be taxation without representation, that jury trial shall be preserved, that private property shall not be taken for public use without just compensation, and the like. The occasional will of the nation finds its expression, as already intimated, in the statutes or ordinances that may be enacted from time to time by some organ or organs of the government established for that purpose.   Whether the expression of national will be in a constitution or a statute, they are relatively to each other only, permanent or occasional.   It might be said, perhaps with greater accuracy, that the only difference is that the constitution is more permanent than the law enacted under it, but both are nevertheless expressions which are subject to changes.   It may be that the same organs of the government which pass the ordinary legislation have also the power to amend the constitution.   This is the case in the German Empire.   Nevertheless there the two wills are still distinct and must manifest their expressions separately, so that it may occur that the occasional will conflicts with the permanent will.   For example, while it lies with the Emperor, the Bundesrath, and the Reichstag conjointly to amend the constitution, they may also together pass an ordinary law.   Each, however, is a separate expression. The ordinary statute, if in conflict with the constitution, falls to the ground ; it does not, because passed by the same organs, operate as an amendment or repeal of the fundamental law.   On the other hand, that body of statutes and old usages which publicists designate as the British Constitution, may be changed by an act of Parliament. In the United States the organs which express the occasional will of the nation are more strictly limited in power, and whenever the statute conflicts with the written constitution it is void.

In a despotic state the power to express the permanent as well as the occasional will resides in the same person, the monarch ; but nevertheless there can hardly be found a polity so primitive but that there is, at least, a substantial body of customs which have consolidated into the similitude of constitutional law and which the most despotic ruler does not invade. These honored usages really indicate the permanent will of the community. In the complex modern states this permanent will expresses itself, as already suggested, in some, in written constitutions ; in others in the departments of government and in maxims of public and private law, established perhaps at remote periods and changed, added to, and modified from time to time by the sovereign, until now they are accepted by the nation as stable. In Great Britain is the most marked instance of the permanent will of a nation, gradually hardening as it were, into a most complicated constitutional structure. Russia is a more modern instance of a land where, theoretically, one and the same man may express both the permanent and the occasional will of the community, and yet where, in fact, an elaborate governmental scheme has grown to express a national will that is practically permanent. In most countries at present, however, there are written constitutions which express the permanent national will.

From the foregoing considerations we reach the conclusion that when we determine, under any system, the person or persons competent to amend the constitution, or change the form of government, that is, with power to express the permanent will, we have defined the sovereign in the nation and have fixed the source of constitutional law.

According to the provisions of Article V. of the constitution of the United States, the power to amend that instrument is given to certain determinate bodies, and in these bodies rest the sovereignty of the nation. In the United States, the sovereign is not the whole body of the people nor the whole body of the voters of the several States. These voters are the sovereign-makers, and can act only when called upon by the proper authority, and when they vote in groups, in districts provided by law.

" We, the people of the United States," who are referred to in the preamble of the Constitution as establishing it for the purposes of a more perfect union and to secure other advantages, were not all the people of the thirteen original colonies, nor is it even clear that they were a majority of them. Each state held a convention, the delegates to which were elected by a majority of votes. The voters were only those who possessed the necessary property or other qualifications. They did not themselves say yea or nay ; they merely authorized certain delegates to speak for them. No doubt the way each delegate would vote was largely determined by the preferences of his constituents. Still, in a general sense, he was a free agent. Assuming, however, that in the conventions each delegate voted as those desired who voted for him at his election, an analysis would show that, in point of fact, a bare majority of the qualified electors accepted the instrument. In some instances, as in New York, the convention finally decided contrary to the expression of opinion at the polls. In that State there were sixty-five delegates, of whom forty-six were elected by the

7

party hostile to the Constitution, and yet at the end it was ratified by a majority of three. In truth, the voters of all States delegated the power of acceptance or rejection to their conventions, and abandoned all control over the question.

The generalization, then, "We, the people," must really be restricted to the several organized political bodies consisting of representatives—theoretically, of the whole body of the people—but, in reality, of the majorities or pluralities of the several political districts which elected them. The whole body of the people was divided, for political purposes, into States ; these States were subdivided into districts and the individual voter was nobody, or, rather, he was somebody only when he spoke by his vote through the instrumentalities of the particular group to which he was attached, and in which he was politically absorbed. Each group had upon that subject, a will, which was expressed by the majority vote. It is true now, therefore, as it was in primitive days, that for what may be called political expression, the individual is nobody. His group, his township, his county, his State, may speak, may act. He alone is merely a constituent, an atom, which may or may not affect the will of the group to which he belongs. The constitution of the United States is a written command or law, adopted by the conventions of the original thirteen States. It expresses at the present, or at any given time, the will of just that number of voters within the limits of the United States, who can elect a sufficient number of representatives authorized to amend it. This year every one in the country may be content with the fundamental law as it stands, but possibly next year there may be a movement for change ; this can be brought about in two ways, either by vote of two-thirds of both houses of Congress, proposing amendments, or by two-thirds of the State legislatures applying to Congress to call a convention.

Let us suppose that the first method is adopted, that the matter of the proposed amendments is agitated sufficiently long in advance so that members of Congress are elected, as for or against them, and that two-thirds of both houses are favorable to the proposition.   It follows, that the proposal emanates from, that the machinery is set in motion by, the sum of the majorities in two-thirds, or, in addition, the number above two-thirds of the congressional districts of the nation which may be favorable. Can we consider these majorities the ultimate sovereign in the nation ?   No ; because it is necessary before the amendments are adopted that they shall be ratified by the legislatures of three-fourths of the States, or by conventions in three-fourths of them.   Neither can we say that the majorities of the several legislative districts which elected the members who voted for the ratification, are, together, the sovereign.   A sovereign must be single or a corporate body, must be an actual or legal person, who can will to do, or not to do, and can make the will effective.   The voters who elect members to conventions or legislative bodies, it is true, exercise their individual wills in the choice they make ; but, having done so, they disappear. They are, in truth, only makers of the sovereign.   They come upon the scene at stated times and then vanish. In the interim they are merely subjects of the superior power.   It is in this sphere of making and unmaking the sovereign in representative governments that political parties act as we shall see later.

Strictly speaking, it is inaccurate to say of a representative republic that the people are sovereign.   While they can, by moral influences, by the use of all those methods of persuasion which bind the consciences of men, influence

their representatives to carry out their wishes, yet so long
as there are no penalties, other than social or moral ones,
attached to violations of promises or expectations, it cannot
be correctly asserted that sovereign power resides with the
voters.

It is assumed that the representative will carry out the
will of his constituents ; ordinarily, in a general sense,
he does; but he is not obliged to do so, and frequently
does not do it. Often questions arise which were not
anticipated before the election. In such an event, the
representative must exercise his independent judgment.
If he is the mere mouth-piece of his electors, then, certainly, he is the servant, and not the master. He goes
to the legislature to deliberate, and to determine as his
judgment is convinced. At least such is the accepted
theory. Actually, in the point of view here suggested,
he is one of a number who help to shape and express,
through certain established channels, and according to
certain forms, the will of the particular political group,
of which the legislature is a part. The fifth article of the
Constitution of the United States provided that amendments might be made in the methods above indicated, with
the proviso that no amendment could be made prior to
1808, which prevented the importation of slaves, or which
imposed a capitation, or other direct tax, otherwise than
in proportion to the census enumeration ; and with the
further important proviso, that no State, without its consent, should be deprived of its equal suffrage in the
Senate. These provisos are, however, instances of a
sovereign attempting to limit by law its own authority,
which it cannot do and remain sovereign. They are to be
regarded simply as pledges on the part of the sovereign
that it will refrain from certain acts within a certain time.

The nation, it is true, by common consent or acquiescence, may change the form of its government. The people of the United States might substitute an aristocracy or any other form for the existing republican government. The change might come about peacefully or through war. Such a fundamental change, or revolution, would be extra-constitutional, or extra-legal, and therefore lies without that field of political inquiry, which assumes, as a starting-point, some government *de facto*. From this point of view we can consider alterations in the form of government only under the limitation that the change be peaceful and normal; that is, either through methods previously provided, or through the gradual steps of natural political growth. It is idle, therefore, to discuss the right of revolution as a political question. It can be examined and discussed only as a question of private morals. Every person who takes part in a revolution must settle with his own conscience, if he succeeds, whether the end attained has justified the bloodshed or misery it has occasioned; and if he fails, he must settle with the penal laws that have been violated.*

---

* Although a political revolution is an extra-legal proceeding, and, therefore, may not properly be considered in the discussion of the nature and organization of the state, yet, by reason of its importance as marking certain crises in political progress, it should not be entirely left out of view in this connection. In a political revolution we observe the operation of a force, or forces, in a manner not provided for by the laws or the constitution, through which the form of the government is changed, or the power of the state is transferred to a different person, or to a different body of persons from that hitherto legally exercising this power. It need not be attended by a violent social agitation, or occupy a conspicuous place in history. The political organization of society tends to become rigid; and when it has ceased to be an adequate expression of the changed political ideas of the nation, and refuses to yield to lawful means of change, or is incapable of being modified

An evolutionary change may be such as has taken place, in large part, in the British system, and in a degree goes on in every government, even in our own. In the sovereign nation there is no legal limitation upon its right to have such form of government as it pleases, and to change it as often as it pleases. To get upon firm ground in analytical politics, we must eliminate morals altogether; morals come into consideration only when seeking to know how the state ought to will, and how to act in any given contingency.

Our American nation, through certain existing political groups called States, which acted in a normal manner through their conventions, accepted the Constitution, and in this Constitution pointed out a method of amendment and the limitations upon amendment. The nation has imposed upon itself this form of government; and, so long as it adheres to it, can only change it, voluntarily, in the way provided in the pact.

The initial question is, who has the power to change or amend this form of government? As provided in the fifth article, it is lodged in two-thirds of both houses of Congress, who can propose the amendment; and in three-fourths of the legislatures, or conventions, as the case may be, of the several States, who can accept it. The fifteen amendments which have been added to the

by methods provided by law so as to meet the actual political demands, the adjustment of political forms to meet the demands will be brought about through extra-legal means, or, in other words, through revolution. Burke, in his *Reflections on the Revolution in France*, says: "The question of dethroning, or, if these gentlemen like the phrase better, 'cashiering kings,' will always be, as it always has been, an extraordinary question of state, and wholly out of the law; a question, like all other questions of state, of dispositions, and of means, and of probable consequences, rather than of positive rights."

THE MAKERS OF CONSTITUTIONAL LAW. 151

Constitution have all been proposed by Congress, and ratified by the requisite number of State legislatures. There never has been occasion to call a general convention for the purpose of amendment, as was expected and hoped would be the case by very many of those who reluctantly accepted the original instrument.

We can therefore assert that in the United States, what may be called the ultimate or primary sovereign, is a collegiate sovereign, made up of two-thirds of the two houses of Congress, and three-fourths of the legislatures or conventions of the States.

In the German empire, amendments to the constitution can be made only by legislative enactment. If there were power in each chamber of the legislature to initiate laws, we could properly say that the two together were the sovereign in the empire ; but as this power is lodged elsewhere, and the legislature is only a consenting body, it occupies merely a negative position. The laws, and also constitutional amendments, are proposed by the Emperor, and submitted to the Bundesrath or Federal Council, or are prepared by the latter body with his consent. The proposed enactment, after being first adopted by the Bundesrath, is by it submitted to the Reichstag, the lower house of the parliament. If, however, there are fourteen votes against the proposition in the Bundesrath it is immediately rejected. If, on the contrary, it is approved, it must also have the approbation of the Reichstag by a majority vote. It is then published by the Emperor. There is, however, a provision that when by the terms of the constitution fixed rights of individual states are established in their relation to the whole, they can be altered only with the consent of the state which is immediately concerned. It thus appears that the power resides in the Emperor to prevent forever any constitutional change, while, if he desires alteration in any particular, it can be accomplished only with the consent of both branches of the legislature. As the test of sovereignty is the ability to command, to will, it is necessarily affirmative, and not a mere power of negation; and as the amendment cannot be made without a combination of the will of the Emperor, of the Bundesrath and of the Reichstag, we may affirm that the Imperial sovereign is collegiate, consisting of these three, and in certain special cases, where certain fixed rights of individual states are to be affected, we must add to this collegiate primary sovereign the specially concerned state.

In France, the constitution of 1875 provides that the two chambers, the senate and the assembly, by majority vote, may, either spontaneously, or upon the suggestion of the President of the Republic, declare that amendments to the constitution ought to be made. (If the prevailing construction of this clause is not misunderstood, it is that this declaration is to the effect that particular amendments are needed, not a general affirmation, that the instrument should be amended.) Thereupon the two chambers unite themselves into one body, and proceed to the revision, which can be accomplished only by a majority vote of the united body.

In the Austro-Hungarian Empire, the constitution emanated from the Emperor, by letters patent of October 20, 1860, and was somewhat modified in 1867. It can be amended only by the vote of two-thirds of those present in the upper and lower houses of the legislature, it being necessary that, in the lower house at least, half of the members shall be present.

In Great Britain, where there is no written constitution, the sovereign is the collective one of the two houses of parliament, in conjunction with the monarch. The actual devolution of the political system of that country has given the paramount authority to the house of commons, in practice. Nevertheless as the assent of the house of lords and the monarch are both necessary to any change of the general system of laws and usages which the British mind contemplates as the constitution, they must be considered as possessing a portion of the sovereignty.

The foregoing analysis indicates where to look in any system of government for the ultimate sovereign, the immediate source of constitutional law. The person, or the body of persons, often designated as sovereign, is not always the real bearer of power. In every nation, this final power of change is lodged somewhere. Technically, it is with the person, or persons who command what the form of government shall be, and who, when it is once established, have power to effect a change. The motive power, however, behind the carriers of sovereignty, in a popular government, is public opinion, as it finds expression at the polls on election days, and through the press, and on the platform ; but as already suggested, we must carefully distinguish, in discussion, the actual legal sovereign, from the individuals who act in constituting the sovereign, and who are represented by the sovereign.*

* Holland, in The Elements of Jurisprudence, p. 249, indicates what from the British point of view, are regarded as the essentials of a national constitution. He says : " It prescribes the order of succession to the throne ; or, in a republic, the mode of electing a president. It enumerates the prerogatives of the king, or other chief magistrate. It regulates the composition of the council of state, and of the upper and lower houses of the assembly, when the assembly is thus divided ; the mode in which a seat is acquired in the upper house, whether by succession, by nomination or by tenure of office ; the mode of electing the members of the house of representatives ; the powers and privileges of the assembly as a

7*

whole, and of the individuals who compose it ; and the machinery
of law-making. It deals also with the ministers, their responsibility and their respective spheres of action ; the government offices
and their organization ; the armed forces of the state, their control and the mode in which they are recruited ; the relation, if any,
between church and state ; the judges and their immunities ; local
self government ; the relations between the mother country and its
colonies and dependencies. It describes the portions of the earth's
surface over which the sovereignty of the state extends, and defines
the persons who are subject to its authority. It comprises, therefore, rules for the ascertainment of nationality, and for regulating
the acquisition of a new nationality by 'naturalization.' It declares the rights of the state over its subjects in respect of their
liability to military conscription, to service as jurymen, and otherwise. It declares, on the other hand, the rights of the subject
to be assisted and protected by the state, and of that narrower
class of subjects which enjoys full civic rights to hold public offices
and to elect their representatives to the assembly, or parliament,
of the nation."

As to the nature of constitutional law, Austin remarks (Vol. I. p.
73), that, " in a country governed by a monarch, constitutional law
is extremely simple ; for it merely determines the person who shall
bear the sovereignty. In a country governed by a number, con-
stitional law is more complex ; for it determines the persons, or the
classes of the persons who shall bear the sovereign powers ; and
it determines, moreover, the mode wherein those persons shall
share those powers. In a country governed by a monarch, constitutional law is positive morality merely : in a country governed
by a number, it may consist of positive morality, or of a compound
of positive morality and positive law.

" Administrative law determines the ends and modes to and in
which the sovereign powers shall be exercised : shall be exercised
directly by the monarch or sovereign number, or shall be exercised
directly by the subordinate political superiors to whom portions of
those powers are delegated or committed in trust. "

CHAPTER XII.

HAVING referred to the general nature of constitutional law and to the power by which it is formed, it remains to indicate the nature of administrative law as the expression of the occasional will of the nation. Constitutional law establishes the political organization of the nation ; while administrative law provides for "the exercise of political powers within the limits of the constitution." In its broadest sense administration includes "the making and promulgation of laws, the action of the government in guiding the state as a whole, the administration of justice, the management of the property and business transactions of the state, and the working in detail, by means of subordinates entrusted with a certain amount of discretion, of the complex machinery by which the state provides at once for its own existence and for the general welfare."* This list of topics embraced within the wide conception of administration defines the sphere of administrative law.

In the modern state, laws of this class are made by the organs of the sovereign, of which, for law-making purposes, there are two—the legislature and the tribunals. "The first organ makes new law, the second attests and confirms old law, though under cover of so doing it introduces many new principles." †

* Holland, " The Elements of Jurisprudence," 251.
† Ibid., 51.

Seeking, with reference to the United States, to determine who forms and expresses the occasional, national
will, we find it provided in the constitution that, "All
legislative powers herein granted shall be vested in a Congress of the United States, which shall consist of a Senate
and House of Representatives."

If we examine a little further, we shall find that the
President is also a factor in legislation, and that the law-
making power is vested in Congress and the President
jointly : "Every bill which shall have passed the House of
Representatives, and the Senate, shall, before it becomes
a law, be presented to the President of the United States ;
if he approve, he shall sign it, but if not, he shall return
it, with his objections, to that house in which it shall have
originated, who shall enter the objections at large on their
journal, and proceed to reconsider it. If, after such
reconsideration, two-thirds of that house shall agree to
pass the bill, it shall be sent, together with the objections,
to the other house, by which it shall likewise be recon-
sidered, and if approved by two-thirds of that house, it
shall become a law."*

Not only bills, but also every order, resolution, or
vote to which the concurrence of both houses of Congress
may be necessary (except on a question of adjournment),
must be presented to the President for approval, and if
disapproved, must be passed again by a two-thirds vote
of the two houses, as in the case of bills.† An exception
has grown up in practice, which is directly in opposition
to this last mentioned clause, and that is, that resolutions
of Congress, proposing amendments to the constitution,
do not require the assent of the President. We thus see
that in legislation the President represents the amount of

* Art. I., Section 7, ch. 2.
† Ib., cl. 3.

power that resides in the number of the votes which
lie between the majority that passed the particular bill,
and the two-thirds necessary to pass it over the veto.
For illustration, let us suppose a majority of the House of
Representatives to be one hundred and fifty-seven votes,
and of the Senate thirty-nine votes, and that a bill passes
by a bare majority in both branches of Congress. We
will suppose the President vetoes the bill. If two-thirds
of the votes of the House of Representatives are one hundred and ninety-six, and of the Senate fifty-one, it follows
that the President's negative represents the quantity between the majority and the two-thirds, that is, forty-nine
votes. In this view, every measure which passes must
receive virtually a two-thirds vote of both houses. The
Chief Magistrate's approval produces the same result as
if he had been present in each house when the vote was
taken, and had given a number of votes for the bill, equal
to the number between the actual majority in its favor,
and the two-thirds necessary to pass it over a veto.

The President is a legislator elected at large, and represents the whole people. He is not an independent element in the government ; he does not represent a distinct
class. He is not supposed to be the conserver of interests
which must be guarded against enemies in the state. He
is not the antithesis of the Demos. He is a legislator
chosen upon a vote of all the electors in the States, who,
during his term of office, possesses a large, though, varying
with the occasion, indeterminate weight in forming and
expressing the occasional will of the nation. In England,
as we know, the monarch possesses an absolute veto upon
legislation. He stands on one side, and the legislature
on the other. He is out of the reach of the people. It
is apparent that there cannot co-exist such an hereditary
monarch with an absolute veto power, and a parliament-

ary system supposed to represent the people, and to be
able to express the national will.   Such a negative upon
the law-makers is absolutism, and therefore in the development of free English institutions, it is as natural that
it should go to the ground as that the claims of divine
right by James I., and the prerogative claims of his son,
should have disappeared.   The assertion, at this day, of
the veto power by the Queen, would be a palpable blow
at popular government.   If the Queen should disapprove
of an Act of Parliament, it would be saying to the English
nation, my will is the ultimate, the sovereign will in the
state ; but when the President vetoes an Act of Congress,
he merely asserts that he casts against the bill the number of votes between the majority and the two-thirds vote.

Under the French Constitution of 1875, the President
of the Republic cannot veto an act of legislation.   He is
rather a moderator.   It is considered that he ought to
have a cooler head than the legislator, and he is therefore
permitted to interfere when there is danger of over-hasty
law-making.   If at any time he judges it necessary, he
may enter the Assembly and take part in the discussion
of a bill pending.   But whenever he desires to do so, he
must send a message to that body indicating his wish to
be heard.   Thereupon the debate is suspended until the
next day, when he is heard, unless a special vote shall
have decided to hear him the same day the message is
transmitted.   After his address, the session is adjourned,
and the subsequent discussion is not in his presence.
Again, each bill must pass through three readings, unless
considered urgent, and those laws which receive the usual
three readings, do not take effect until a month after
their passage, while those which have been declared urgent, go into operation within three days.   The constitution, upon this view of imposing moderation, rather

than a check upon the deliberative branch of the government, permits the chief magistrate, when a law has been declared urgent, and passed without the three readings, to resubmit it for a new deliberation to the Assembly, and in those cases where the bill is going through the usual course of three readings, he may interpose after the second reading, and postpone the third reading for a month. He has in effect only a deliberative, counselling function in the making of the laws ; is a sort of prime minister without a vote.

The constitution of the German Empire is somewhat vague on the point in question : It nowhere, in terms, authorizes a veto, or any interposition, by the Executive, in the deliberations of the Reichstag. The only provision which refers to the laws when they come from the legislative body, is that : "The laws and regulations of the Empire shall be published in the name of the Emperor, and require for their validity, the signature of the chancellor of the Empire, who thereby assumes the responsibility." This last clause immediately suggests the query, to whom is the chancellor responsible ? He is appointed by the Emperor, and is alone removable by him ; he cannot be impeached by the Reichstag or any other body. His responsibility is solely to his Imperial master. In effect, therefore, when the Emperor disapproves of a bill, his chancellor refuses his signature to it, and it is absolutely vetoed. If it so happen that the chancellor is the strong man, and the head of the state merely a weak instrument of his will, then of course, the minister is absolute master of legislation. It does not seem to have occurred to the Germans, that this requirement of the signature of the chief minister was not mandatory upon that officer, or that it really was putting an absolute veto into the hands of the Emperor until recently, when Bismarck told the Reichstag in his usual blunt fashion, that he, the chancellor, really controlled legislation.*

The President of the United States has not, it is true, the right of initiating legislation by the submission of bills, as every member in the Senate and House has. He is confined to general recommendation of measures, which may or may not be heeded ; but he is as much a part of the legislative as of the executive branch of the government through his qualified veto.

In this view, he is clearly not confined, in a proper exercise of his power, to an examination merely of the constitutionality of a measure before he signs the bill. He is to "approve" or not to "approve" the measure as he sees fit, and has the same range of considerations to review, before reaching a decision, as a member of either branch of Congress. He is, in effect, elected as a co-ordinate member of Congress for a term of four years, with a varying number of votes at his command ; while the Senator is chosen for six, and the member of the House

---

* Bismarck made a speech in the Reichstag, in which he defined the position of the chancellor, in the Imperial system, and in doing so explained the system itself in a way that astonished even the natives. He said it is the duty of the chancellor to submit to the Reichstag the decisions of the Federal Council, and for the performance of his duty he is responsible ; but he need not do it, if he does not think best. He may tell the Emperor that he does not think the bill a good one, and refuse to sign it ; and the only way out of the difficulty for the Emperor is to get another chancellor. But the Emperor need not get another chancellor unless he pleases, and in this way may veto all legislation, for legislation must originate in the Federal Council. Thus it appears that the chancellor really controls legislation. He is not responsible to either house ; no one but the Emperor can dismiss him.—See *The Nation*, No. 820, March 17, 1881, p. 179.

of Representatives for two years, with but one vote each.

In a moral point of view, he has no more right to use his power for bad purposes, or to be influenced by unworthy reasons, than the Senator or Representative, but constitutionally there is no limitation on the veto.

The three factors of legislation, then, the President, the Senate, and the House of Representatives, form and express the occasional will of the Union.

But why two Houses of Congress? Democracy being the basis of our institutions, and representatives being merely elected because of the physical impediments in the way of legislating *en masse*, it would seem natural, at first blush, that there should be but one National Assembly, proceeding directly from the people. There is a certain degree of plausibility in this view; it has a palpable logical completeness, which has always been attractive to idealists in government. The French Democrats, who are largely of this kind, always attempt the single assembly system when they have the upper hand, and always with a disastrous outcome. And though in the British system, one branch of the legislature is practically supreme, yet with all its limitations, the House of Lords is still a serious counterpoise to the Commons. It furnishes something of what Bagehot aptly terms the "dignified parts" of the British constitution, which are as valuable as what he styles its "efficient parts." The principal reasons which controlled the Constitutional Convention of 1787 in providing for a Senate, were, the examples in the mother country, and most of the colonies, of an upper and lower house, one, more or less permanent in its constituents, and the other the product of general suffrage; further, because the equal votes of the States in this body is a recognition of their equality, and it was

anticipated that the supposed disposition of the larger
States to oppress the smaller ones would thus be counter-
vailed ; and lastly, two houses would be a check upon
hasty legislation, especially as it was believed that the
Senate would be composed of picked men, of more enlarged experience in statesmanship, and certainly more
conservative in consequence of their longer tenure of
office and method of choice by the State legislatures.

The government established in the United States was a
more or less ingenious adaptation of that of the mother
country to the new circumstances arising out of the colonial growth. In England, at that day, the House of
Lords was a more important factor in legislation than it
is now, and especially it represented the aristocratic
idea, which even on this continent had a firm hold
on our young society, until the death of Washington.
The greater part of the framers of our constitution were
in fact, really afraid of the people. They were conscious at the same time of the profound hold which the
sentiment of equality had on the masses, especially in
New England, and which had grown rapidly throughout
the Middle, and Southern States, during the Revolutionary War. The problem with them was, to introduce a
conservative element, as a check upon the passions of democracy, and this, it was believed, might be accomplished
by a sort of artificial selection, of the conservative men
for the Senate through a second vote, one remove from
the people ; as it was also thought, a more capable man
could be chosen for President, through a similar removal
of the electoral body one step from the voters. In both
instances the results have been flat contradictions of their
theories. The fear that the larger States would oppress
the smaller is also proven to have been a phantom.
These able men were as wise as any of their day ; but

they, or the most of them, experienced the difficulty which is the greatest of all in statesmanship : that of knowing the significance of contemporary events ; of measuring and comprehending present social tendencies. It is easy to devise what should have been the laws two generations ago, but it requires more than ordinary insight to frame a constitution which fits in exactly with the social conditions of the present, and is equally well adapted to the inevitable future. The major part of the Convention of 1787 did not see that there was a young *nation* without their doors awaiting governmental organization ; that there was a society which had grown over the narrow colonial limits, and was fused into one organic being. Hamilton almost alone, fully comprehended it. When a national government was furnished, State jealousy, and State pride had nothing to stand on. What afterwards occurred in the way of the hot controversy of the North and the South, was a social conflict originating in causes foreign to the form of the government, but in which the South seized upon, and artificially nourished the old colonial and early State jealousies, and finally turned them into articles of political faith.

CHAPTER XIII.

THE BICAMERAL SYSTEM OF THE MODERN LEGISLATURE.

THE division of the legislature into two houses, as is the custom of most representative governments, rests on ideas of political organization, which were characteristic of the primitive Aryans, and which have become the common heritage of the Aryan stock. The full realization of these ideas was hindered in the middle ages by the existence of distinct social classes, which constituted the basis of the political organization of that period. The ideal legislature of the middle ages involved a distinct representation of each of the several classes. The upper house, in the bicameral system of modern times, represents either a privileged or a conservative element in the nation, or is a means of recognizing the individuality of the minor social groups which have joined to form the larger whole ; while the lower house represents the great body of the people enjoying political rights, and is the exponent of the political unity of the nation.

The tendency of modern nations to maintain, or to return to, the essential features of the primitive Aryan government has already been briefly illustrated. After the fall of paganism and the rise of Christianity, the church, as the organized body of Christians, acquired an individual existence. The affairs of religion ceased to be merged in the affairs of the state. The ecclesiastics appeared as a class in society and demanded an equal political recognition with other classes. The political system of the middle ages was based on the recognition of the individuality of the several classes, as the nobles, the clergy, the burghers, and the peasants. In the cities and towns, moreover, men of like pursuits were associated in guilds. The fundamental principle of social organization was found in class distinctions. Even individuals, as princes, and corporations, and institutions of learning, were treated as classes by themselves. Delegates received instructions and commissions from their principals, as to their votes and actions. And as late as the meeting of the three estates of France at Versailles in 1789, under the summons of Louis XVI., the delegates received instructions. The nobles, the clergy, and the deputies of the people, the "third estate," were separately summoned, and it was when their instructions were thrown away that a complete breach was made with the class system. Every class voted individually, and could authorize a representative to vote for the whole class. The delegates of the classes were responsible to their principals, and were paid for their services by the latter. The classes first considered their own interests, and secondly, the general welfare. New taxes were granted by the different classes, and frequently upon conditions, as, that the country should not be mortgaged or alienated to a foreign prince, or, that their consent should first be demanded before a war was declared.

The classes held fast to the principle of making treaties with the prince, and their homage was sometimes made to depend upon guaranties of their rights and privileges. An example of this is Magna Charta, which was a treaty between John and the barons. Frequently, as independent powers, the classes counselled and aided the prince, and often, standing committees were appointed by the classes to assist in the government.*

It is not strange, in view of these mediæval conditions, that there has descended to modern society, by way of survival, the belief that, wherever there exists a legalized aristocracy, it has separate political interests, which should be guarded by a separate legislative branch. We may even go further, and say that much of modern thought about society is largely controlled by the class ideas of the middle ages. We still ideally divide society into classes, and our speech only follows our thought, when we speak of the rich class, the poor class, the middle class, the educated class, and even the criminal class.

It is clear, moreover, that as long as the rigid distinctions of mediæval classes were maintained, the bicameral system had to yield to a legislature composed of several houses. But the union of the privileged orders, on the one hand, and the fusion of the unprivileged orders, on the other; or the destruction of all marks of class distinction save the political privileges of the nobility; or the union of minor political bodies in the formation of a nation, were conditions favorable to the existence of a bicameral legislature. The upper house in many modern states is composed of those whose right to membership rests on the same basis as the privileges of the noble class, namely, the favor of the crown. In other states, as in the United States or in Sweden, the upper house derives part of its significance from the fact that it is a recognition of the individuality of the subordinate political bodies in the nation.

In Austria, by the constitution of 1861, as modified in 1867, the upper house consists of the princes of the im-

* See Bluntschli, " Lehre vom modernen Stat." Vol. ii., Ch. iii.

perial family, who have reached their majority ; heads of noble families, nominated by the emperor ; archbishops and bishops, having the title of prince of the empire. In addition, the emperor can, without limitation as to number, nominate eminent men who have signalized themselves by services to the church or to the state, or in science or art. In Hungary, the chamber of magnates is composed of feudal nobles. In Prussia, the members of the upper chamber are chosen by the king from among the candidates presented by the different bodies of the state, or classes of citizens, such as : (1) the members of the nobility called by the ordinance of February 3, 1847, to a seat in the chamber of nobles ; (2) the class of counts having a fief in one of the provinces ; (this class in each province can present a candidate); (3) the assemblage of families with large landed estates invested by the king with the right of presentation ; (4) the families with landed property anciently confirmed ; (5) the universities ; (6) the cities to which the right of presentation has been granted. In Italy, according to the terms of the Sardinian constitution of 1848, which has been successively applied to the provinces annexed, the senate is chosen from a great variety of persons. All the royal princes who have reached the age of twenty-one years are members, but they cannot vote, until they have reached twenty-five. In addition, an unlimited number can be nominated by the king, but must be chosen from the following categories : (1) archbishops and bishops ; (2) president of the chamber of deputies ; (3) deputies who have had six years experience in three legislatures ; (4) ministers of state ; (5) secretaries of state ; (6) ambassadors ; (7) envoys extraordinary, who have been in commission within three years ; (8) the superior presidents of the court of cassation, and of the court of accounts; (9) the superior presidents

of the court of appeal ; (10) the advocates-general of
the court of cassation, and procurers-general, who have
had five years' experience ; (11) presidents of the courts
of appeal, who have had three years' experience ; (12)
councilors of the courts of cassation, and of the chamber of accounts, in office within five years ; (13) advocates-general, and fiscal officers of the courts of appeal,
in office within five years ; (14) general officers of the
land and sea forces ; (15) councilors of state who have
acted within five years ; (16) the members of the councils
of division, who have been three times elected to the
presidency ; (17) general intendants, who have been in
service seven years ; (18) members of the royal academy
of sciences, nominated within seven years ; (19) ordinary
members of the superior council of public instruction,
of seven years' experience ; (20) all those who, by eminent services, or talents, shall have merited well of the
country ; (21) those who have within three years paid
3,000 livres of direct taxes upon their goods or business.

This breadth of choice certainly gives the opportunity
for the formation of an upper chamber, which shall represent all the conservatism and intelligence of the country,
though at the same time it puts it in the power of the
monarch, if he has any special end in view, to fill the
Senate with his own tools.

In Portugal the constitutional chart of 1826, as supplemented in 1852, provides that the Chamber of Peers
shall consist of members, whose tenure of office is for life,
and hereditary members ; both of which classes are nominated by the king, without limitation as to numbers,
and without restriction as to choice. It shall contain,
also, certain members holding their positions *ex officio*, or
by reason of birth, as bishops, and the royal princes.

In Sweden, since 1866, the members of the upper

THE BICAMERAL SYSTEM. 169

house are elected for nine years by the provincial assemblies (Landstingen), and by the municipal councilors of those cities which do not take part in the provincial assemblies. Each of these assemblies, and each city having the right, elects a member for every 30,000 inhabitants. To be a member of the upper chamber, the person must be thirty-five years of age, and have possessed for at least the three preceding years, real estate, assessed at $2,280, or shall have paid within the same period, a tax upon a revenue of at least $1,144 per annum, derived from his capital or occupation.

In Denmark, according to the fundamental law of 1866, the upper chamber (Landsthing) is composed of sixty-six members, of whom, twelve are nominated by the king, seven by the city of Copenhagen, forty-five by electoral districts, and one each by the islands of Bornholm and Faröe. The royal deputies are nominated for life, from among those who have been members of the representative assemblies, and the remainder are elected for eight years; one-half being elected every four years. Their election, however, is not directly by the people, but by a body of secondary electors, elected by the people, by a somewhat complicated proportional system of voting, intended to give the minority a share in the representation.

In Holland, the constitution of 1815, as modified in 1840 and in 1848, fixes the number of the upper chamber at thirty-nine, who are elected by the provincial states for nine years, and every three years one-third go out of office. The only conditions of eligibility are, to be a citizen of good repute, and thirty years of age.

In Belgium, by the constitution of 1831, the Senate consists of a number of members equal to one-half of the number of members elected to the lower branch of the

8

legislature. They are elected for eight years, one-half
every four years. In order to be eligible to the Senate,
the candidate must be forty years of age, and pay a direct
tax of at least 1,000 florins (about $480), and every
Belgian, twenty-one years of age, who pays a tax of eight
dollars and a half per year can vote.

In France, during the second Empire, the Senate was
composed of the princes of the imperial family, the car-
dinals, marshals, and admirals, and of such citizens as
the emperor nominated to be senators, not to exceed one
hundred and fifty, who were appointed for life ; but the
constitution of 1875 established a popular basis for this
body. It enacts that the Senate shall be composed of
three hundred members, of whom two hundred and
twenty-five are elected by the departments and colonies,
and seventy-five by the National Assembly ; the latter
for life. The only conditions of eligibility are, that the
senator shall be a French citizen, and at least forty years
of age. The senators not appointed by the Assembly
are elected for nine years, by electoral colleges, in each
department, one-third retiring every three years. These
colleges are composed of the deputies elected to the Assembly, the members of the council-general, and the
members of the councils of the several departmental districts (arrondisements), together with a delegate from
each municipal council in the department.

The federal republic of Switzerland is peculiarly constituted. By the constitution of 1874, a national council
or lower house, and a council of states, or upper house,
exercise the legislative power ; and these two, together,
elect seven persons who constitute a federal council, which
possesses the executive power. The members of the
council of states are elected by cantonal laws which are
not uniform. In some cantons, as Glavis, Uri, and

Appenzell, the members are chosen in a democratic assembly of all the people; in others, by grand councils; in Zurich, by direct suffrage. The only voting qualifications are, to be twenty-one years of age, and not excluded from active citizenship by legislation of the canton.

The upper chamber, the Bundesrath, or federal council of the German Empire, is really no more than an assemblage of ambassadors from the several kingdoms, duchies, and principalities, each having a fixed number of votes, which are cast by each delegation as a unit. The delegates are paid by the States sending them, and are subject to recall and substitution. They represent the States of the confederation, as distinct political entities, and not any special class interests.

The English House of Lords is composed of spiritual and temporal peers. The spiritual are, the archbishops and bishops, who in 1878 numbered twenty-six; the temporal in the same year, were 5 peers of the blood royal, 21 dukes, 19 marquises, 115 earls, 25 viscounts, 248 barons, together with 28 representative Irish peers, elected for life by their fellows, and 16 Scotch peers, elected for the term of Parliament by their order.

The permanent tenure of the upper house of parliament has evidently influenced the principal British dependencies in their legislative arrangements.

By the act of parliament of 1855, establishing a form of government in New South Wales, an upper house, called a legislative council, is provided for. The crown, by an instrument under the sign-manual, authorizes the governor, with the assent of the executive council, to summon to the first legislative council not less than twenty-one persons, as he shall deem fit. At least four-fifths of these persons shall not be office-holders under

the crown.   The members of this first council were to
hold their seats for five years, while those summoned
afterwards were to hold for life.

In Victoria, by an act of parliament, in the same year,
1855, there is provided an upper-chamber, also called
the legislative council.   It consists of thirty members,
who are elected in districts, called electoral provinces,
five to each of the six provinces, into which the colony is
divided.   It is so arranged that a member from each
electoral province shall retire every two years, and a new
one shall be elected in his place.   The qualification of a
councilor is, that he shall be at least thirty years of age,
and the owner of a landed estate, of the value of five
thousand pounds sterling, or, of the annual rental value
of five hundred pounds sterling.

The British colonies, in upper and lower Canada, were
consolidated into a federal union in 1867, and subsequently the other colonies and possessions as far as the
Pacific ocean were added.   This federation consists of
the provinces of Ontario, Quebec, Nova Scotia, New
Brunswick, British Columbia, Manitoba, and Prince
Edward Island.   The executive authority is a governor-
general, nominated by the Queen, who acts under the
advice of a privy council, appointed and removable by
himself with the assent of the federal house of commons.
The legislative department consists of a senate and house
of commons.   The senate consists of 78 senators.   The
senator is appointed for life by the Governor-General; he
must be thirty years of age, the owner of a freehold estate
of the value of $4,000, or possessed of real and personal
property of the same value above his debts, and must be
a resident of the province from which he is appointed.

This brief reference to the present constitutions of the
upper legislative chamber in the principal civilized states

shows that, for the most part, the members hold their seats either as a political privilege by appointment of the crown, who is the source of the political privileges enjoyed by a nobility, or through an indirect election or an appointment, in which prominence is given to certain subordinate groups within the nation. In Austria, Hungary, Prussia, Italy, Portugal, and England, their authority rests on the will of the king, and, as a privileged element, or as an aristocracy between king and commons, are inclined to be conservative, and to prevent power from falling exclusively into the hands of the crown or of the people.

Through the upper house in the German Empire, Switzerland, Holland, Sweden, the United States, and in France to a certain extent, the individuality of social groups subordinate to the nation is recognized, and a certain balance is established between local independence, on the one hand, and the extreme of centralization, on the other. The upper house in Belgium, Denmark, France, and the British provinces falls, to a certain extent, under each of the foregoing descriptions.

The lower house of the modern legislature, on the other hand, stands for the popular assembly of the primitive state. The ancient popular assembly, in which all freemen participated, ceased to be a part of the legislature of sovereign governments, not through the growth of a sentiment hostile to government by the people, but because of that extension of sovereign dominion which rendered the meeting of the whole people impracticable. At an early stage in the growth of the nation, through the union of communities or through the extension of the dominion of a single community, a point was reached where it was no longer possible for the whole body of the freemen to meet in a common assembly ; and at this point the legislature lost its popular branch, which remained in some cases the assembly of the subordinate political division of the nation. The introduction of representation made practicable an assembly in which the mass of the people, through their representatives, might have a voice in the political affairs of the nation ; and there grew up by the side of the exclusive council, a body to take the place of the ancient assembly of the freemen, and to represent the unity of the nation, as opposed to the upper house, the exponent of class or territorial divisions.

In addition to the survival of primitive and mediæval political methods, there may be perceived in these modern arrangements two fundamental ideas ; the one is, that society contains within itself two antagonistic elements, conservatism and radicalism, which, like the old conceptions of good and evil, are supposed to be always present, and always secretly or openly in conflict ; and the other, that if you push the selection one or two removes away from the body of the people you will be apt to get wiser representatives than by direct, popular vote. Where there are distinctly defined classes, as there were in mediæval times, each class is conservative as to itself ; that is, it wishes to preserve its own privileges, and whichever class forms and expresses the state will and uses the state force, will of course be the conservative one in the state. It will be the class that, having the greatest number of advantages to be derived from the use of state power or the greatest number of interests to suffer by a change, will be opposed to modifications of existing conditions. But break up these mediæval classes ; take the individual out of his class, and merge him in the nation ; make the social body a collection of units, with individual relations directly with the

state, and then we find that those persons are the conservatives who have the most to lose through change ; or,
where their interests are not apparently affected, who by
temperament, or education, or surrounding influences are
averse to new experiments. Conservatism, then, is not
necessarily identified with a class, fixed within well-defined
social limits, at points where you can, as it were, put
your finger upon it. Every question that comes up
in the state for determination is advocated or resisted,
as it affects actual or supposed interests, or personal
views or prejudices, by each citizen. In short, every question has its radical and conservative aspect, and every
citizen is both a radical and conservative, as the occasion
urges him to act. In our modern conditions of society,
and especially as they have developed in the United States,
we cannot create a legislative branch on purpose to represent a special conservative class, much less to represent
conservatism in the abstract. Political parties are now
the instrumentalities which take up and advocate any
special interest, or set of opinions.

Can we, then, by selecting representatives out of particular categories of men, or by electing them at second-
hand by a selected body, as, for instance, by the State legislature, expect to get together the wisest of the community,
for a separate legislative house ? We could, if every one
having a voice in the choice of representatives, whether
the primary, or the secondary elector, should be, not only
disposed to look around for the wisest man, but should
also have an opportunity to vote for him when found.
Unfortunately, neither of these conditions ordinarily exists;
most voters, in fact, look at candidates as instruments to
carry out particular views ; they seldom measure their
fitness by the general test of ability to do, at the best,
whatever work the state may have to do. Then again,

the necessity of concerted action through party, forces
upon the voter the choice between the man whom his
party proposes, whether wise or not, and the man whom
the opposite party puts forward, who, though he may be
the better man, is pledged to forward measures the voter
deems hurtful.

The theory is, that a legislature is a deliberative body,
which debates about, and finally judicially decides upon,
measures. This, we know, is only partly true in fact.
The judicial tone is maintained upon secondary, unimportant questions ; but the partisan spirit is apt to pre-
vail upon those where parties are divided.

Experience shows that the composition of a legislative
body, elected by an extended suffrage, whether universal
or approximately so, is governed by those who control
the primary movements of political parties, or what perhaps may be designated as the springs of party organization ; so that the legislature may be above, or on a level
with, or below the average wisdom, culture, and honesty
of the community, as these controllers of party are in
these respects above, below, or on a level with the community. It may be considered, however, that the tendency is generally towards a representation of the average
ability of the majority of the voters.

In the United States, universal suffrage has become
the rule. Fixed, legal, class distinctions do not exist ;
those which inevitably grow up through differences in
wealth and culture, are very mutable ; sometimes lasting
two, seldom three generations. There is, therefore, no
reason for a legislative branch to represent especially
the conservative classes. As we have seen, even if such
were the occasion of its formation, the inevitable tendencies in a democratic system would bring it under the
control of party and the people. A democracy will not

tolerate any intermediary between its representatives and itself. Our Federal Senate, as experience has shown, is not necessary as a shield for the little States against the large ones, nor is it possible for it to rise higher than its source, and be wiser or better than the average of those who elect its members.

Theoretically, in a homogeneous nation like ours, there should be only one legislative body, elected directly by the people, and capable of promptly expressing the national will ; but in practice it is found that there is a reason for an upper as well as a lower house. The department of the government which expresses the national will should form its judgments with the greatest possible deliberation. Now, observation proves that when a measure is passed upon by two distinct bodies of men, deliberating separately, it will receive more. criticism and consideration than if acted upon by the same number of men united in one body. It is a psychological fact, that one's individual will is merged into the common will of an associate body, in which he is called upon to act ; and the larger the body, the less voluntary his action. At least, the sense of personal responsibility is diminished in proportion to the number of those who are jointly responsible. And again, every separate deliberative body is more or less, consciously or unconsciously, in antagonism with co-ordinate bodies, and for this reason, there is a sort of corporate impulse to an independent judgment. Hence, there is an advantage in two legislative houses. Even if the people elected all their delegates at once, for the same terms, it would be better to separate them into two chambers than have them all act together.

There is, moreover, an advantage in electing one house for a longer term than the other, and in having it consist of fewer members, simply because, as suggested, the

8*

sense of responsibility increases in the inverse ratio of numbers, and it may be added that a certain independence of judgment is secured by length of official tenure.

In this view, we may conclude that, though the election of the members of the Federal Senate, by the State legislatures, does not necessarily secure the choice of conservative men, or assure any more wisdom than should be found in the House of Representatives ; yet, because it is a body separate from the lower house, and because its members have a longer tenure of office, and are fewer in number, there is the possibility of an enlarged sense of responsibility, and the advantage of the deliberations of a more restricted body.

The lower legislative house is supposed more especially to represent the mass of the people ; but where the upper legislative house proceeds from a popular vote, as is the case in the several States of the United States, and also where its members are elected by a second body of electors, as in the case of our Federal Senate, and the upper houses of some of the European States, it is only closer to the people, because its members usually hold their positions for shorter terms, and consequently more frequent elections are necessary. For this reason, the House of Representatives in our system, may be said, every two years, to be an expression of the immediate will of the people, because voters for its members must have the qualifications requisite for electors of the most numerous branch of the legislature of the State from which they come.

CHAPTER XIV.

THE INITIATIVE IN LEGISLATION.

In order that the political power of a nation may be in a state of equilibrium, the right to initiate laws, and the right finally to pass them, should both be lodged in the same department of government. If the right to initiate is in one person or body of persons, and the right merely to accept or to reject is in another person or body of persons, then there is a practical division of the national will, which, being an abnormal condition of things, will produce a struggle in the state to bring about a re-union of the two rights in one person or in one department.

The permanent will of the nation expressed through its constitution designates, among other things, the persons or bodies of persons who shall formulate its occasional will, with reference to the two sets of relations with which the state deals—those between the nation and other foreign political bodies, and those between the individual citizens of the nation itself; and also defines the limitations within which these persons or bodies of persons shall move. The departments of government do not act spontaneously. They proceed in a predetermined way when set in motion by duly authorized persons. When a foreign nation is to be spoken to, it must be by the president or monarch, through the department for foreign affairs, or the ambassador. When laws are to be passed, the project or bill must be introduced by a person authorized to do so. This leads to the important question, who can set the

casual will in operation ; or, in other words, who can take
the initiative in legislation and in the management of
foreign affairs ?

It will be found that the possessor of the power of initiating legislation, or treaty-making, has command of the
sources of what may be called creative politics.

After the constitution and form of government have been
settled, a great deal of administration is routine work,
but constantly there are arising new circumstances, new
demands, new contingencies to be dealt with. These
require lines of policy to be determined upon ; and if the
matter in hand concerns the external relations, it becomes
important to know who can initiate the policy and the
diplomacy necessary to the occasion. In our own system,
this is a function which pertains exclusively to the President. The Senate, as to the foreign policy, acts as an
advising and consenting body.

A treaty is a contract made by the nation with a foreign
power. Under our constitution, it becomes, "the supreme law of the land." If it does not require any legislation to carry out its provisions, it is in effect a law made
by the President and Senate. And it is to be remarked
that the initiative, in this law-making, is entirely with the
President, through the ambassador. The Senate cannot
set on foot a treaty; it can only adopt or reject one
already made ; it cannot even amend the one presented.
When we recollect that there have been instances in our
history when the laws of states have been abrogated by
treaties, as, for instance, those precluding the inheritance
of real estate by foreigners, it is apparent what an enormous power is thus deposited in the hands of the Chief
Magistrate and Senate. In 1794, when Jay's treaty was
finally approved in the face of bitter popular opposition,
and the House of Representatives was asked to adopt ap-

propriate legislation to carry out its provisions, also subsequently in 1815, at the time of the treaty of peace with
Great Britain, and more recently at the time of the purchase of Alaska from Russia, the question was much discussed whether Congress was morally bound to execute
those provisions of a treaty which require legislation to
make them effective.   It has not been, and probably
never can be, definitively settled, for the obvious reason
that there is no tribunal whose decision can be in any
sense authoritative.   But there is no question that, when
a treaty has been made by the President, and approved by
the Senate, the United States is bound, by the rules of international law, to live up to its terms, and if it fails to do
so, because of the refusal of Congress to furnish the
necessary legislation, the foreign power, the other party
to the contract, has cause of war.   It is certainly no
answer to the demand for fulfillment of its terms, that the
legislative branch of the government is displeased with
the treaty, and properly cannot be so considered, because
the entire political society called the United States is, in
its international relations, an organic, single, political
being, which through its President and Senate expresses
its will and assent in the form of the given treaty.

We have thus the anomaly in our system, that a
"supreme law of the land" may be initiated by the
President alone, and may be finally enacted by him, with
the advice and consent of the Senate.   The treaty repeals
all laws which are in conflict with it ; but on the other
hand, an act of Congress may virtually abrogate the
treaty, if its legislation comes into conflict with it.   As
the supreme court of the United States announced : "A
treaty may supersede a prior act of Congress, and an act
of Congress may supersede a prior treaty." * Our Constitu-

* The Cherokee Tobacco case.   11 Wallace Rep. 621.

tion, as to the treaty-making power, is a compromise
between two ideas ; the one that the nation can speak
to, or treat with other nations only through the executive ; and the other, that the legislative body is the proper
organ to express the national will. The first is a survival of absolutism, of the form of government which was
personified in the prince ; and the second is the outgrowth of modern representative government. We do
not accept either theory in its entirety. The inclination
is, however, rather to the old one, because we entrust to
the President the power to initiate and provisionally conclude the treaty, and put the Senate in the attitude of
a privy council, or cabinet, to assent to, or reject it.
Many plausible reasons were advanced during the debates
of the Constitutional Convention, and, in the discussions
pending the adoption of the Constitution by the States,
and have been since advanced, in vindication of this feature of our system. It was, and is claimed, that treaty-
making pertains strictly to neither the executive nor the
legislative branch ; that its objects being to make contracts with other nations, it properly appertains to a department by itself, and moreover that dispatch and secrecy,
which are often necessary, would be impossible if the
treaties should be publicly discussed in both houses.   It
may be answered that many other acts of government are
better accomplished under an absolute monarchical than
under a representative system, but we are fully committed
in the United States to the latter.   We, as to other matters, lodge the will-expressing power in the legislative
branch ; that is, in the President and two Houses of Congress jointly.   Why another rule in this case ? Our Constitutional defect is, that we attempt to divide, as it were,
this will. We say, as to our foreign relations, the President
with the assistance of the Senate shall express it, and by

the same act he shall also create a supreme law of the land ; and we say as to our internal relations, that only the ordinary representative body in conjunction with the executive shall be omnipotent.

It is true, that international intercourse is largely carried on as though profound secrecy were absolutely necessary, and publicity destructive of its objects, but it may be seriously asked, whether this is not a mistake ? In an age when so much of the business of government is accomplished through discussion, why should those things which affect nations in their relation to one another, and wide circles of interest, be kept secret until they are accomplished facts, or, if discussed at all in advance, discussed upon surreptitious information, or half-true guesses ?

The treaty-making power is, in Great Britain, subject to the action of parliament, in so far as it trenches upon the legislative domain ; in this respect being analogous to our system ; though with us, there is this essential and very important difference, that the treaty may override or prohibit all State legislation upon matters which otherwise would be solely within the competence of the State.

In the constitution of the German Empire, it is provided that all treaties with foreign States, which refer to matters within the control of the legislature of the Empire shall require for their validity the consent of the Bundesrath, or federal council, and of the Reichstag. Within this category would come all commercial treaties. As an extended reference has been made to one power of our Federal Senate, it may not be out of place to refer briefly to other functions of that body which ally it on one side to the executive, and on the other to the judiciary.

The necessity of requiring the assent of the Senate to all appointments to office, by the President, naturally limits the latter in his choice, and practically puts the appointing power in the hands of the Senate. It has led to what is euphemistically termed " the courtesy of the Senate," through which a division of appointments to the offices among the different members is accomplished. If the function of the President is to see that the laws are executed, and he is to be made responsible therefor, then clearly he should have the power of appointing all subordinates. As it is, he must have the assent of the Senate to the appointment, and by the tenure of office act of 1867 he cannot remove even the heads of departments without the assent of the same body ; during a recess, he can only suspend an officer until the next session of the Senate, and fill only vacancies caused by death or resignation.

It is not necessary now to allude more fully to this extraordinary control of the Senate over the executive department, except to illustrate the real departure from what is popularly supposed to be the distinguishing feature of our new system, the rigid separation of the executive and legislative departments.

The function of the Senate as a court to try cases of impeachment, and especially to sit in judgment on the President, when charged with high crimes, still further enlarges the power of that body over the executive.

If domestic interests, or any considerable number of people in the country, demand legislation upon any given subject, the same question arises, Who can initiate the laws?

The demand and the supply in legislation and foreign policy give rise to all the movement of the current politics of a country. Now, where in any government the right to initiate the laws and policy, and also finally to pass or make them effective, are both lodged in the same

person or body, there, at that point, will be found what
may be styled the balance of power ; and it can be further said that that particular government is politically
matured.   It may be an absolute despotism or a pure
democracy, and yet it will be in a condition of equilibrium, and not in a transition stage.   The equilibrium
may not continue very long, and the balance of power
may again commence to move to some other part of the
organism ; but while it lasts, these two powers, the right
to initiate and the right to pass or finally adopt, must co-
exist in the same person or body.

It will probably be found that all revolutions, whether
gradual or sudden, have had for their ultimate object the possession of one or both of these rights.   Of course this object
is very seldom, if ever, thus distinctly formulated in the
minds of the actors, particularly at the outset.   It is only
after the first resistance to acts of oppression, or the first
outbursts of passion have been succeeded by organized
conflict, that the aim to control the law-initiating and
law-passing power clearly appears.   We have had, however, in recent times a striking example of a single con-
spirator deliberately planning to control this initiatory
process in the government, and completely succeeding.
The French constitution of 1848 provided that the President of the Republic should be elected for four years, and
should not be re-eligible until after an interval of four
years.   It also required that propositions to amend the
constitution could only proceed from the national assembly, and the amendment for its adoption had to be accepted by a three-fourths vote of that body.   Louis
Napoleon, as his term of office as first President was ap-
proaching its end, caused his friends in the assembly to
propose a general revision of the constitution, in order to
permit him to be re-elected immediately.   The proposi-

tion did not receive the necessary three-fourths vote of the assembly, and was consequently defeated; but, notwithstanding, Napoleon, a few months later, having the army on his side, dispersed the assembly, and submitted for adoption or rejection to the vote of the people this *plébiscite :* "The French people wish the maintenance of the authority of Louis Napoleon Bonaparte, and delegate to him the powers necessary to establish a constitution upon the basis proposed in the proclamation of December 2, 1851." The people having adopted the *plébiscite* by a large majority, Napoleon promulgated a constitution which confided to himself for ten years the government of the Republic, and which expressly provided that he should have the sole initiative of the laws.

It was the assertion and final seizure of this initiative power by the assembly in the first French revolution which lifted the grand movement of the people out of the lower regions of blind rage and resistance ; and when they added to it the prerogative of adopting the laws of their own initiation, the revolution was politically completed.

Louis XVI. called together the Estates General of France in 1789. The convocation was of the three classes, the clergy, the nobility, and the third estate. When the attempt to deliberate by the orders separately failed, the third estate, with a few of the clergy, constituted themselves a national assembly, and proceeded to reorganize the government. The legal revolution was accomplished when the king assented to a constitution which provided that the National Assembly should be permanent, though renewed every two years ; that the right to propose the laws was exclusively vested in the assembly, though the king should have a suspensive veto, that is, his veto should suspend the law until two succeeding legislatures had acted upon it. When Louis abandoned the

power of initiating legislation, he had completely surrendered himself to the revolution.

In England, the movement has been a slow continuous
one, which has transferred the initiative power from—to
use again the language of Mr. Bagehot—the dignified to
the efficient parts of the British system.   It was a very long
time ago when only the king could propose the law.   In
those days the Commons petitioned the monarch, in the
words of the bill which they wished to become a law ;
and even the form of royal assent which is now used,
"the king wills it," indicates the ancient combination of
the proposing, and the enacting power in the crown.

We are so accustomed in our American life to the spectacle of any member of a State legislature, or of Congress,
who has a particular idea which he wishes embodied in
a law, framing a bill for himself, introducing it in the
body of which he is a member, and if possible, persuad-
ing the majority to adopt it, that we are apt to assume it
is the only way in which representative government can
be carried on ; but for long periods, and in many countries even now, a parliamentary system has been, and is
practiced, in which the representatives merely assent to, or
reject the project of laws prepared by the head of the government.   In effect, this is the case in Great Britain to-
day, with relation to all questions of national importance.   The old power of the monarch to prepare the law
and propose it to parliament is now exercised by the
cabinet, which consists, as we know, of the leaders of the
party in power for the time being.   They prepare the
law, introduce it to the Commons, and the obedient
majority approves it.   The single member of the house
has the right, with the leave of the house, to offer any
bill he pleases, but it is a barren privilege, when party
questions are up ; the initiating power is then, practically,

solely in the hands of the few leaders, and sometimes the single leader of the party. It is not to be supposed that any bill, for instance, on the Irish land question, would have been received in the House of Commons in 1881, except from Mr. Gladstone, or one of his cabinet with his sanction. This practice is one of the distinguishing features between party government in Great Britain and this country. The causes of this difference, we shall discuss later. A point to be noted is, that where the right to propose the law is in one person or department, and the mere right to approve or reject is in another, the political system where such is the case is in a transition stage, and not in a condition of equilibrium. It is manifest that under these circumstances, there must be a conflict between departments of the government. The creative power, which is the effective one, the one most eagerly sought for, and without which needed changes cannot be accomplished, must be supplemented by the ability to formulate the power into a command in order to insure perfect harmony in administration. Most Continental nations are now going through the transition stage between absolutism and representative democracy. We must not be misled by name and forms ; by the " dignified parts " of a system. We must go below these, and inquire where is the balance of power ? Let us again look at the conditions in the new German Empire, because they illustrate quite distinctly the conflict alluded to.

The constitution, as previously remarked, enacts that the right to prepare the laws pertains to the Emperor. It is further provided that the Bundesrath, or federal council, shall take action upon the measures to be proposed to the Reichstag. This latter body, it is true, may propose a law by way of petition to the Bundesrath ; but that body is not compelled to act on the proposal.

The Reichstag is elected by universal suffrage ; so that we see, on one side, the crown proposing bills to a popular parliament, and the latter merely saying, yes, or no, to them. Naturally, out of this, there is a constant recurrence of strife.   In the language of diplomacy, the relations between the two ends of the system are always more or less strained.   A man like Bismarck may give more emphasis to the antithesis, which, however, is outside of the man ; it is in the system.   We may expect, therefore, in Germany, continuous movement ; whether it will be forward to a combination of the two powers in the Reichstag, or back to the monarch ; or, whether it will be accomplished peacefully, or after bloodshed, cannot of course be predicted.   It is clear that the present division of powers promises only temporary repose.   The whole set of political power, at this day, is towards that branch of the administration in every European country, which most immediately represents the body of the people ; and hence, we may safely assume that the Reichstag, if the Imperial system continues, will gain in power ; that its voice in the proposition of laws will be more and more listened to.

This power to propose laws, and the power to adopt them, though, as we know, separable in the practice of many countries, is essentially so single in its nature that when divided into the two parts, tends always to become united in a single person, or the same governmental department.   The absolute veto power in the monarch indicates, in the system where it exists, the same division of the two powers spoken of, as in the system where the initiative is in the monarch, and the assembly, or parliament, approves or rejects.   We find, therefore, a political system to be in the transition stage, where the absolute veto exists and is practiced.   Legally, the monarch of

Great Britain may veto an act of parliament, but in fact, the right is not exercised, and has not been since 1707, because the balance of power, or rather the once separated powers of proposing and approving the laws, have been finally, in practice, united in parliament.

In France, as we have seen, the President cannot veto a law passed by the legislative body. Under the constitution of 1852, of the Second Empire, the right of initiating the laws was solely in the Emperor ; but when liberalism gained head, and it could no longer be avoided, he submitted to the people the *plébiscite* in virtue of which the modified constitution of May, 1870, was adopted. This gave the initiative of the laws to the three branches of the government ; the Emperor, the Senate, and the Corps Legislatif; but still requiring the sanctioning of them by the Emperor. Thus, practically, the powers were divided as before ; while the lower house might initiate, the monarch could reject. The only improvement gained by the new system was in adding to the moral force, or weight, of the legislative branch, because it requires greater courage in an executive to veto a law absolutely than to neglect to initiate the legislation demanded. The veto is an open affirmative act of opposition to the will of the representatives, while the omission to propose a needed law is merely a neglect of duty ; and the human mind is so constituted that action impresses the imagination more vividly than inaction.

The constitution of the United States provides that : "all bills for raising revenue shall originate in the House of Representatives ; but the Senate may propose, or concur with amendments, as on other bills." This exclusive power of initiating laws for supplying money to carry on the government gives the command of position to the lower house of Congress ; for confessedly in modern days,

a government will very soon fall to pieces without taxation.   At the same time, it must be conceded that, as
the President can interpose his qualified veto to the
revenue bill, there is a separation of the two powers of
initiation and approval.   With reference to revenue bills,
the President does not stand in precisely the same attitude
that he does with reference to other proposed legislation.
In other cases, both the Senate and the House can initiate, and the President in his assent to the measure,
merely adds, or, as it were, votes, as we have seen, the
number of votes, or quantity of power, represented by
the number between the majority of the two houses
which passed the bill, and the two-thirds necessary to
overcome a veto.   But in the case of the revenue bill,
the House may initiate a law, which the Senate by uniting
with the President may absolutely veto.   It is true, this
absolute negative may be pronounced as to any bill originating in the House of Representatives; but this would
have no special significance, because, in effect, the two
houses are one body in such cases, with the form of
deliberating separately, and in succession upon a measure
which, indifferently, may have originated in either.   As
to revenue, however, the functions of the houses are distinct; one has a power which the other has not, and consequently when the Senate alone, or in combination with
the President, can absolutely veto the affirmative action
of the initiating body, then, as to that function, there is
clearly a separation of the power of legislation into two
parts, and consequently, as to that function, the system
is in the transition stage.

Here again, the practical working of the British constitution has united these two powers in the House of
Commons.   The Lords, it is true, have the right to reject,
though they cannot amend supply bills; but this privilege

of rejecting has been substantially abandoned, so that, in effect, the ruling party proposes, and also agrees to the revenue measures.

As above remarked, the initiative power in law-making is the creative force in the politics of a country. It has under its control all the possibilities of the future, and is the central lever which must be grasped by the person or body that would control the state.

In our American system, the initiatory power is limited and defined by the Constitution. The powers of Congress are enumerated. Eighteen sections state what this body can do, and eight what it cannot do.

In addition, there are the limitations imposed by the articles embodying the clauses concerning personal rights and privileges. The range of legislation is much wider in those Continental countries which have written constitutions, because in none of them are personal rights and privileges so carefully guarded as in Great Britain and the United States.

CHAPTER XV.

THE separation of a government into three branches, the executive, legislative and judicial, is not a necessary condition of free institutions ; it is simply a convenient and natural specialization of the functions which are developed as a nation grows in numbers and in the volume of its business. In the nature of government, the will or law-making power must be superior, and the executive power subordinate. This necessarily must be so, because the will must first express itself before the act willed can be performed. In a highly developed political system, a law is first formulated, and then the designated functionary executes it. The whole circle of governmental activity is comprised in command and performance. That the same person both wills and commands through a law, and also executes the law, in no wise affects the essential fact of the duality of the processes, and the further fact that the command must precede the action which is commanded to be done. Hence that department of any political system which expresses the volition of the state, is the central and superior power in the state. The ministers or functionaries who obey this volition are merely its servants.

The tendency of civilization is towards the specialization of functions ; in enconomical affairs to division of labor ; in political administration to the separation of the law-making department, from the departments which ex-

9

ecute the laws. If this differentiation is carried out to
its extreme limits, one set of men will be exclusively engaged in formulating and expressing the will of the nation in laws ; another in executing them, while a third
will occupy themselves in judging of individual cases of infractions of the laws or of disputes, to the adjudication
of which the laws are to be applied. There is, thus,
in the course of time, partly in consequence of the increase of the business of government, partly through the
consolidation of antagonistic social forces, an assumption
by different individuals of the law-making, the law-execut-
ing, and the law-judging functions. The separation and
distribution of these various functions to different individuals is only for the convenient, practical working
of the government ; and when constitutional writers in-
sist that a division of government into three departments,
the executive, legislative and judicial, is of the very
essence of free institutions, they put mere form for substance. It is by no means incompatible with the liberty
of the citizen that the law-making body should be also
the executive body, and even the judicial body.

We see in the actual working of the British system a
practical consolidation of the legislative and executive
functions in the dominant party in the House of Commons. The cabinet, which is no more than a committee
of this party, prepares legislation of national moment,
obtains the assent of the party to it, and then executes it.
In truth, it may be asserted, that the development of
government among civilized peoples, as the nation becomes homogeneous, is towards the concentration of the
legislative and directing, executive functions in the same
person or body of persons. The details of execution,
the subordinate work, must of course be done by a multitude of persons, who for convenience of administration,

must be divided into departments, boards, and single offices.

Even Montesquieu reasons in a circle when discussing the necessity of the separation of powers. He asserts that when the executive and legislative powers are vested in the same person or the same body, there is no liberty, "because," as he says, "it is to be feared that the same monarch, or the same senate, might make tyrannical laws in order to execute them tyrannically." And he further adds : "There is no liberty if the power to judge is not separated from the legislative and the executive power," because, as he continues : "If it were joined to the legislative power, the power over the life and liberty of the citizen would be arbitrary, for the legislator would be a judge."* It is obvious that whatever of tyranny there may be will exist in the law itself, and not in its execution. If Congress passes an act, supposing it to have the constitutional power, that every pauper shall be executed, the tyrannical act is complete ; nothing is added to or taken from the tyranny through the obedience of the sub-

---

* "Lorsque dans la même personne ou dans le même corps de magistrature la puissance législative est réunie à la puissance exécutrice, il n'y a point de liberté, parce qu'on peut craindre que le même monarque ou le même sénat ne fasse des lois tyranniques pour les exécuter tyranniquement. Il n'y a point encore de liberté si la puissance de juger n'est pas séparée da la puissance législative et de l'exécutrice. Si elle étoit jointe à la puissance législative, le pouvoir sur la vie et la liberté des citoyens seroit arbitraire ; car le judge seroit législateur. Si elle étoit jointe à la puissance exécutrice, le juge pourroit avoir la force d'un oppresseur. Tout seroit perdu si le même homme, ou le même corps des principaux, ou des nobles, ou du peuple, exerçoient ces trois pouvoirs : celui de faire des lois, celui d'exécuter les résolutions publiques, et celui de juger les crimes ou les différends des particuliers."—*De L'Esprit des Lois.* Livre xi. Chap. vi.

ordinate functionary in carrying out the law. Its odious-
ness may be more palpable to the senses because of the
execution of some particular pauper. And so, a law may
be arbitrary in and of itself; its application by the judge
to a particular case in no wise alters its character, nor does
it appear that it is any more or less arbitrary because the
same person may be first a legislator and then a judge.
It may be said here, upon this last point, in passing, that
the reason why, in a country where legislative powers
are limited by a written constitution, the judge should
not at the same time be a legislator, is not because
he might be more arbitrary, but because he might,
through pride of opinion, be disposed to decide a law
which he had had a voice in passing not to be in conflict
with the constitution ; and because he would be indis-
posed to hold that he had violated his duty when a legislator.

The confusion of thought on the subject of the separation of powers grows out of the failure, when actually
contemplating its government, to separate the will of the
nation from the force of the nation. There is no difficulty in the conception ; the trouble is to keep it always
before us when looking at the practical working of any
system. We are apt to have an ideal in our minds, with
well-defined parts, but we discover very soon that it seldom fits in with any particular system. In every government the will power is really distributed, in greatly varying
degrees, over every part, and so is the national force.
There cannot, in the nature of things, be any conflict
between the will power and the executive power, because
the one is superior to and distinct from the other, though
they may both reside in the same person. When, therefore, there is talk about a conflict between the executive
and legislative branches of a government, it means really

that the one is attempting to wrest from the other some portion of the national will power which it is exercising. It means that in that government there has not been an actual separation of functions ; that the power to make commands has not been exclusively devolved upon one person, or organized body of persons, and the duty of executing these commands upon another. The long dispute between King and Commons was no more than the working out of this differentiation. It is the dispute which is going on in every country where the monarch retains a certain portion of the legislative power, and the representatives of the people the remainder ; as, for example, in those instances which have been referred to, where the initiative is in the monarch, and only the right of approval or rejection in the representative branch.

Our Federal Constitution attempted a stricter division than can be found elsewhere, which, however, yet it is not so complete as to exclude conflict. It is divided into three parts, which provide for the legislative, the executive, and judicial departments. It says: "The executive power shall be vested in a president of the United States of America ; " and also : " he shall take care that the laws be faithfully executed."

This is very clear. It limits him to the execution of what the legislative department has commanded. As the executive officer of the nation, the President would be its spokesman with foreign powers ; and the chief representative of the national force both within and without. The field of conflict, however, is prepared when the President is also made a legislator, through the effect of his qualified veto, and through his right to initiate, and with the aid of the Senate, to adopt treaties which shall become the supreme law of the land. At this point, there is a union of the functions of two theoretically distinct departments, which *a priori* should produce conflict, and which in fact have produced conflict. On the other hand, the executive competency is seriously impaired by the interposition of the Senate in the confirmation of purely executive officers, thus investing one-half of the legislative body with the power to interfere in the executive department, by dictating who shall be the instruments through whom the President shall take care that the laws are faithfully executed.

It is intended, however, at this moment simply to call attention to these variations from the theory of a strict separation of powers, and also to call attention to the subordination in fact of the executive officers, to the legislative branch, except in those matters where there is a division of the willing power, and that it is just at those points that there is strife.

The judiciary, under our system, is elevated to the position of a distinct department in the constitutional system, while in other governments, it forms no part of the political system, but confines itself to the interpretation and application of the laws, in cases of disputes between individuals.

When there is a written constitution, and the legislative power is limited to certain enumerated subjects, the question will naturally arise, who shall determine when the occasional will of the nation conflicts with its permanent will ? If the decision is left to the legislative department, the legislature will naturally, by construction, extend its powers. And again, under a federal system, there must be some one to determine controversies which will be sure to arise between State laws and Federal laws.

In the constitution of the German Empire, there is a somewhat clumsy contrivance to meet this requirement. It provides :

"Article 76. Disputes between the different states of the Union, so far as they are not of a private nature, and, therefore, to be decided by the competent courts, shall be settled by the Bundesrath, at the request of one of the parties. Disputes relating to constitutional matters in those of the states of the Union whose constitution contains no provision for the settlement of such differences, shall be adjusted by the Bundesrath, at the request of one of the parties ; or, if this cannot be done, they shall be settled by the legislative power of the Empire."

This clause is somewhat obscure, but it is obviously based upon the confederate character of the empire, in which the states, through their ambassadors in the federal council, agree to settle their disputes by friendly arbitration among themselves. Our federal system is more than a league of states ; it contains a central government, which is in daily contact, directly, with every citizen, and whose laws and constitution constitute a jurisdiction to which he and not his State, is immediately subject.

The citizen of the United States is amenable to two jurisdictions, the Federal and the State, and it is an admirable contrivance to furnish a tribunal to which he can appeal when his rights under the one or the other are in question, or when State passion or prejudice may threaten them because he is a resident of another State, or because the matter in controversy is within admiralty jurisdiction. Our judicial system has been termed the balance-wheel in both the Federal and State governments. Whatever it may be figuratively, in fact it is a great political power. Under the guise of interpreting the constitution and laws in disputes between citizens, it is constantly laying down rules of action to be imposed upon future legislative bodies. It prunes and revises legislation, and thus hedges about and limits the exercise of the national will in its expression in its appropriate department, and thus, in effect, usurps a portion of the prerogatives of that will.

Theoretically, courts only declare what the law is ; but in the broad and somewhat vague regions of what is known as the "common law," there is an opportunity of judicially legislating, which courts in England and in the United States have embraced ; so that "judge-made-law" certainly exceeds all other in volume. It may be this constant tendency on the part of common law courts actually to make new laws, under the assumption of only applying old ones, has developed a striking difference between the methods of legislation in English-speaking countries and continental Countries.

An English or an American statute goes into the fullest details ; every possible contingency is anticipated and provided for ; as little as possible is left to discretion. The result is that our courts are called upon to listen to the most minute criticisms of acts of the legislature, and frequently decide cases upon the collocation of a phrase. It may be, that beyond what has been suggested, a further reason for this disposition can be found in the strong incentive for the legislative branch to draw to itself the exercise of the whole law-making power, and its reluctance to concede any of the will-power of the state, or any independent judgment, to another branch of the government. It wishes to prescribe everything. It is in part caused by the frame of mind, which has come down to us, of presuming everything in favor of the liberty of the subject and of freedom of action, and hence of allowing only the positive words of the law to limit them in any direction. Out of this conflict between the judicial and legislative departments has sprung the growing practice of codifying the laws, by means of which the latter department is constantly narrowing the field in which the former

can act.   On the contrary, in the Continental states of
Europe the statutes are mere outlines, furnishing only
general directions ; the details are left to be worked out
through the rules and procedure of the executive officers.
Take, as an illustration, the law passed by the Senate
and Chamber of Deputies of France, in December, 1880,
concerning the secondary education of girls.   It consists
of nine short sections, establishing no more than the outlines of a new system.   The same subject would have
been elaborated by an American legislature into a statute
copious in details, of at least five times the length of this
one.   The French statute, however, is merely a skeleton.
It will, in practice, be filled out by regulations prescribed
by the Bureau of Education.   The French method in this
regard grows out of the fact that, until recently, the whole
power of the state was in the monarch, who announced
his will in the most general form, leaving to his subordinates to attend to details.   Now his power has gone over
to the legislature, which, however, has not yet taken to itself
the functions of the monarch's subordinates.   In this respect there is still a practical division of the will power,
which will no doubt, if legislative supremacy continues in
France, concentrate more and more in the Chamber of
Deputies and Senate.   At the same time, the traditional
habit of mind there, as in our country, has much to do
with the French style of framing laws.   Those presump-
tions in favor of the liberty and innocence of the subject,
which are so familiar to us as to seem a necessary part of
political and juridical thought, are there unfamiliar to the
general mind.   Moreover, the executive has hitherto been
so overshadowing, and has for so long a time made and
construed the laws, that it seems natural that the representative body should merely sketch them, and leave the
details of execution to be accomplished in the old way.

9*

As suggested, it is really a division of legislative power, and as the representative branch becomes more and more conscious of its true position in the government as the possessors of the balance of power, it will more and more absorb the whole will-power of the state, and, by degrees, elaborate its statutes, so as to leave as little as possible to the discretion of the executive. The absence of a system analogous to the common law, and the practically large share of the executive in law-making, has reduced the Continental courts to a subordinate position, especially as compared with those of the United States.

CHAPTER XVI.

A POLITICAL system cannot be said to be established in a normal condition until all parties agree upon the fundamental principles of government, on which the system should be founded.

There is always a tendency to concentrate the supreme will or controlling power of the nation at some point in the government, and to draw after it, necessarily, the executive power, which, as we have seen, waits upon it. It is, however, only a tendency. The history of every sovereign political community shows a constant series of external and internal events, which interfere with the normal current of purely political devlopement. Every nation is a growth ; usually a fusion of a series of small communities, which retain a portion of their original law-making power, but transfer the superior will to the larger state. As we have seen, local and finally national institutions take their peculiar shapes as a consequence of this fusion. We therefore find, especially at the beginning of the history of the great modern nations, a mass of heterogeneous institutions, customs, and laws. But, out of this confusion, as the nation grows in distinctness, there is a concentration, as it were, of the national will ; that is, there is a growing submission to one person, or to one department, as the exponent of the national will. But as social forces within the nation distribute and redistribute themselves, there is apt to accompany the movement a shifting of the balance of power from one part of the social organism to another. In this latter case, there will probably be a dispute as to the foundation principles of the government. Such a dispute must first be settled before there can be normal political development.

It is very important for the peaceful living, and hence for the healthful social growth, of a people, that there should be a common agreement, not only as to the form of the government, but also as to the general methods of adminstration. Without this harmony of opinions, without a community even of sentiment in this respect, there are the possibilities of violent collisions between parties, because they will be divided, not upon mere questions of expediency in legislation, but upon the fundamental theories as to how the government should be constituted.

Two questions must be settled in the nation before the danger of civil war is removed. First : the form of the government ; that is, shall it be monarchic, or oligarchic, or aristocratic, or democratic ? Second : in which of the governmental departments is the ultimate power lodged ? Until these questions are disposed of, it cannot be said that the particular nation is in a normal political condition. Its social development may be the most advanced ; its administraton of private law, its methods of, and efficiency in, preserving order, its civil and military service may be wise, thorough, and economical, and its intellectual life may move upon the highest plane, and yet it may be in a politically abnormal condition. As long as its people are divided on the form of its political administration, or are in dissension as to where in the governmental framework the supreme power should be manifested, so long is there danger of convulsions affecting the very foundations of the state.

France has been in this abnormal condition since the breaking out of the Revolution of 1789. It is true that, since the Franco-German war, the largest party has been in favor of the Republic ; but there are strong and influential bodies of the people, which aim to revolutionize the existing form of government. The legitimists would restore the Bourbons to the throne, which of course, means a return to the mediæval idea of the divine right of kings and to the concentration of power in the king supported by the old aristocracy. This party does not profess absolutism ; it even concedes that the modern demand for constitutional guaranties must be respected, but it does not admit that the lawfulness and continuance of its powers depends upon the consent of the governed. Its theory is, that whatever part in the administration is exercised by the people, is a concession from the monarch. The Orleanists, on the other hand, would introduce the quasi-constitutional methods of Louis Philippe, a halfway resting-point between Bourbonism and republicanism. The Imperialists demand a centralized personal government, founded on universal suffrage. These three sections are really revolutionary parties seeking the overthrow of the existing régime, and until they disappear, and the bulk of the people are finally agreed upon the form of government, there will be abnormal political conditions in France.

Great Britain, on the other hand, presents the example of a country all of whose people agree, not only as to the form of the government, but also as to which department of it shall exercise supreme control. Its geographical position and social conditions have been such as to permit a steady, or nearly continuous political evolution for

several hundred years.   For over six centuries it has had
its three factors, the executive, the upper house, and the
lower house, and we may add, for a portion of the time,
its independent judiciary rigidly divided.   What has been
the result?   All power has been finally concentrated in
the House of Commons.   On this point Frederic Harrison
recently wrote : "In the course of centuries, everything
in the working of the complex machinery of this nation
has become concentrated in, or absorbed into, the House
of Commons.   The House has, in fact, become the most
gigantic and heterogeneous bureau that the world ever
saw.   *   *   *   This conversion of one of the two legislative chambers into an irresponsible executive has grown
up insensibly and gradually out of two main functions,
into which it may still be conveniently grouped.   The
first is the time-honored right of criticising the executive ;
the other is the modern habit of giving a legislative form
to purely executive details.   The history of the process
is one of the most curious and subtle in our long constitutional development.   One sees how the body, which was
once the sturdy petitioner of the Plantagenets, the obse-
quious tool of the Tudors, and the undaunted opponent
of Stuart misgovernment, gradually became the Mayor of
the Palace to the Hanoverian Fainéants, and now in this
century has become a despot more autocratic than any
Czar—a despot with an unbounded power of meddling,
and an inexhaustible gift of prolixity." *

It is only within a century, or rather one may say, during this century, that the centre of power has finally
lodged in the House of Commons ; and less than a century and a half since the country was split asunder by a
dispute over the succession to the throne.   The deposition
of James II., in 1688, and the Declaration of Right,

* *Nineteenth Century*, Sept., 1881, pp. 318, 333.

which recognized and legalized the accession of William
and Mary to the throne, was a violent breach of the traditions to which the Stuarts had sought to give additional
force. It introduced a dynastic question, which divided
the nation, and as long as the non-juring party was
sufficiently numerous seriously to divide public opinion
upon the duty of allegiance to the occupant of the throne ;
as long as there was a party which recognized as its
sovereign a person who could not enter the country, except as an invader, there could not be said to exist normal political conditions.

The Revolution of 1688, moreover, established the
doctrine that the English government rests on the consent of the governed. It is interesting to observe how
Burke in his "Reflections on the Revolution in France"
labors almost fiercely to disprove the assertions of his
adversary, Dr. Price, that by the Revolution of 1688, the
people of England acquired three fundamental rights : 1.
the right to choose their own governors. 2. the right to
cashier them for misconduct ; and 3, the right to frame a
government for themselves. He endeavors to show that
there was only a small and temporary deviation from the
strict order of succession ; that it was an act of necessity,
and merely a provision by parliament for an emergency.
We must recollect in reading this strange reasoning, that
at the time when these Reflections were written the comprehensive, philosophical perception of Burke in political
things, was sadly obscured by his bitter hatred of the new
doctrines of equality and fraternity, and by the barbarities
of the French revolutionists.

It has been the good fortune of England that, for so
many centuries, there has been a substantial agreement
among its people as to the form of its government. The
departments and forms of government have undergone

but little alteration since very early times, but gradually the centre of governmental power has gone from one extreme to the other.

The political evolution in a nation appears to be always towards the concentration of the law-making power and the control of its physical force, or the executive power, in one and the same person or department.   .

If this be so, then the attempt to create an artificial system of checks and balances in government, as was the case in framing our federal constitution, is futile, because this constant tendency to the lodgment of all power in some particular part of the system will either entirely destroy resistance, or, what is more likely, will direct the forms to other purposes than those originally intended. And it is very fortunate for a nation if its government is flexible enough to permit the centre of gravity to pass through old forms from one department to another without civil war.

In tracing the history of a government, one is often struck with the fact, that at one peroid, the balance of power is in one person, or branch of the administration, and at another, in another ; and that it is difficult to point out the steps by which, in the interim, the power has been absorbed by the one, and lost by the other. And again, that all the time the same offices and departments continue apparently unchanged. It is related that Lycurgus constituted a Spartan senate, whose members voted in conjunction with the two kings who sat with it, and that with this there were combined periodical assemblies of the Spartan people, though no discussion was permitted at these assemblies, as their functions were limited to the simple acceptance or rejection of the previous resolves of the senate. It appears that about a century after the establishment of this system, a change was made by which an executive directory of five Ephors, could be chosen from the body of the citizens. While it is not certain what were the original powers conferred upon this new body, the subsequent history of Sparta shows that the Ephors gradually drew to themselves the most extensive and commanding functions of the state, and limited "the authority of the kings to little more than the exclusive command of the military force." *

In the Continental states of Europe, the absorption of power by the monarchs, and its gradual re-distribution in this century to the people, is marked, it is true, by occasional violent transitions, but still, on the whole, in the long course of the years, the change has been accomplished through a multitude of petty encroachments, first on one side and then on the other. In England, as already re-marked, the movement from one part of the system to the other has grown up "insensibly." The causes which are always and everywhere operating, are to be found in certain qualities of human nature already referred to. The corporate impulse, like the individual impulse, is constantly in the direction of enlarging jurisdiction. If we look closely we shall see that, almost without excep-tion, the conflicts between officers and departments of government are over the exercise of the will-power, or power to make effective commands, and seldom, if ever, over the effort to obey commands, or the mere executive power. An individual, or the body of individuals, has the right to make a law or regulation on a given subject, and another person has a right to make a rule or com-mand, which, by construction can extend over the same subject. Here is an opportunity for strife, and in the end, one or the other will be sure to dominate.

* Grote, " History of Greece," II., 345-347.

Of course, it cannot be asserted that there is always open, or constant strife. On the contrary, more commonly, one official or department, little by little presses back and circumscribes another, because, possibly it possesses more personal vigor, or more persistency, or greater opportunities. No doubt, in the division of power in the German Empire, between the Emperor and the Federal Council on the one side, and the popular Reichstag on the other, the personal weight of Bismarck may keep the balance on the side of the crown. But when the sturdy Chancellor disappears from the scene, it is possible that a weaker successor may not be able to hold it there, against the steady pressure of four hundred or more representatives of the people, who are constantly seeking to grasp power. The solution of the question as to which branch of the administration will be likely finally to be dominant in a constitutionally free system controlled by political parties, depends upon which has the command of position. This command of position is owing to so many and such a variety of conditions, that it cannot be accurately defined in advance. We must examine the particular government by the light of the principles already discussed, in order to discover the point to which power naturally tends. The law-making power of the United States is distributed among three departments. As we have seen, the President has a share, both by means of his treaty-making capacity, and by means of his qualified veto ; the two houses of Congress have a large share, and even the Courts are really law-makers, though theoretically, only its interpreters.

The first business devolving on Congress was to organize the administration of affairs. The attempt was made, and very successfully, to define precisely the limits of the several departments. As early as 1793, the question came up as to the separate functions of two of them. An act of Congress concerning pensions, imposed certain duties upon circuit courts, and made their decisions revisable by the Secretary of War, and afterwards by Congress. The chief justice and the justices of the New York circuit, and the Pennsylvania and North Carolina circuit judges, declined to act, on the ground that the duties were not judicial, and therefore could not be imposed upon the judicial branch. They all agreed that, by the Constitution, the government of the United States is divided into three distinct and independent branches, and that it is the duty of each to abstain from and oppose encroachments on the others. Theoretically this rule has never been controverted ; but, as we know, the theory and practice of a government are frequently widely different.

The important question, already referred to, as to the power of the President to remove an officer appointed by him, without the consent of the Senate, was only decided by the casting vote of the Vice-President, John Adams, in the Senate. At that early day, it was merely a theoretical question ; but later, at the close of the civil war, when it became a practical one, and party passions were high, Congress passed the Tenure of Office Act of 1867, which has turned the Senate into an oligarchy for conferring official appointments.

Another important question arose during Washington's term. Jay's treaty with England was ratified by the Senate in 1796, and Washington proclaimed it as the law of the land. The treaty was very unpopular, and a majority of the House of Representatives were bitterly opposed to it, and to the administration. A motion was made, calling on the President for his instructions to Jay, with the correspondence and other documents relating to the

treaty.   The reason advanced by the mover was, that
the house was vested with a discretionary power whether
or not to carry the treaty into execution.   It was claimed
in support of the motion, that as treaties became the
law of the land, and the legislative power was in Congress, the House, as the branch of that power, had a voice
in the enactment of every law, whether by treaty or when
proposed in Congress itself. This extreme ground, however, was not strongly urged.   The more reasonable one
was taken, that, as to those provisions which required the
aid of Congress to carry them out, this body could
furnish aid or not, as it pleased and thus control the treaty.

Washington declined to furnish the demanded papers,
upon the explicit ground that the House of Representatives had no voice in the treaty-making power, and he insisted in his message, " that the boundaries fixed by the
Constitution between the different departments should be
preserved."

The practice, however, has become well established,
notwithstanding the continued reservation of the right to
the contrary, for the executive to furnish diplomatic
papers upon the call of the House, sometimes even while
negotiations are pending with a foreign country.   The
actual power of the House of Representatives, in refusing
its aid to enforce treaties, is so great that it compels the
President, in negotiating a treaty to guide himself by its
temper and views.   This furnishes a sort of moral coercive power, which strengthens the dominating attitude of
the lower house.

The purely executive functions of the presidential
office can be so guided and limited as to be substantially
under the control of Congress.   As commander-in-chief
of the army and navy, his duties can be accurately
marked out.   We have an instance of the extreme point

to which this can be carried, or rather attempted, in the
Act of Congress, in the time of Johnson, requiring the
President to transmit his orders through the general of
the army, who could not be removed for disobedience to
them without the consent of the Senate. His cabinet
can even be kept in place against his wish. Every movement he makes in the direction of executive duty is prescribed by law. He is, in that regard, merely the chief
servant of the legislative power. It is at the points where
he is invested with a portion of the will power of the
nation that the possibilities of struggle for dominance can
arise. This explains very much in our political life which
appears obscure if we do not keep in view the fact that
the President is both a maker and an executor of the
laws. And this being the case, we cannot keep the
departments of the government separate, for the reason
that they are not essentially entirely separable. The
framers of the Constitution were impressed with the conviction that in the British system there was actually
present a separation of legislative, executive, and judicial
functions, and that each moved within an independent
circle of its own. They were not in a position accurately
to determine the full force of the set of power, both
legislative and executive, into the House of Commons.
Personal government, as exhibited in the constant interference of George III. in the conduct of affairs, and
always for the purpose of oppression, had inspired them
with a dread of a strong or willful executive. They were
afraid to give the President an absolute veto. If they had
given him this power the issue would, no doubt, at a
very early day, have been forced and settled between the
chief magistrate and Congress by the practical dominance
of the latter, because the power of impeachment would
have been used without mercy. As it was, the executive

was to be a check upon Congress, and the latter a counter check upon the chief magistrate, while each branch of
Congress was to be a check upon the other, and the
judiciary a check upon all the co-ordinate branches.

The importance, therefore, of the President in our system is not as the republican symbol of the king, not as
the personification of the national unity, but as a legislator
elected by the people at large, with a voting power nearly
equal to one-third of the two houses of Congress. The
attitude of mind of the colonists towards the British executive, and the theories which grew out of it, prevailed
until the disappearance of the generation of the Revolution ; in truth, they color even yet the thought of very
many of our people. This thought is, that the President
is one of the guardians of the Constitution ; that he stands
as a national conservative to restrain popular passions ; a
wise man in a possible access of folly. The actual constitutional position of the chief magistrate had a flood of
light thrown upon it by the doings of Jackson. Jackson
took his presidential position literally as it was. When
he made his warfare upon the Bank of the United States,
he assumed the attitude of a tribune of the people, pro-
tecting them against the machinations of the rich. In
his message vetoing the bank charter, he asserted : "The
Congress, the executive, must each for itself be guided
by its own opinion of the Constitution. Each public
officer who takes an oath to support the Constitution
swears that he will support it as he understands it, and
not as it is understood by others."

This has been much criticised, but if we limit its assertion of independence of judgment to acts proposed,
and not to acts accomplished, it is unassailable. The
Supreme Court of the United States only passes judgment
upon existing facts, and applies the constitutional test to

a case already made. But the important functions of the President and Congress, in the exercise of legislative power, are to be applied to acts proposed which relate to the future. In this field, each must necessarily construe the Constitution for itself. Then again, in what is called purely political action, that is, the choice of means to accomplish a constitutional end, the action of the particular department charged with a duty must be guided by its own judgment; for instance, if a national bank is constitutional, what shall be the details of construction; or it may become necessary, before a power can be exercised, to determine and declare that a certain state of facts exists, as, for example, that there is an actual state of war. Jackson, however, really went further; he took the position of the chief representative of the people in law-making. He quietly swept aside the theory that the people were only indirectly the choosers of the executive, and appealed directly to them, claiming that his second election was a popular endorsement of his policy. Since his day, the position of the President in our system has been more distinctly brought out. The point of inquiry, however, to which it is desired to direct attention is that regarding the inherent probabilities of the absorption of power, as between the President and Congress. This turns, as already suggested, on the constitutional advantages of position. Which of the two can draw most from the common reservoir of will-power? It is apparent that Congress has at least two advantages—it has the initiative in legislation, and it can prescribe the manner and time of presidential acts in domestic affairs. The right of initiation, however, loses somewhat of its value, because of the veto power, and when Congress is anxious to carry out particular legislation, it may be forced to go to the President in advance to know what form of bill will meet

his approval. This has frequently been done. Jackson
intimated that he possibly might approve a bank measure,
if made to conform in advance to his views; a claim,
which particularly excited the anger of Clay and Webster.
Tyler was consulted as to the form of the bank bill prepared after his first veto, and even altered the phraseology
of particular sections; and in other instances, the views
of the executive have been ascertained before introducing
a bill.   Nevertheless, even with these qualifications, the
power of initiating measures gives an immense advantage
in the choice of time, subjects, and method. Add to this,
the power of hedging the chief magistrate about with
restrictions, supplemented by the power of impeachment,
and it may be safely asserted that, in the long run, Congress
will encroach upon, and reduce the President to a secondary position.

The impotency of this officer, when in opposition to a
hostile Congress, animated by strong passions, was strik-
ingly illustrated in the controversy between President
Johnson and the legislative branch.   There were fundamental differences between them, going even to the theory
of the relations of the States to the general government,
which, however, might have been bridged over; but the
irreconcilable antagonism grew out of the attempt of the
President to carry out a policy contrary to that of Congress.
He proposed on his side, and they on theirs, to exercise
the will-power of the nation.   In the meantime, the
people stood by, and looked on.   In a contest of this
kind, the legislative branch of the government has such
an enormous advantage that in the end it will be sure
practically to dominate the executive.

The judicial branch of the government has apparently
an independent position.   If it really possessed the powers
it theoretically possesses, of being the final arbiter between

the occasional and the permament wills of the nation; if it could without restraint, absolutely veto legislation upon the assertion that it contravenes the Constitution, then it would, certainly, become the dominant branch of the government.   But, actually, it can be held in check by the legislative branch.   The Supreme Court cannot be abolished, nor can its jurisdiction be impaired ; but the number of judges is in the control of Congress.   If a decision is contrary to its views, it can increase the number of judges and thus bring about a reversal, as was actually done when the greenback cases were before the court. Or the amount in controversy required to authorize an appeal can be made so high as practically to cut off resort to the court in most cases.   The whole scope of the inferior judiciary is so entirely in the control of Congress that this body may make and unmake the courts almost at its will.   Then, again, the action of the courts is only upon individual disputes; and, while its decision in a particular case may in effect nullify a statute, it is rather a definition than a limitation of the will-power of the nation.   Whenever the court steps outside of the case before it, to decide political questions agitating the country, it not only loses in moral weight, but its decree falls dead upon the subject-matter itself.   The Dred Scott decision was a most flagrant instance of judicial assumption, and a most lamentable example of judicial impotence.   Chief Justice Taney labors through three or four pages to show that Dred Scott could not maintain his action in the United States Courts, because, being a negro and the descendant of slaves, he could not be a citizen, either of a State, or of the United States.   Having reached the conclusion that Scott had no standing in court, the proper course would have been to go no further, and dismiss the case.   But the majority of the court was so

10

anxious to throw its weight into the controversy which was then raging over the question of slavery in the territories, that it proceeds, unnecessarily, to hold that the Missouri Compromise was void, and that slavery could be introduced into all the territories. Read now coolly, after the slave controversy has become a matter of history, this opinion shows the absolute perversion of sound judgment, which is apt to exhibit itself in the judicial mind, when dealing with questions about which political passions are raging. Instead of terminating the angry debate over slavery in the territories, this opinion added fuel to the flame, and no doubt was potent in hastening the inevitable war.

Our history has clearly demonstrated that the judiciary cannot make itself felt as a balance wheel between parties. It invariably loses the respect in which it ought to be held, when it takes hold of living political issues, and its judgments never lead to an adjustment of them. The judiciary, in a government based upon a written constitution, is valuable in defining the limits within which the different departments shall work, and gradually it gives, through its exposition, greater precision to the different parts. The legislative branch has its defined limitations, but its tendency always will be to construe for itself the scope of its competency, and it is to be expected that, from its greater command of resources, it will be inclined to impose limitations upon other departments, and to aggrandize itself. These results in the normal action of the government come about slowly, so that it may be a long time before the legislature absorbs most of the functions of government.

The tendency in our federal system is plainly to establish Congress as the means for expressing the will of the nation. The inevitable drift of Congress is toward the exercise of powers not expressly given, nor ancillary to any enumerated in the Constitution ; powers which Judge Story styled resulting powers, arising from the aggregate of the powers of government, and Congress will be always naturally inclined to push its claims in those fields of legislation, constantly widening under the general clauses of the Constitution, where the judiciary from a very early day have decided that it is the judge of what is "proper and necessary." It may and probably will be a very long time before there will be such a concentration, as we see in Great Britain, in the House of Commons. The old forms and theories will remain substantially the same, but the substance of power will be in Congress. As between the Senate and the House, the tendency will naturally be towards the House, for one, if for no other reason, because it possesses the great power of initiating all revenue measures.

The tendency to differentiation of functions in government is not in conflict with the one already described as leading to a concentration of all directing power in one person or department. Naturally, as a community grows older and more complex, there is an increase of the departments of government, but it does not necessarily follow that there will, at the same time, be a corresponding division of the dominating will-power. A division of will-power may come about from other causes than the mere growth of the social body ; perhaps through the slow operation of a variety of causes, as in England ; or possibly in consequence of a grant of limited representative institutions from a king, as when Frederick William IV., in 1850, gave a constitution to Prussia. When this dominating will-power is divided, from whatever causes, whether through external wars or social or political revolutions, or by design, in written constitutions, there are new forces set in motion, which inevitably tend to reunite it. Moreover, the work of governing, as it increases, demands a continually increasing number of departments, boards, and officers, to perform the routine and other duties mapped out by the law-making power. At the outset, when the United States contained about four millions of inhabitants, it was found sufficient in organizing the government to create only three departments : one for foreign affairs, another for war, and a third for the treasury. Now there are eight principal, and several minor departments. There are the departments of State, of the Treasury, of the Interior, with its subordinate divisions into the General Land Office, Pension Office, Patent Office, Indian Office, Bureau of Education, Census Office, besides various minor offices ; there are also the departments of War, of the Post-Office, of the Navy, of Justice, and of Agriculture. In addition to these, there is attached to the Treasury Department an elaborate system of offices for the collection of internal revenue. Not only are the departments more numerous, but there has also been an enormous increase in the number of persons employed in them, and, moreover, a more specialized division of duties. This has all occurred with us in less than a century, the specialization being all in the direction of the details of labor. In all legislative bodies, there has also been a division of labor through committees, and through the growth of a complex system of forms. In the original assembly of the people, the body acted directly in making the law, but now, a bill introduced into Congress must go through certain readings, be referred to certain committees, and be acted upon in certain prescribed ways, before it can be published as the law of the land.

It is one of the results of social specialization that men

accomplish their ends by indirect expenditures of their individual forces. We see this prominently illustrated in the economical relations ; how men labor at one thing, in order to accomplish another. In the political relations also there is a division of labor, and the national as well as the individual force expends itself through various devious and intricate channels before it reaches its object. What is popularly sneered at as " red tape " becomes really inevitable.

The differentiation of government from its simpler forms into distinct executive, legislative, and judicial branches is a natural process, as governments become popularized ; that is, as the number of those increases who have a voice in saying how the government shall be conducted, and as the work for the government to do enlarges. The increase in the number of those who can decide how the government shall be conducted means, of course, that the supreme directing power is not exclusively in the one, or more than one who may have originally possessed it, but is shared by many. Under these circumstances, the laws producing a division of labor will operate, and one function will be exercised by one person, and another by another. If a hundred men set about the accomplishment of a given task, they will very soon divide the work into convenient parts, and though all may at the outset be on an equal footing as to the methods of reaching the desired end, it will very soon result that the directing will will be lodged in one, or a specific number of the body. So those social ends which can be accomplished only through government are reached in very much the same way. As all cannot, from day to day, assist in the making of laws and the execution of them, the work is naturally divided and assigned to different persons ; but if, in this distribution, the supreme

directing power is also divided, then there is, according
to the degree of division, an abnormal political condition, which in the healthy vigorous community, naturally
tends to become normal again through concentration of
this supreme, controlling power.   At the time our Constitution was framed, the balance of power had not completely gone over to the House of Commons, as has since
been the case.   There was still much of the " personal
government " of the king.   The Cabinet had not become so
entirely the pivot of affairs as now.   There was supposed
to be, by the admirers of the British constitution, a
happy balance of powers which kept the whole scheme of
administration in a beautiful poise, neither inclining
too much to absolutism nor too much towards democracy.

Impressed with these beliefs, the makers of our Constitution attempted to make firm and stable by positive,
written law, what in truth was in the mother country in
a transition stage.   Consequently one of the political tasks
of the century has been, and continues to be, to twist
and construe and practically work the Constitution, so as
to concentrate the directing power in the House of Representatives.

The separation of the departments of government into
legislative, executive, and judicial has, at bottom, no other
significance than as a convenient working scheme for the
administration of the complex affairs of a complex
society; and in so far as the attempt in separating them is
also to distribute among them the law-making power,
which is the final expression of the supreme national will,
to that extent are the occasions of strife introduced, leading to more or less open conflict between the departments, which will end only with the final concentration
of this supreme power in one or another.

CHAPTER XVII.

A CONFEDERATION of states is necessarily short-lived ; if it does not go to pieces, it can be considered only as a transition stage between smaller single states and a larger single one. In like manner also the federal state represents merely a further stage of development toward the single state.

Thus far the analysis has been confined to the single, complete, or, as it is usually denominated, sovereign state ; and the nation has been treated as embracing such a state. The aim has been always to keep in mind a single, organic, political body, and to discover, if possible, the elementary forces which are operating in every such body. The special manifestations of these forces in particular forms of administration have been only incidentally adverted to, and by way of illustration, because, if we can make clear to our minds the general principles upon which all governments are constructed, we are in a position to study properly any particular government.

We must now go a step farther, and examine the character of the governmental relations which arise when two or more states join themselves together and form a new government. It is not within our scope to consider the maxims of international law, which furnish rules of conduct and bind sovereign states together into a world-community. These maxims belong to the domain of positive morality, and the rights and obligations which arise under international law are moral rather than jural. Nor is it proposed here to consider those temporary alliances of states, which are the result of treaties, but rather those permanent alliances through which the governments of the individual states are more or less affected. There may be merely a personal union, as where a prince becomes, by descent or other means, the governmental head of states permanently allied. We have examples of this personal union in the Empire of Charles V.; also in the cases of William III., King of England and Stadtholder of Holland; and of George I., King of England and Elector of Hanover. Or, at the other extreme, there may be the federal state, like the United States. Between these, there may be, as there have been at various times, several forms of federations. They have even been carefully classified, as alliances, confederacies of states, federal states, real unions, personal unions, and incorporations; but it is impossible to put in definitions the precise differences. One shades off into the other, and a combination of states may present the characteristics of two or more of these classes. German writers, for purposes of analysis, distinguish among them two kinds : the *Staatenbund* (confederacy of states), and the *Bundesstaat* (federal state). This is probably the most comprehensive and best classification.

We cannot expect, even as to these, accurate definitions. In a general way, it may be said that both, as to other states, in external relations, or foreign affairs, present the form of unity. There must be a central organ which speaks for the entire body, as one political being. It is in the relations between the central power and the citizens that the essential distinction manifests itself. In the confederacy of states, there is a central government created by agreement between the states, and the laws of this central authority are to be obeyed by the several states as states ; that is, the individual states as sovereignties are to see that the laws are executed.   The relation of the citizen to the central government is only indirect, through his state.   The federal state is also an association of states, by agreement, in which, however, the central government, by its own laws and officers, acts directly upon the citizen, without the interposition of his state.   Under this system, the citizen owes a double allegiance—directly to the central government, and also directly to his state.   In the federal state, the objects over which the central power has jurisdiction, and the methods of exercising this jurisdiction, are defined in the written constitution, and all powers not conferred upon the central government are reserved to the states.   It is commonly said of the federal state that its powers are enumerated, while those of the component states are sovereign, except where surrendered to the central authority.

A very good example of a confederation of states is found in the union of the colonies during the Revolutionary war, under the Articles of Confederation adopted July, 1778 ; and the most complete instance of a federal state is that of our Union, formed in 1787.   The Articles of Confederation were more like a treaty than a scheme of effective government.   The third article provides that "the said states hereby severally enter into a firm league of friendship with each other, for their common defence, the security of their liberties, and their mutual and general welfare, binding themselves to assist each other against all force offered to, or attacks made upon, them, or any of them, on account of religion, sovereignty, trade, or any other pretence whatever."

10*

This is the language of independent sovereignties, combining for purposes of mutual defence, against a common enemy.

In order to promote intercourse between the citizens of the different states, certain privileges are accorded to all alike concerning ingress and egress, commerce, and other matters. In all these things, the Articles do not go beyond an ordinary treaty. The characteristics of a common government appear, in the provision that delegates should be annually appointed to meet in Congress, in such a manner as the Legislature of each state should direct. These delegates were rather plenipotentiaries from the governments of the different states than representatives to a parliamentary body. Each state could send such a number of them as it pleased, not less than two, nor more than seven, and could recall them at any time and send others in their stead. Each state paid its own delegates, and upon the adoption of measures each state had only one vote; thus putting them upon a plane of equality. In these respects, the Congress of the states was very much like the present Bundesrath, or federal council, of the new German Empire. This body consists of delegates from the governments of the several principalities composing the empire; the maximum number which each shall send being fixed by the constitution, but all the votes of each State can, however, be cast only as a unit.

Our American confederation confided to the general Congress all the powers of the common government, with authority to appoint a committee to sit during its recesses, called "a committee of the states," consisting of one delegate from each state, which had power to manage the general affairs of the confederacy to the extent prescribed in the Articles.

The essential characteristic, however, of this confederacy was, that the central will-power acted upon the states, and not directly upon their citizens. The central government, politically, did not know of any citizens, except as they were mentioned in the Articles, as having certain rights as citizens of a state ; it knew only the states as political organizations.

The new conception embodied in the Constitution of the United States, which brings the central government into direct relations with all the citizens, and at the same time leaves them subject to the jurisdiction of their several states, which makes each person a citizen of the United States, and at the same time a citizen of his own state, is justly claimed as an American discovery. It certainly must be considered as a remarkable instance of that political sagacity by which the Anglo-Saxon is led instinctively, as it would seem, to adapt his political action to his particular present needs.   But to speak of it as the *ultima Thule* of political discovery, is exaggerated praise. Political evolution proceeds in the direction of the fusion of heterogeneous political particles, and their expansion into a homogeneous body which, as a political organic being, constantly tends to make one organ pre-eminently the exponent of the common will.   The occasions, causes, and methods of fusion or expansion vary according to the accidents and circumstances we see depicted in history.   We have not yet reached that condition of positive knowledge—and perhaps we never shall—when we can say with assurance of correctness how much of the progress toward national growth is due to early and later environment alone, and how much to innate special race qualities.   It is, however, certain that running through political phenomena there is a general logical sequence of events in view of which it can be affirmed that the order of progress is from the political unit, the family, or tribe, or city, as the case may be, through fusion and expansion to the nation ; that, hence, a confederacy of states and the federal state, are but transition stages of development ; and that, in the order of development, the federal State is but a step beyond the confederacy, and a step behind the fully developed nation.

The legal theory of our American federal state is, that it contemplates as of its essence the balancing of the governments, national and State, so as to hold them forever in equipoise.   Let us look into its actual constitution and operation in order to see whether such an equipoise has been or ever will be reached.

We must start from two facts : 1. that the people inhabiting the territory claimed by the colonies which had combined to free themselves from Great Britain were socially an embryo nation ; 2. that at the close of the Revolution they were divided politically into separate groups.   Madison states that prior to and at the time of the Revolution the current theory was that there was only an executive sovereignty in England, and that each colony was sovereign in legislation within its own limits ; that in matters of foreign trade and external relations parliament might pass laws, and that certain general legislation by the Parliament for the colonies in their relations to each other, had been permitted by the latter. As a fact, the colonies never were, at any time, up to the Declaration of Independence, and the Articles of Confederation, a little later, actual sovereign states.   They were dependencies of the mother country, and politically subject to it, and yet they were so far distinct from each other that when the tie with the parent government was severed they stood apart from each other, as distinct political beings.   While the pressure of the war was the occasion of the joining of forces for the common defence, it cannot be said to have been altogether the cause which induced the new states to enter into the Articles of Confederation. They do not seem to have been in very great haste to come together into close political union, for the Articles were not adopted until July, 1778, three years after the war commenced ; and they were not accepted by all the States until the actual fighting was nearly over, in March, 1781, some seven months before Cornwallis surrendered. The two opposite impulses, that involved in the State-rights ideas, and that growing out of the national feeling, which have been such powerful factors in our political life, were then suddenly brought to light, and stood in opposition to each other.   The experiences of the war probably turned the scale in favor of union, overcoming colonial pride and the narrow prejudices of provincial communities against each other, which were then rife, and also overmastered the latent antagonisms which were then smoldering in the North and South, and which afterward developed into the war between these two sections.   The instinct of a common nationality was pushing in one direction, and the jealousies and fears of small independent states in another.

Whatever the facts as to actual sovereignty were, the Constitution which was framed for the new political body, the United States of America, was, undoubtedly, a compact based upon a supposed and accepted sovereignty in each of the thirteen states.

Prior to the accession of Jefferson to the Presidency and the triumphs of his school of politics, the prevailing opinion was that the Constitution created a national federal state ; but after that, with very little question, until Jackson's time, and following that period down to the breaking out of the civil war, with occasional doubts

and fluctuations, the State-rights ideas were in the ascend-
ant.   On this point, however, there was a division, the
South tending to the extreme view of State-rights, the
North to the moderate national side.   Whether the increased profitableness of slavery and its fostering of indus-
trial and social conditions divergent from those where free
labor prevailed, occasioned the opposite tendencies, in
the two sections, need not be discussed here.   We know
that in the South the extreme State-rights doctrines were
developed, and that in the North they were so much weakened that the first shock of the civil war may be said to
have swept them away.   Certainly during the war they
entirely ceased to be an active political force.   We can
now see that with the body of the Northern people, they
were rather abstractions than realities.   There was among
the people of the North a breadth and strength of national
feeling of which they were not fully conscious until it
was seriously proposed by the South, arms in hand, to
act as it believed.

This new American conception of a great confederation
of states, with a central government, supreme in its special
sphere, and acting without the intervention of the several
states directly upon their citizens, and at the same time,
a congeries of sovereignties, each supreme in its sphere,
and also acting upon the same citizens, involved an in-
congruity, which it might have been affirmed *a priori*,
would have evolved radically opposite theories, leading,
according as the one or the other prevailed, to disrup-
tion or consolidation.

THE political history of the United States from 1787 to
1865 is filled with the great debate on the question :
What is the Constitution of the United States ?   It may
not, therefore, be out of place to examine somewhat
closely the opposite views which, at an early day, made
their appearance, because they illustrate what, necessarily,
will be the divergent lines of argument, when a com-
posite system like ours comes under discussion.

The advocates of State-rights said, substantially, that the
government of the United States is Federal, as distinguished from National, and also as distinguished from
that of a confederacy.   It is Federal, because it is the
government of a community of states, and not of a single state or nation.   They affirmed, moreover, that the
delegates to the Constitutional Convention were appointed by separate states ; that the question of acceptance or rejection was presented to separate states, and
the adoption was by separate states, and was only effected
between those adopting.   It is thus, they conclude, apparent that the act of ratification did not make the government national.   Is there anything in the Constitution
which makes it so ?   If, by ratifying this instrument, the
states have divested themselves of their individuality and
sovereignty, and merged themselves in one great community or nation, it is clear that sovereignty would reside in the whole, or what is called, the American people,

and that allegiance would be due to them ; that the general government would be the superior, and the State government the inferior, and that the people would be united socially and not merely politically.

The whole action of the colonies, in adopting the Declaration of Independence, the Articles of Confederation, and the Constitution, was, as distinct political communities, independent of each other. In order to be effective, the Constitution had to be ratified " between " nine states; consequently it was not "over" them. " Between " implies a compact.

" We, the people of the United States," in the preamble, means no more than the people of the several States, speaking through their states. If the names of the several States had followed this phrase, there could not have been any question ; they were omitted because it was not known how many, and which, states would ratify. The expression " ordain and establish " is qualified by "to form a more perfect union," indicating, not that a new government was ordained and established, but that an old one was made more perfect.

The Constitution everywhere recognizes the existence of the states. The Senate is elected by states; the states as such are districted for members of Congress. The President and Vice-President are chosen by Electors in states. Amendments are consented to by states, as such. As the Constitution became effective as to each particular State when ratified by it, it is only by compact that they agree to modify or restrict themselves in the power of amendment ; that is, when all the states promise that they will be bound by amendments to which only three-quarters may agree, it is still a compact.

All delegated powers are delegated in trust, wherefore it is absurd to say that the states are federal as to reserved powers, and national as to delegated powers. The reservation to the states, or to the people respectively, of powers not delegated to the United States, nor prohibited to the states as provided in the 10th Amendment, means that of those powers which remain after the delegation to the United States some go to the states and the remainder are still in the people of the states.

It is true that sovereignty is single, and cannot be divided, but the *exercise* of sovereign powers may be divided, so that some will pertain to one, others to another agent. If this indivisible something is transferred to the government then it is gone from the states and from the people, which certainly cannot be the case, because contrary to the fundamental theory that sovereignty is in the people. It cannot be transferred to the people of the United States in gross; consequently, it must remain unimpaired in the people of the several states. The solution of the apparent anomaly is found in the doctrine that the sovereign people delegate certain powers in trust to both the State and federal governments. Nevertheless, politically speaking, there is no such community as the people of the United States regarded as constituting one nation. The great change effected by the constitution was in introducing a government in the place of a Congress of diplomatists from the states. These states, after severing their connection with England, had severally the treaty-making power, and could therefore enter into the Articles of Confederation, which constitute a mere league; but when it became necessary to form a new government, they could not do it because beyond their power. Then the people of the several states, as the sources of power, had to be consulted. Under the Confederation the states were superior, and the central government inferior. Under the Constitution the two are co-ordinate.

The federal and state organizations divide between them the delegated powers appertaining to the government ; and as of course each is divested of what the other possesses, it necessarily requires the two united to constitute the entire government.   Each has paramount and supreme authority within its sphere, and they are to this extent equal, and sustain the relation of co-ordinate governments.

Federal powers extend generally to the external or foreign relations of the whole United States, and to the relations of the states with each other.   It cannot be claimed that under the general provision " To make all laws which shall be necessary and proper for carrying into execution the foregoing powers, and all other powers vested by this constitution in the government of the United States, or in any department or officer thereof," * Congress may legislate except in aid of the enumerated powers.

So far, theoretically, the whole circle of governmental action, both as to external and internal relations, is harmoniously filled, but there are certain disturbing influences growing out of human nature and human conduct which interfere with the practical working of the scheme.

The state governments and the federal government are administered by different persons ; the objects to be acted upon by the reserved powers of the one, and the delegated powers of the other, may be claimed by both. Moreover, there is an inherent tendency of one to encroach upon the other.   The domain of the reserved powers of the states may be said to be the battle-ground.

Up to this point, the State-rights argument has certainly great cogency.†   But, if we follow it to its logical

* Art. I., Sec. 8, Cl. 18.

† In this résumé of the State-rights doctrines, extensive use has

conclusion, we cannot avoid ultimate dissolution. This was clearly seen by its advocates. Time and experience very soon taught them that the antagonism which existed in theory was developing in fact, and would reach its climax when the majority of electors and the majority of states should fall together on one side of a geographical line, and the minority should consider their reserved rights as states, about to be, or actually, invaded. The crucial question, if there is conflict, who shall decide ? had to be answered. Can a state oppose rightfully, sufficient resistance to the strong tendency on the part of the federal government to encroach upon the reserved powers a tendency which, undoubtedly, is continuous ? The answer was : Under our system, the powers of government are divided ; one portion is delegated to the federal government, another to the state, and that not especially delegated, remains with the state. The two governments are co-ordinates, not superior and inferior ; and therefore to give one the power to judge, not only as to the extent of its own powers, but also as to those of its co-ordinate, and to enforce its decision, would destroy the equality between them ; would deprive them of the attribute common to all governments, that of judging in the first instance of the extent of its own powers, and would reduce them from the position of equals, to that of superior and subordinate. Each has an equal right to

been made of Calhoun's " Discourse on the Constitution and Government of the United States," and occasionally his exact language has been used. It furnishes, certainly, the clearest exposition of the full length and breadth of that side of the great national debate which engrossed so much of political discussion for three-quarters of a century, but which, after all, continually ranged backward and forward, over the same narrow ground. In what follows, the language of Jefferson, Madison, and Hayne is sometimes quoted.

judge of its powers. If each can judge of the powers of the other, then the umpire must be brute force, and necessarily the end would be, either consolidation or disunion, and a destruction of the system ; a conclusion incompatible with the idea of the perfection of the organism.

The federal government in carrying out its powers, can only pass laws " which shall be necessary and proper for carrying into execution the foregoing powers ;" and the determination whether a law is necessary and proper cannot rest with the power making the law.

The judicial branch cannot decide upon the extent of the powers of the states, and of the United States. It constitutes one department only, which is merely co-ordinate with the others, whose decisions within their spheres are equally conclusive. Moreover, there may be instances of usurped powers, which the forms of the Constitution would never draw within the control of the judiciary, because the courts can only decide upon isolated cases, as they arise, between citizens ; but as neither the United states, nor the states, can be made defendants without their consent, there cannot be any decision which will bind them specifically. The question, then, naturally suggests itself, what prevention is there against encroachments on either side? The answer is, that the only protection is, for each to have a negative upon the acts of the other when they come in conflict. The qualification upon this right is moral, not legal ; the negative should be only in cases where there is a deliberate, palpable and dangerous breach of the Constitution. Will this, necessarily, lead to conflict? No, if we assume that reason is to sway, and the two opposed powers are anxious to find a way out of the difficulty. In the event of a negative interposed by a state to an alleged usurping act of the federal government, the latter should invoke the amending power, and call all the states in consultation, and so amend the Constitution as to meet the difficulty.   If no such course is taken, what then ?

This brings the State-rights position to its inevitable outcome.   The state may secede from the Union.   The ultimate sovereignty lies in the people of the several States. In their primal capacity within the states, they created the Constitution, and as between them, in this capacity, the Constitution is but a compact.   "Hence," to use the words of Calhoun, "a state, acting in its sovereign capacity, and in the same manner in which it ratified and adopted the Constitution, may be guilty of violating it *as a compact*, but cannot be guilty of violating it *as a law*.   The case is the reverse as to the action of its citizens, regarding them in their individual capacity." Therefore, a state can interfere within its own limits, for the purpose of arresting an act of the federal government, in violation of the federal Constitution, and to prevent the delegated from encroaching on the reserved powers, and the state can decide on the mode, and also the measures to be adopted to arrest the act.   It must be borne in mind, that whenever there is a conflict between the delegated and the reserved powers, the majority of states and also of population will be on the side of the party in power, which has control of the departments exercising the delegated powers which may be brought in question ; and the resisting state or states will be in the minority, so that the stress will naturally be on the side of the federal government.

As to the individual citizen, it is true, he owes obedience to both governments.   Why ? because his state commanded him to obey ; but the state can determine in the last instance whether his obedience shall be withdrawn

from the federal government. The state is the authority
which commanded him to obey the federal Constitution ;
that is, the state did so by its ratification ; and by an
analogous process, that is, through a state convention, it
can command him to withdraw his obedience.

It is thus plain that following the " compact " theory,
we are landed irresistibly in the doctrine of secession.

The opposite view of the federal government may be
very briefly stated in the form of affirmations of general conclusions drawn from the history of the country
up to the time of the adoption of the Constitution, and
from the whole of the instrument construed together. It
has, perhaps, never been more succinctly presented than
by Webster, in stating his main propositions, when
answering Calhoun in the Senate in February, 1833, at
the time the latter presented his nullification resolutions.

1. " The Constitution of the United States is not a
league, confederacy, or compact between the people of the
several states in their sovereign capacities ; but a government proper, founded on the adoption of the people, and
creating direct relations between itself and individuals.

2. " No state authority has power to dissolve these relations ; nothing can dissolve them but revolution ; and
consequently, there can be no such thing as secession
without revolution.

3. " There is a supreme law, consisting of the Constitution of the United States, and acts of Congress passed
in pursuance of it, and treaties ; and, in cases not capable of assuming the character of a suit in law or equity,
Congress must judge of, and finally interpret, this supreme law so often as it has occasion to pass acts of legislation ; and in cases capable of assuming, and actually
assuming, the character of a suit, the Supreme Court of
the United States is the final interpreter.

4. "An attempt, by a state, to abrogate, annul, or nullify an Act of Congress, or to arrest its operation within her limits, on the ground that, in her opinion, such law is unconstitutional, is a direct usurpation on the just powers of the general government, and on the equal rights of other States; a plain violation of the Constitution, and a proceeding essentially revolutionary in its character and tendency."

Strange as it may seem, this long controversy as to the essential character of our institutions owed much of its intensity to the peculiar fact that the structure of the government was shaped under the eyes of those who commenced the debate, and only one generation removed from those who pursued it most bitterly. Jefferson and Hamilton began it, and Webster and Calhoun continued it up to within a decade of the civil war. Both sides overlooked the historical truth that every great commonwealth is made up of an aggregation of what, at some stage, were smaller sovereignties, and that in the ordinary course of normal development, time itself, and the operation of universal laws, will bring about the merging of one into the other, or, a fusion of all into one. They saw too closely the processes through which the two opposing forces, which always exist at some stage of every national growth, those of repulsion and those of integration, adjusted temporarily their differences, in the attempt permanently to arrest the nation at what is, after all, only a transition stage, by establishing a state midway between a confederacy and a nation. They were powerfully impressed with the purely legal questions involved; they were haggling over the debates of the Constitutional Convention, and the very words of the bond, but failed to cast their eyes back over the whole course of colonial growth during the one hun-

dred and sixty-eight years between the landing at
Jamestown and the skirmish at Lexington, and note
that every important political change was a step in the
growth of a nation.   In looking back now over this debate, one cannot but be struck with its narrowness.   It
moves over a very restricted surface, and yet, perhaps, it
could not have been otherwise, in view of the necessity
all parties were under to look to a written instrument
as the final test of their opposing arguments.*

* As early as 1798 the Supreme Court of the United States had
occasion to pass on the relation of the States to the Federal Government.   In the case of Calder *vs.* Ball (Dallas Rep. III. 387),
Justice Chase, speaking for the Court, said : "It appears to me a
self-evident proposition, that the several state legislatures retain all
the powers of legislation, delegated to them by the state constitutions, which are not expressly taken away by the Constitution
of the United States.   The establishing courts of justice, the appointment of judges, and the making regulations for the administration of justice within each State, according to its laws, on all
subjects not entrusted to the Federal Government, appears to me
to be the peculiar and exclusive province and duty of the state
legislatures.   All the powers delegated by the people of the United
States to the Federal Government are defined, and no constructive
powers can be exercised by it, and all the powers that remain in
the state government are indefinite."   Again, in 1837, in Briscoe
.*vs.* Bank of Kentucky (Peters Rep. XI. 317), it was said : "The
Federal Government is one of delegated powers.   All powers not
delegated to it, or inhibited to the states, are reserved to the
states or to the people."   Chief Justice Marshall said, in the case
of M'Culloch *vs.* the State of Maryland, in 1819 (Wheaton IV.
405): "This Government is acknowledged by all to be one of
enumerated powers.   The principle that it can exercise only the
powers granted to it, would seem too apparent to have required
to be enforced by all those arguments which its enlightened
friends, while it was pending before the people, found it necessary to urge.   That principle is now universally admitted.   But
the question respecting the extent of the powers actually granted is
perpetually arising, and will probably continue to arise, as long as

Our American constitutional system rests upon the claim that the citizen is subject to two sovereigns, the

our system shall exist." In 1865, the same court, in Gilman *vs.* Philadelphia (Wallace Rep. III. 730), said : "The states may exercise concurrent or independent power in all cases but three : 1. Where the power is lodged exclusively in the Federal Constitution ; 2. Where it is given to the United States and prohibited to the states ; 3. Where, from the nature and subjects of the power, it must necessarily be exercised by the National Government exclusively." In 1868, the question came before the Supreme Court, as to the effect of an ordinance of secession adopted by a state at the outbreak of the rebellion, followed by actual war, the final subjugation of the state, and its reconstruction in the union ; and on this occasion Chief-Justice Chase, in Texas *vs.* White (Wallace, VII. 724), said : "The union of the states never was a purely artificial and arbitrary relation. It began among the colonies, and grew out of common origin, mutual sympathies, kindred principles, similar interests, and geographical relations. It was confirmed and strengthened by the necessities of war, and received definite form and character and sanction from the Articles of Confederation. By these the union was solemnly declared to be " perpetual." And when these Articles were found to be inadequate to the exigencies of the country, the Constitution was ordained, to form a more perfect union. It is difficult to convey the idea of indissoluble unity more clearly than by these words, What can be indissoluble, if a perpetual union, made more perfect, is not ? But the perpetuity and indissolubility of the Union by no means implies the loss of distinct and individual existence, or of the right of self-government by the states. Under the Articles of Confederation each state retained its sovereignty, freedom, and independence, and every power, jurisdiction, and right not expressly delegated to the United States. Under the Constitution, though the powers of the states were much restricted, still, all powers *not* delegated to the United States, nor prohibited to the states, are reserved to the states respectively or to the people. * * * When, therefore, Texas became one of the United States, she entered into an indissoluble relation. All the obligations of perpetual union, and all the guarantees of republican government in the union, attached at once to the state. The act

11

state and the United States. Taking away the word sovereign, which imports the highest power, we may say, instead, that the citizen is subject to two jurisdictions. But is it not the case in all governments that the citizens are under two, and sometimes more than two, jurisdictions? For instance, within a state, a person may be subject to the jurisdiction of a city, and, at the same time, of a county, and finally, of the state itself. As to two of these, the county and the city, they are acting within a limited range of authority, and cannot legally overstep it. Even the legislative, executive, and judicial branches of the state are laboring under restrictions. As to all the inferior jurisdictions to which the citizen is subject within his state, the legislature *may* change them unless there are prohibited clauses in the state constitution. So that for the highest and final authority we must go back to the people. We reach this point, then, that the people write down in their state constitution the particulars of the government which they themselves are willing to submit to, and they submit themselves to a variety of jurisdictions, of which the departments of the state governments are some among many. This occurs in all the states. In addition, the citizen is subject to the jurisdiction of a number of federal departments and officers. Now, it must always be borne in mind, that it is a fundamental right, not only of individuals living under Anglo-

which consummated her admission into the union was something more than a compact; it was the incorporation of a new member into the political body; and it was final. The union between Texas and the other states was as complete, as perpetual, and as indissoluble as the union between the original states. There was no place for reconsideration, or revocation, except through revolution or through consent of the states." The ordinance of secession was held to be null, and Texas continued to be a state of the union notwithstanding the rebellion.

American, but we may say under all civilized institutions, to challenge every person who demands any duty from, or claims any right against him, to show the law which sustains the claim, and if he disputes its applicability, or denies that the supposed statute is a law, he can have the question decided by some competent court.

Government is not a series of abstract propositions, but a practical working system.   A great number of people are living together within a certain territory, having intricate relations with one another.   Each act of every body of persons in authority, whether called a congress, or a state legislature, or a board of aldermen, or selectmen, or superiors, or school trustees, or of a single person, whether called a president, or governor, or mayor, or sheriff, stands by itself, and when brought to bear upon the citizen, must, if questioned, find its authority in some delegation of power from the people.   It therefore becomes purely a question of construction in each case. If the power comes from the state legislature, the inquiry is, Has the state constitution prohibited the legislature from passing the particular act? If the power comes from Congress, the question is, is it within the enumerated grants of power in the Federal Constitution ? And, descending in the scale, if a power is exercised by a city, or a county, or a township officer, its source also must be found in a previous grant of authority.

The fundamental idea which underlies our whole governmental system is, that its jural relations are not between itself and masses of citizens as masses, whether in states, counties, cities, or smaller subdivisions, but between every individual and the particular department and officer who exacts obedience from him.   States, counties, and cities are organizations arranged conveniently to express the political will of the particular groups within their limits upon those subjects which are within their jurisdiction, or are instrumentalities to execute the sovereign will of a higher power in the general State.   In short, the government, whether general or local, is on one side, and the citizen on the other as to jural relations, and at every step of the former the latter may challenge its right.

As between the Federal Government and the states, it is no part of the duty of the State to keep general watch and ward over its citizens, to see that the federal authorities do not oppress the citizen, nor to warn off trespassers upon the reserved rights of the states.   Each act of all the branches of government, from the highest to the lowest, necessarily implies subject and object ; that is, an act to be done by some one upon some one or some object ; and the relationship which is established is between the body of persons, or single officer, who wills the act, and the person who executes the act or upon whom it is to be executed.

The State-rights theorists insisted upon viewing the relations of the citizen to the Federal Government as passing through the state organism.   Metaphorically, there was in their view a wall of state jurisdiction around the confines of the state, and the federal edicts could only reach the citizens within by going through the gateways, and after passing the inspection of the watchers posted there by State authority.

The extreme State-rights theories were so purely abstractions that they would very likely have died out without assuming the importance they did assume, had it not been that they very early became the refuge of the slave States.   These states very soon felt, though unwilling for a long time to admit it, that they were falling to the rear in wealth and population.

Their leaders of political thought seized upon and
nourished the extreme views of the sovereignty of the
states as a shield to their weakness. Calhoun very clearly
comprehended that a dominant party is always in favor of
an enlargement of delegated powers, and that strict construction was only a weapon of defence in the hands of
the minority ; so that as long as states were divided by
opposing parties, the danger of violent collision was remote. What he feared was, that the numerical majority
and state majority would both concentrate in the North,
and he distinctly predicted that when this occurred there
would be a crisis. If the social and economic causes
which mainly contributed to bring on the civil war had
not existed, it is highly probable that the consolidation of
the·system would have gone on with ebb and flow of gain
between the delegated and reserved powers, but the tendency, from the very nature of the conditions, could not
have been otherwise than toward the supremacy of the
central power, and for various reasons.

The business of any government, within the limits of
its territory, is with the relations of its citizens to each
other, or those actions which are entirely personal to the
individual that may eventually affect the relations of
citizens to each other. For instance, as an example, as
to relations between citizens, a law may provide a punishment for stealing ; this regulates a relation that may arise
between A, the owner of property, and B, who steals it
from him ; or, the mere existence of the law may prevent
B from an act, the stealing, which he would otherwise be
guilty of. An example of a law affecting only the person
might be one which compels a child to attend school between certain ages.

The theory of our dual system is that the citizen has
two sets of relations and interests : one which he has in

common with the other citizens of his own state, and
another which he has in common with all the citizens of
the United States ; and also that frequently the same relations and interests have a double quality : are common
at the same time to the state and to the Federal Union.
Now, if the proportion between the relations and interests
of individual citizens, which they have only in common
with the other citizens of their state, and the relations and
interests which they have in common with all the citizens
of the United States, had remained always the same, the
federal would not have grown at the expense of the state
government ; but, through the consolidation of the population, the bringing remote points of the Union together
by railroads, so that it now requires less than one-half the
time to go from San Francisco to New York that it took
Jefferson, in 1790, to go from Monticello to the latter city ;
through the localization and specialization of industries ;
through the extension of sympathies, and religious and
intellectual bonds of fellowship, the duties of the Federal
Government have been enormously extended. The relations and interests range through the whole life of the
people. In regulating commerce, Congress has to deal
with new factors, the railroads and telegraphs, and in
consequence of the expansion of inter-state water trans-
portation, it and the courts have been obliged to stretch
their jurisdiction farther and farther into state centres.
Necessarily, banking has become national, and so, no
doubt, many other things that now are supposed to be
entirely within the purview of state authority, will be
taken hold of by the Federal Government.

A noticeable recognition of the contraction of state
and the expansion of national relations and interests, is
manifested in the opposite characters of the changes which
have taken place in the Federal Constitution, and many of

the State constitutions. The earlier state constitutions contain little more than a bill of rights, in addition to the outlines of the departments of government. Since 1868, fourteen of the *ante-bellum* states have entirely remodeled their constitutions ; all, except Pennsylvania, Illinois and California, it is true, because of the social and governmental changes consequent upon the war of the rebellion. In all of them, nevertheless, the salient modifications have been in the remarkable limitation of legislative power. The tendency is, to throw purely local affairs back into the hands of the townships, counties, and cities. For example, in the new Constitution of California, there is a specification of thirty-three classes of subjects, concerning which the legislature cannot make local, or special laws.

In that State the volume of statutes of 1877–8 contained about eleven hundred pages, and that of the next year after the adoption of the new Constitution less than two hundred, showing an extraordinary diminution of legislative activity. It is true, that the extent of the law-making power in the state is not diminished. The change indicates that the people wish to keep the greater part of the power, which usually is exercised by the state legislature, in their own hands, because it concerns only those relations which extend to the circle of the township, the county, and the city.

On the other hand, since the addition of the first twelve amendments to the Federal Constitution shortly after its adoption, the changes made by the thirteenth, fourteenth and fifteenth amendments have extended the power of Congress.

Again, the tendency of the departments exercising delegated power on behalf of all the states, and all the people, will be to enlarge their powers by construction. That great reserve of power, which is the background of every

government, and which with us lies in the whole body of
the people, and is to be used by them in case of need,
will be drawn upon more and more in aid of the majority
which for the time being controls the Federal Government.

Under the authority granted by the Constitution to
Congress, are the following powers:

"To levy and collect taxes, duties, imposts, and ex-
cises, to pay the debts, and provide for the common
defence and general welfare of the United States."

"To borrow money on the credit of the United States."

"To regulate commerce with foreign nations, and
among the several States, and with the Indian tribes."

To establish "uniform laws on the subject of bank-
ruptcies throughout the United States."

"To establish post-offices and post-roads."

"To declare war."

"To raise and support armies."

"To provide and maintain a navy."

"To provide for calling forth the militia to execute the
laws of the Union;" and finally, the comprehensive
power, "To make all laws, which shall be necessary and
proper for carrying into execution the foregoing powers,
and all other powers, vested by this Constitution in the
Government of the United States, or, in any department
or officer thereof." Under these powers, the area of congressional action will be continually enlarging, because,
in the first instance, Congress must decide as to whether
the subject-matter to be accomplished is within their
grant of powers, and secondly, whether the means proposed are also within the same limits. Hence, two results are sure to follow: a tendency in Congress to enlarge
its powers, and the claim that it is the *sole judge* of the
means to be used to carry its express powers into effect.

Under the claim that it is the only judge of the instrumentalities to be used to carry the express powers into operation, an enormous extension of power can be had by Congress. The courts cannot interfere upon the ground that the means are not appropriate; they can go no farther than to define the limits of the power. Then again, Congress is also the sole judge whether a proper state of facts exists calling for the exercise of any of the enumerated powers. It can, for instance, as previously suggested, decide as a fact whether a war exists, and then can call into exercise the vague but almost unlimited mass of war powers. It can go to almost any extreme in deciding what relates to inter-state and foreign commerce. Upon those subjects which are purely political—that is, those which touch more particularly the relations between communities, as distinguished from those rights which are purely personal ; as, that no one shall be deprived of life, liberty, or property, without due process of law, the Federal Government can, by construction, stretch its jurisdiction to almost any extent within the range of political action. Hence, the inevitable normal tendency, under a system like ours, is, to the absorption of power in the central government, and the breaking down of state lines. The civil war played sad havoc with all the previous abstractions that had puzzled our politicians. Theoretically, the several states in rebellion were never out of the Union, and although their citizens had banded together in insurrection, they were only individual criminals, and, as soon as the war was over, should have been allowed to resume their old relations, and should have been permitted to send members of the House of Representatives and of the Senate to Washington, though, at the same time, these law-breakers could be individually pursued and punished. It is evident that, under all the

10*

novel circumstances, the old theories were at fault. It was necessary to find a new standpoint. The fact had to be recognized that there was a nation, and that one-half of it was prostrate, disorganized, socially and politically. Congress did what it always will do when there is a crisis : it was its own judge of the extent of its political powers, and it stretched those powers so as cover the exigencies of the case in hand. We may say that this makes of the Constitution but a sheet of rubber, to be stretched to suit every occasion. In a sense, it is. It will always be worked in the interest of those having control of the federal government. In times of peace, the encroachments will be step by step, in one instance after another, perhaps at long removes. The States as States will imperceptibly lose power and importance, and the federal government will as imperceptibly become stronger and more important. Forms will remain, but the substance of power will concentrate in Congress. The gravitation of power will continually be toward this common centre.

A pure confederacy is necessarily short-lived, because the enforcement of the central authority can only be upon a whole community, an entire political body ; in other words, war has to be declared, if the community disregard the law. In a war, all the people of the opposed community become enemies, and in the recalcitrant member of a confederacy, all become delinquents. The real aim of every war is the destruction of the opposed community. Humanitarian or international considerations may restrain the victor, but these only abridge the exercise of his right. War within a political organism to enforce a law, is practically suicide.

The Constitution of the new German Empire provides that : " If the States of the Union shall not fulfil their constitutional duties to the Union, proceedings may be instituted against them by execution. This execution shall be ordered by the Bundesrath, and enforced by the Emperor."

This is a continuation of a power vested in the old Bund, and its attempted exercise against Prussia brought on the war of 1866, between that kingdom and Austria, and the south German States. When, however, several states, before sovereign, unite for political purposes, and invest the central authority with power to make laws, which act directly upon individuals within the States, and abandon their sovereignty so far as to permit the central power to enter within their borders, and take hold of the individuals who disobey the laws, and punish them for their disobedience, then the State has abandoned the chief element of its sovereignty, and the combined States constitute no longer a confederacy.

As suggested above, the confederacy, and all its modifications, are but transition stages in political growth, from the smaller single to the larger single state ; they are only artificial ways of bringing about that expansion and fusion which exterior accidents, as wars, or interior accidents, as revolutions, may arrest or destroy, but which ordinarily go on by slow and natural processes in the formation of every great nation.*

* It is worth noting, as illustrative of the vast change in the general estimation concerning Federal and State official honors, between the present time and the early days of the republic, that Washington at times met with difficulty in filling the public offices. When Randolph resigned the Secretaryship of State, the President offered the office to Patterson, King, Patrick Henry, Charles Cotesworth Pinckney, and others. It was almost impossible to find a person to accept the war department. While Jay was engaged in his mission to England, to undertake which he had resigned the Chief-Justiceship of the United States Supreme Court, he was elected Governor of New York, and returned to take that

place as one of greater honor than any he could receive under the
federal government. (Charles Francis Adams : " The Life and
Works of John Adams," I. p. 483.)

When it was hinted that Washington intended to appoint John
Quincy Adams United States District Attorney, his father wrote
to his wife that he hoped their son would not accept the office,
saying that he did not wish him " to play at small games in the
executive of the United States ; " and adding : " I had much rather
he should be the State attorney for Suffolk." (Ibid, I. p. 463.)

In the work already cited, p. 449, it is remarked : " Throughout the administration of General Washington there is visible
among public men a degree of indifference to power and place
which forms one of the most marked features of that time. More
than once the highest cabinet and foreign appointments went
begging to suitable candidates, and begged in vain."

The incident is familiar of the disputed point of etiquette which
arose when President Washington visited Boston, whether Hancock, the Governor of the State, should come without the city to
meet the Chief Magistrate of the republic, or, whether the latter
should go into the city and first call on the governor. Hancock
had the good sense to give way. It is evident that such a question
could not have arisen had there not been a strong support in
public feeling for the attempted assertion that the State was the
superior, and the Federal Union the inferior. At the present day,
federal positions outweigh in honor those of the State. Governors
eagerly resign their offices to go to the United States Senate ; and
the chief-justice of the highest court of the largest State in the
Union has been recently seen to resign his position in order to
accept a precarious cabinet appointment. These things in the
earlier days of our history would have been incomprehensible.

It is hardly to be doubted that the honor in which all State
officials are held has, within half a century, diminished enormously.
While it is true, we cannot attribute the falling off to any one
cause, yet it may perhaps, in large part, be ascribed to the diminished importance of the State governments in the affairs of the
people.

CHAPTER XIX.

A GLANCE at the history of other federations furnishes additional illustration of the proposition already stated. The great historical confederations, in the course of time, have either drawn the federal bond tighter and tighter, or gone to pieces, and in their disconnected parts laid the foundations of independent states. The most important of these, besides the United States, are the Achaian League, the Swiss Cantons, the United Provinces, the German Confederacies, and the German Empire. A map representing the political divisions of ancient Greece in the last decades of its independent existence, would show nearly the whole territory partitioned among a number of leagues—the League of Achaia, the League of Bœotia, the League of Euboia, the League of Phokis, the League of Akarnania, the League of Thessaly, the League of Magnesia, the League of Perrhaibia, and the League of Epeiros. But of the political history, or even of the governmental organization, of the minor Grecian leagues, we have only little information. Some of them, as for example Phokis, Akarnania, and Epeiros, had strictly federal governments, yet of the history of all of the leagues, with the exception of Achaia, we lack data sufficient to determine whether the federal bond in them grew stronger or weaker. The League of Lykia, outside of the limits of Greece, possessed at one time a federal government, to which Montesquieu has referred as a model of a federal republic ; but of its origin and internal development no account has been preserved. It is, therefore, chiefly from Achaia that we must learn whatever antiquity has to teach us concerning the general tendency of power in the history of federal government.

Even before Macedonia became the dominant power in Greece, the foundations of a federal government were laid in Achaia by the union of twelve democratic cities. Although no details have been preserved of this "old Achaian constitution," yet "at the same time," as Mr. Freeman suggests, "it is easy to believe that the federal tie may have been much less closely drawn than it was in the revived confederation of after times."

The new league of Achaia, beginning about 280 B.C., grew, from a union of small towns, to embrace the whole of Peloponnesus. Its constitution was not a loose bond of alliance, but the fundamental law of a state. "The federal form of government now appears in its fullest and purest shape. Every city remained a distinct State, sovereign for all purposes not inconsistent with the higher sovereignty of the federation, retaining its local assemblies and local magistrates, and ordering all exclusively local affairs without any interference from the central power." * The State was a federal democracy, but without a system of representation. The national assembly, although any citizen of the league was privileged to attend it, was in practice composed of those citizens "who were at once wealthy enough to bear the cost of the journey, and zealous enough to bear the trouble of it." It tended, therefore, to become an aristocratic body. It had two regular sessions yearly, but extra sessions might be called by the executive branch of

* Freeman, "History of Federal Government," I. 255.

the government. The limitation of the session of the assembly to three days, taken in connection with the fact that the initiative in legislation was always in the hands of the executive, gave to the executive the preponderance of whatever power the central government possessed. This government consisted of ten ministers, who formed the Cabinet of the President, or general of the Achaians, as he was called. These and the President himself were chosen directly by the Assembly for a specified time, namely, for one year, and there were no constitutional means for removing them before the expiration of their term of office. Being elected by the Assembly, there was likely to be harmony of views between the two bodies. The Assembly would therefore be disposed to accept without question the propositions of the executive, and thus were established conditions most favorable for the encroachment of the central power on the authority of the local governments. Power drifted toward the centre. One after another the cities of Peloponnesus were drawn into the league, and out of them grew a single great nation. They were subjected to the increasing power of the national government, and to the assimilating force of the national spirit. "The tendency to assimilation among the several cities was very strong. In the later days of the League it seems to have developed with increased force, till at last Polybius could say that all Peloponnesus differed from a single city only in not being surrounded by a single wall. The whole peninsula employed the same coinage, weights and measures, and was governed by the same laws, administered by the same magistrates, senators, and judges. * * * The Achaian League was, in German technical language, a *Bundesstaat* and not a mere *Staatenbund*. There was an Achaian nation, with a national assembly, a national **government**, and national tribunals, to which every Achaian citizen owed a direct allegiance."[*]

The federal government grew strong at the expense of the local governments; and in the central government itself, the executive department, which possessed the initiative in legislation, became practically supreme. The national assembly retained its right to appoint the members of the executive department, and also to give or withhold its assent to legislative propositions. Owing, however, to the shortness of the sessions, which rendered all discussion of these propositions impracticable, the participation of the assembly in legislation grew, in the course of time, to be little more than a mere formal act of registering the decrees of the president and his ministers.

A further illustration of the same purport may be drawn from the political history of Switzerland. The earliest union of cantons of which we have documentary evidence was that of 1291. This, like the still earlier union to which tradition points, was simply a defensive alliance. It formed no central state, nor deprived the cantons of any of that power which they had hitherto exercised. It was a pledge of mutual protection. They agreed to unite their efforts to resist "all who should do violence to any of them, or impose taxes, or design wrong to their persons or goods." Disputes arising between them were to be settled by arbitration. The three cantons of the original alliance were joined by five others early in the fourteenth century. The eight cantons thus brought into union agreed to maintain peace among themselves, and to join their forces in defence against their common enemies. In the course of time the several cantons extended their dominions, and gradually drew

---

[*] Freeman, "History of Federal Government." I. 259.

together into a closer union ; still, in the fifteenth century Switzerland had not advanced politically beyond a league of cantons for mutual defence. The cantons might form separate alliances with foreign states, and even make war on one another. In the convention of Stantz, however, in 1481, they agreed to lay aside this latter right ; but the agreement had only a moral force, and was broken by the cantons, as in the period of the Reformation, as soon as it was found to conflict with their individual interests or aims. The nature of the confederation, prior to the recent changes, is described by May as follows : "Originally it was little more than an alliance, offensive and defensive, between particular cantons; and until recent times, the union continued far too loose for the effective purposes of a confederation. Its main objects were mutual defence against foreign enemies, and internal tranquillity. The confederation had no powers—either legislative, executive, or administrative—binding upon the several cantons : no federal army : no public treasury, or national mint : no coercive procedure : not even a paramount authority to enter into treaties and alliances with foreign powers—some of the cantons having reserved to themselves the right of forming separate alliances with other states."* The diet had no definitive powers in legislation, yet the habit of deliberating together on questions of common concern developed a certain unity of political sentiment, which manifested itself later in strengthening the national as opposed to cantonal institutions. A step in this direction was taken soon after Switzerland had gained a recognized position among the independent powers of Europe at the peace of Westphalia. It was the establishment of the so-called "Defensional." This provided that the diet should have power,

* "Democracy in Europe," I., 373.

in cases of great danger, to call upon the cantons for
stipulated numbers of troops to defend the confederation.
It provided also for military discipline, for the appointment of officers, and for the general direction of the
army by means of a council of war.

While the Swiss were thus slowly advancing toward
national unity they were overwhelmed by the revolutionary influence of France. Their independent political
growth was suddenly interrupted, the old confederation
was swept away, and the Helvetic republic, modeled
after the then existing French republic, was set up in its
place. The new government was to be based on popular
sovereignty. It was imposed upon the people by a
foreign power; it disregarded their ancient cantonal
divisions and their ancient political traditions, and was
consequently met with vigorous resistance. In 1803,
the Swiss accepted the Act of Mediation rather than suffer
the alternative of loss of independence under the government of France. By it the former cantonal division was
renewed, and a federal government established. This
remained in force till the fall of Napoleon. Then in the
general political reorganization of Europe, which followed
the Congress of Vienna, Switzerland adopted a new constitution, somewhat reactionary in character, apparently
taking up the thread of constitutional growth where it
was broken off by the interference of the French.

The submission of the Swiss to the federal government imposed upon them by the Act of Mediation, cannot but have been influential in directing their attention
to the benefits of a closer union ; and the Constitution
of 1815 bears evidence of the progress of their ideas on
this line. Finally, in 1848 a constitution was adopted,
in which the federal principle triumphed, and in 1874 a
new constitution was proposed essentially identical with

that of 1848, but enlarging still farther the federal authority. This was carried and became the fundamental law of Switzerland, by the vote of fourteen out of the twenty-two cantons, or by a majority of 142,000 votes out of a total of 538,000. We observe, then, throughout the history of Switzerland, the gradual development of the central power, justifying the statement of Mr. Freeman, that "the Swiss confederation—in its origin a union of the loosest kind—has gradually drawn the federal bond tighter and tighter, till, within our own times, it has assumed a form which fairly entitles it to rank beside Achaia and America." *

The history of the Netherlands shows the union of several provinces for the purpose of achieving their independence, and, moreover, the gradual development in them of a central power which finally became hereditary and a permanent part of the political institutions of the country. The government grew into a monarchy. This result was the outcome of the relation of the provinces to foreign powers. The need of resistance, first to the arbitrary rule of Spain, and later to the encroachments of the French, made unity of action and of organization an essential condition of their independent existence. But there was in the several provinces, in their early history, a strong antagonism to any central authority. The tendency of the political development of the provinces toward unity was determined, therefore, rather by their peculiar external relations than by the growth of any strictly national spirit.

The Holy Roman Empire, during its history as a feudal institution, illustrates the movement of power in the opposite direction. The declaration of the electoral union at Rhens, in 1338, that it was by election "that the sover-

* " History of Federal Government," I. 6.

eign obtained his right to the title of king and emperor,
and that in consequence he did not need to be approved
or confirmed by the apostolic chair," virtually marks the
separation of Germany and Italy. During the next three
hundred years the provinces and states of Germany grew
into practically independent sovereignties, and their independence was formally recognized by the Treaty of Westphalia, in 1648. By this treaty they were permitted to
contract alliances, either among themselves or with
foreign States, and also to make war, provided the empire were not the object of attack. But before the end of
the eighteenth century this last provision had come to
be entirely disregarded, and although the empire continued to exist in name, there had grown up within its
borders a large number of practically sovereign states.

In 1815, after the empire had passed away and Germany had been freed from the dominion of Napoleon,
an attempt was made, through the Federal Act, to bring
the several states into union. The history of the German confederations and the empire, since 1815, illustrates
to a certain extent the political tendency we have observed in the history of other confederacies. But according to the Federal Act the members of the confederation
retained those rights which they had had confirmed by
the Treaty of Westphalia. They might form alliances
with foreign powers and with one another, provided such
alliances were not detrimental to the general interests.
That the union effected was simply a loose confederacy
may be seen from the eleventh article of the Federal Act :

"Every member of the confederation promises to protect all Germany as well as each individual confederate
state against every attack, and to guarantee mutually to
each other all their possessions comprised in the confederation. When war has once been declared by the

confederation, no member can enter on individual negotiations, or conclude a truce or peace individually. The
members of the confederation retain the right of forming
any alliance, but bind themselves not to make any engage-
ment directed against the safety of the confederation, or
any of its members. The members of the confederation
engage not to make war on each other on any pretext
whatsoever, nor to settle their differences by force, but to
lay them before the diet. It then becomes the duty of
the latter to attempt a reconciliation through a commission, and in case this attempt should fail and a
judicial decision become necessary, to bring this about
by a properly instituted Austrägal Tribunal, to whose
sentence the contending parties are bound instantly to
submit."

In spite of the great expectations that had been enter-
tained of the Congress of Vienna, the bond of German
union was still very weak, and it was clear that unless
the central power was strengthened the confederacy would
go to pieces. In May, 1820, the draft of the so-called
Final Act of Vienna was completed by representatives of
the several German governments, assembled at Vienna.
This was ratified in the following month and became a
part of the fundamental law, of equal authority with the
Federal Act. It described the confederation as "an international society of the German sovereign princes, and
of the free towns, for the preservation of the independence and inviolability of the states which compose the
confederation, and for the maintenance of the internal
and external security of Germany. This union, with regard
to its internal affairs, is a corporation of self-dependent
and, with regard to each other, independent states, with
mutual treaty rights and obligations; and is, with regard
to external affairs, a politically united power."

The Final Act strengthened somewhat the central
authority, but it failed to satisfy the growing desire for
national institutions ; in fact, there were serious obstacles
to bringing the German people under a single government, even into a single federal state ; and prominent
among these was the existence of two great rival states,
Austria and Prussia, of practically equal powers. The
governmental unity of the German people was impossible without the subordination of one of these
states to the leadership of the other. In their mutual
jealousies lay the main difficulties of Germany's political
problem. It was in great measure the embarrassment
presented by the rivalry of these states that negatived the
vigorous attempts of 1848 and 1849 to set up a government for united Germany, and necessitated a return, in
1851, to the old order of things, under the German confederation. But the co-operation of Austria and Prussia
was now out of the question. The year 1859 brought
a change : Austria was defeated in the Italian war, and
by this lost prestige as a leader ; and at the same time
the triumph of the French made the Germans feel the
need of union under a more trustworthy head. When it
became evident that no peaceful solution of the problem
was possible, Prussia took the lead, broke with Austria,
and established the North German Union. Into this
union all the German States except Austria were finally
drawn and their mutual adherence confirmed by their
common participation in a great victory ; and out of the
Union grew the Empire.

If we were now to compare the present imperial government with the central government of confederate
Germany at any period since the overthrow of the Holy
Roman Empire, there would be left no room for doubt
that Germany illustrates the political tendency already

observed in the history of confederations. The central
government has tended to become stronger and stronger,
in comparison with the power of the subordinate States ;
and with this point determined, it is a matter of no great
moment in the present inquiry whether the Empire is to
be regarded, in its present form, as a *Bundesstaat* or
merely as a *Staatenbund.*

Not only does the history of Germany under its confederations show a gradual strengthening of the general
government, but there are, moreover, provisions of the
present imperial constitution which indicate the continuance of this drift toward centralization. In the first place,
according to the second article, the '' laws of the Empire
shall take precedence of those of each individual State.''
In the second place, in maintaining the constitution and
in making the laws, the Emperor has the advantage of
position. In the Bundesrath there are fifty-eight votes,
divided among the states in such a manner that Prussia
has seventeen, Bavaria six, Saxony four, Würtemberg four,
Baden three, Hesse three, Mecklenburg-Schwerin two,
Brunswick two, and seventeen smaller States one each.
It thus appears that in the Bundesrath, Prussia's power is
superior to that of any other State. The union of German Emperor and Prussian King in one person adds further importance to Prussia's position. As King of Prussia he can appoint seventeen members of the Bundesrath, and as Emperor may rely on them to carry out
his will in matters of imperial policy. Now, since fourteen votes in the Bundesrath may negative any proposed
amendment to the constitution, the Emperor through his
control of the seventeen votes of Prussia may prevent any
change in the constitution, even were such change desired
by all the other states in union. It is, therefore, impossible, without the consent of the Emperor, to take away any

of that power which the imperial government at present exercises. But the history of other confederations shows clearly that it has hitherto been impossible so to balance in them the centrifugal and centripetal forces as to place the government in equilibrium between these forces. It appears, then, that since the power of the central government cannot be lessened except by the consent of him to whom such diminution would be a loss, it must inevitably grow stronger. And, moreover, the extensive powers already granted through the constitution, together with the fact that the initiative in legislation rests with the Emperor and Bundesrath, indicate that, in the future, the strictly constitutional growth of the Empire is likely to result in a still greater development of the central power as compared with the power of the individual States.

CHAPTER XX.

POLITICAL parties necessarily arise in the nation with a representative government. If the power to initiate laws, and also to adopt them, is possessed by the same persons and these persons are elected, then two great parties will arise ; and the aim of each will be to obtain and hold the law-making power and, through it, the executive power. Where, however, the power to initiate legislation is in an irremovable monarch, and merely the power of acceptance or rejection in an elected assembly, there only fractional groups, not effective political parties, will exist.*

Within the party, just as within the state, there is a constant tendency to the lodgment of supreme control in one person, and also to rigidity of organization. This is met by a resisting impulse or disposition on the part of the members to be free, so that, where there is free movement in political life, parties always tend to an equilibrium.

Within the great organic being, the state, there is continual movement as there is within the life of the individual man. With both the question is constantly recurring, What shall I do ? The man listens to the pleadings of his feelings, his prejudices, his experiences, his judgment, and his wishes, decides, and then executes. When

* Interesting in the literature of this subject is Bluntschli's "Charakter und Geist der politischen Parteien," Nördlingen, 1869. This treatise was later embodied in " Lehre vom modernen Stat." constituting the twelfth book of the third volume.

12

life is at its prime these debates with self rage frequently and fiercely, and often his whole being is endangered by them ; but as life declines they become less frequent ; the needed decision is postponed, that repose may not be disturbed, and the tyranny of daily habit at last usurps the enfeebled will.

Within the state the answer to a similar question is also constantly demanded. In the free state the debate is by political parties. The feelings, the judgment, the experiences, and the prejudices of the community find expression through them ; and at last the decision is by that organ in the state which makes the law. In the vigorous state the pleadings of political parties will be vehement, often passionate; it is only when the fatal lethargy of corruption creeps over the nation that parties disappear and despotism reigns.

Without parties the currents of political life would become stagnant, and free government would cease to exist. But what is a political party? How does it come into being? and what are its aims? In order to answer these queries we must recur again, at the outset, to the fundamental principle so frequently referred to, that the will power in every state—that is, the right to make effective commands and to use the physical forces of the state to enforce them—is always lodged in one person or in a body of persons. Now if the whole of this will-power, or any part of it, is exercised by a person or a body of persons who are representatives of other and larger numbers of persons, in short, if any part of the government is representative, then political parties will arise among those who have the right to be represented. This will be the case both in those states in which the will-power is divided into two parts, as in Germany, where the monarch proposes the law and parliament accepts or rejects it, and in those other states in which the will-power is practically centralized in the legislative body, as in Great Britain, or is distributed, as in the United States, in the President and the two houses of Congress.

Wherever we find that any portion of what has been termed the ultimate sovereignty is in the people, or in any considerable number of them, we may be sure that political parties will come into existence. And if these conditions exist either in the whole of the state or only in some subordinate circles of administration, the same results follow. The will-power concerning the general affairs of a nation may be vested in a single person—in such case we need not look for national political parties. But this single ruler may grant self-government to a subdivision of his empire, as to a city or a commune ; in which case political parties will come into being in such subdivision. The aim of the political party is to obtain and hold possession of that organ in the state which expresses the will of the state, as well as those organs through which the force of the state is exercised. When successful in these points it has accomplished the end of its existence. Whether it uses its power for good or bad purposes does not concern the aim which the party has in view when it organizes and strives for victory, namely, the possession of the government.

In a narrow sense political parties exist under all forms of government. If the monarch is even an absolute despot there will be combinations of persons about him seeking to control his political action, and to mold the will of the state through him. These, however, are merely court factions ; or even if a large fraction of the people combine together to persuade, or influence, or oppose this absolute monarch, the combination lacks the true elements of a political party, because it cannot possess the instrument of power. In the despotism such combinations usually take a revolutionary attitude ; their effort is not so much to possess as to destroy the existing government. Properly speaking, such a combination is not a political party; it is rather a revolutionary party, and is without the range of inquiry when we are investigating the normal action of political systems, for revolution is without the sphere of normal political growth and action.

When the government is working normally, and the reserve force of the nation has shifted over to a sufficiently large body of its members to render combinations on a large scale effective in securing the control of this force, or, as stated above, effective in obtaining possession of the organs of will and force in the government, then a true political party comes into the field.

A political party may be defined to be an association of subjects or citizens in a state, entertaining common views, or having similar opinions as to a given subject within the scope of state action, who have joined themselves together for the purpose of exercising the combined power of the state to accomplish the desired object ; in order words, to control and wield the will and force of the state. The members of the party must necessarily, therefore, be confined to those in whom reposes some part of the political force inherent in the particular community. In this view, then, it follows that all persons who do not have a potential voice in public affairs cannot with propriety be said to belong to a political party, however much their sympathies and efforts may go with it. For instance, under the systems generally prevailing in the several states, women, children and aliens are in the category of exclusion. The essential attribute of a member of a party is, that he must hold somewhat of that political force which is inherent in the community of which he is a part. The voters are those who constitute the party, and the party which has possession of the government is really, for the time being, the ultimate sovereign in the state.

How is the party formed? What are its processes of growth? Like the state, the party is founded in the essential attributes of human nature. Its growth proceeds from the interaction of the love of domination and its antithesis, the disposition to be free. It is possible to imagine that all the inhabitants of a country may agree upon all the lines of policy to be pursued, and thus decide without dissent upon the laws to be made; but taking men as they are, and as they always have been, this Arcadian unanimity may be looked for only in the realm of imagination. While the great diversity of intelligence, of culture, of passions, desires, and interests continue, so long will men be divided on all questions which can come within the purview of governmental action, and so long as there are two opinions on any political question, there is at hand the nucleus of two political parties.

A body of voters actuated by common interests, or by the same opinions, and a common desire to control the will and force of the state in order to carry out their particular views, if few in number, seek in the first instance to dominate the minds of a sufficient number of other voters to obtain a numerical majority, and thus to be in a position to seize the central power. Common conditions in the administrative or social affairs of the whole country will often produce what appears to be a spontaneous community of desires and opinions in a large number of voters. These desires and opinions lie in many minds perhaps unexpressed, or only half expressed, but finally

are voiced and directed to action by a leader.   Often a
very small band of men hammer away at a reluctant community until they communicate to it the heat that glows
in themselves, thus forming a political party actuated by
their desires and opinions.

Whatever may be the precise cause of this integration
of men with common desires and opinions, it is clear
that if their objects are obtainable through governmental
action, and they are sufficiently numerous to hope for
success, they will combine to accomplish their objects.

Why men join this party or that, depends upon a great
variety of circumstances.   By some it is supposed there
is a tendency in nations enjoying political liberty to
divide into conservative and radical parties.   Macaulay
speaks of the distinction between the two great parties
which, in England, have alternately held power since the
time of the Long Parliament, as one likely always to exist;
"for," as he says, "it had its origin in diversities of temper, of understanding, and of interest, which are found in
all societies, and which will be found till the human mind
ceases to be drawn in opposite directions by the charm of
habit and the charm of novelty."

Others have advanced the theory that youth and those
who, though of advanced years, have still the temperament
of youth, will combine together in a party of progress;
and those who have the caution of age, whether young or
old, will fall into the opposite party of resistance to
change.*   Both these views are fanciful.   Men act with
political parties because of the most diverse causes, but
seldom by reason of temperament alone.   A few go with
a particular party, because they reason on broad general

---

* This theory and other theories concerning political parties
are discussed in "Friedrich Romer's Lehre von den Politischen
Parteien," durch Theodor Rohmer.   Zurich, 1844.

grounds with reference to its aims. Some, because their supposed interests lie with the party ; but the mass through the influence of association, neighborhood, family, or of their calling in life. Mere association, rather than original thought or temperament, keeps the greater number in a party which is established. Why is it that the majority in one village will be with one party and the majority in the next village will be with the other party? Or, why is it so often the case that the political views of the father will be taken up by the sons successively as they become old enough to feel an interest in them, if it is not that the social environment is the determinant ?

When the party is established, that is, has sufficient numbers and coherence to aim distinctly at the possession of the government, then a process of development manifests itself within the party analogous to that within the state. Leadership is evolved, which is the equivalent of sovereignty. This is but natural, and, we may say, entirely human. At some point within the party, supreme power will be lodged either in one person or in a small body of persons. In political integration and evolution, there is a constant gravitation toward the despotism of one, or of a few. At the same time, its antithesis, the resisting instinct which impels men to be and remain free, is excited ; and where the two activities are nearly equally balanced in the community, we have the conditions of a vigorous, stable, free state.

In its earlier days, and while the new party is in the minority, the leaders are those who take their position through their greater ability or zeal in the cause, because new parties generally attract, in the first place, men of ideas, though sometimes, it is true, they only draw those of strong and similar prejudices. Nevertheless the formation of a new party upon any basis, however narrow, implies the breaking up of old combinations, and affirmative, original action.

Let this new party be successful in obtaining power, and then there is developed a rapid tendency to the domination of not merely one, or a few individuals, but a domination of principles and forms, or what is termed "organization." Even if the party suffers defeat, and it is not dissolved, the organization retains its despotic rigidity. The party develops a self-consciousness, a spirit, which becomes more arbitrary and aggressive the longer the party exists. The most remarkable illustration of these various tendencies is seen in the history of the Roman Catholic Church. Looking at the Church simply as a combination of persons, whose object it has been and is to induce mankind to lead holy lives, to believe in certain doctrines, and to earn a happy immortality, we are struck with the completely human way, so to speak, in which, through the centuries has been evolved and elaborated a most comprehensive and rigid organism, which has at last been able, in the dogma of infallibility, to furnish the most extreme instance of intellectual and spiritual despotism that can be conceived on earth.

It has required fifteen hundred years of historical development, full of strange events and wonderful vicissitudes, to accomplish this end. The point which attracts attention is, that human nature itself is so constituted as to make results analogous to this the inevitable outcome of combinations of men, if long enough continued.

Possibly the reason why combinations with religious aims can continue longer to develop in organization, is, because their claims extend into the intangible regions of faith, and, therefore, cannot be subjected to those visible tests of fitness which are applied to all working social and governmental schemes. A political party proposing a plan for the temporal betterment of the people of a state is, immediately it comes into power, put upon trial, and if its scheme is unsuited to the people or the times, the failure is soon discovered, and the party falls into disfavor ; but to the claims of a religious sect no such gauge can be applied. New parties are formed by the men in whom the resisting element predominates. These men are generally active and pugnacious; they have, or think they have, new ideas, better plans, for the amelioration of some evil ; they combine, they agitate, mold public opinion, and finally succeed. As the party enlarges, it embraces more and more of those who are influenced by mere family or neighborhood or social influences, and by the strong disposition to imitate the leading type. Let two parties live side by side for twenty years, and a whole generation of voters has grown up, and the greater part of these will be of one party or the other because of their environment.

The influences within the party, as it grows older, settling steadily toward dogmatism and despotism, tend to drive off into opposition, or to the formation of a new party, those in whom the resisting quality is most active. It is for this reason that we sometimes see the leaders in the creation of a new party afterward becoming enemies of its organization. Then again the general public, forming the loose outskirts of parties, become surfeited with the ideas and measures of a party, and there is a temporary reaction, and afterward reflux. This has been repeatedly seen in our political history. Very often, the Congressional elections, after a heated presidential contest, will show a vibration over to the side opposite to the administration, and then at the next presidential election a full return of party strength. This is often seen in

12*

England also, where liberals and tories go in and out of power, in a sort of see-saw way.

We thus reach the point at which we may safely formulate the proposition that in a free state, political parties are constantly tending to an equilibrium. No matter what the principles may be, whether embracing all that is most favorable to the growth of the highest civilization, or counseling a stationary, or ultra-conservative policy, the parties which support either class of measures will expand, or contract with almost regular alternations, now supported by enthusiastic majorities, now dwindling away to weak minorities. This view by no means imparts the belief that political movements must necessarily go around in a circle; on the contrary, there may be continuously a slow advance, but the currents will at times rush headlong over rocks and boulders, and then in a little while spread out into quiet eddies, and apparently even flow backwards.

The political party generates within its bosom the faction which is a combination of those who seek to control the supreme power within the party; so that factions are parties, and the law of their origin, growth, success, and defeat is the same as that of parties themselves.

There is the same tendency in parties as in all bodies of men acting in a corporate capacity, whether departments of government, or associations for spiritual or political or business aims, to enlarge the area of their determination. This is curiously illustrated in our own history. The great line of division in our politics from the first term of Washington down to the breaking out of the civil war, and in a less degree to the present time, was between strict constructionists and liberal constructionists. In the view of one, no legislation could be had by Congress which did not find its support in the very words of the Constitution, or which was not indispensably necessary to carry out its express grants; in the view of the other, Congress has all the general powers which are necessary to execute the specific grants of the Constitution, and can exercise its own judgment, and very liberally too, as to what laws "shall be necessary and proper for carrying into execution the foregoing powers," and also as to what may be best "to form a more perfect union, establish justice," etc., and especially "to promote the general welfare." At the session of Congress in 1790, Hamilton, as part of his general financial scheme, proposed the establishment of a National Bank. Jefferson opposed it in the cabinet as unconstitutional. Washington called for the written opinions of these leaders of the two new parties which were then in course of consolidation, the Federalists and Anti-Federalists, or Republicans. The difference in this, as in nearly every subsequent case of dispute, turned upon, whether the object was *necessary*, or whether it was only *convenient*. But beneath the apparent narrowness of the issue, there was really involved the significant question of centralization or State autonomy—whether a national government should grow at the expense of that of the States, or not. The rising democracy adopted the strict constructionist view of Jefferson. He and his followers firmly believed that there was a party which was aiming to introduce monarchy, and they looked upon Hamilton as one of its leaders. It is evident that most of the prominent men of the Federal party distrusted the capacity of the people to carry on government; but there is no evidence of any design on their part to change the form of the government. It must be borne in mind that this was in Europe a transition period. The Revolution, then under full headway in France, had already caused a strong reaction in the opinions of social and political leaders in the other countries of Europe towards absolutism, and these opinions were reflected in this country in a marked distrust, by the leading Federalists, of the capacity of the people for self-government. On the other hand, the democracy were stimulated to enthusiasm by French ideas, and fearing a concentration of power in the central government, adopted the strict construction tenets in order to avoid centralization. They came into power in 1801, with Jefferson. But how was it then? Whatever their abstract views of the Constitution, the Jeffersonian democrats obeyed the inevitable impulse of a party in command of the government to stretch its authority. In 1803, France offered Louisiana for sale, and Jefferson bought it for the United States. He and his party conceded that there was no direct warrant in the Constitution for such a purchase. They were driven to shelter themselves under the treaty-making power, a clear evasion of their principles. Jefferson, in a letter to Lincoln, of August 30, 1803,* writes : "The less that is said about any constitutional difficulty the better " ; and a few days later, in a letter to Nicholas, he enlarges on the necessity of a vigorous construction of the Constitution, affirming that the treaty-making power should not be too broadly construed, but he urges that the treaty concerning the purchase of Louisiana be ratified without too much debate, and to prevent the treaty being quoted as an example of broad construction, that an appeal should be made to the people for new powers in a constitutional amendment. This was but a repetition of the defence of a higher necessity ; a defence often made by other governments when they violate their constitutions, and then ask for indemnity. Again, another instance of the disposition to sacrifice ab-

* Works, IV. p. 505.

stract principle to power is found in the establishment of
the embargo in 1807. In answer to the bitter opposition
of the Federalists, the Jeffersonian party pointed to the
preamble of the Constitution as the source of the power—
a method of interpretation which that party had always
rejected with pronounced asperity. Afterwards, at the
close of the war with England, Calhoun brought in a bill
for a national bank, and in its support the members of
Congress of the strict construction party quoted from the
report of Hamilton to Washington in favor of such a bank,
and Madison approved the bill, although in 1799 in his
report on the Virginia Resolutions of 1798, he had ad-
duced the establishment of a national bank as a prominent instance of the usurping tendencies of the Federal
government. So, with the questions of internal improve-
ments and the tariff, the constitutional gauge was applied
to them, broad or narrow, very much as the party in
power found it best suited their interests. When it became the interest of the democratic party to acquire Texas,
a foreign state, it was found constitutional to do so by
joint resolution. And, when the Civil War came on, the
" war power" was stretched by the dominant party to
cover whatever it found necessary and convenient to do
to carry out the policy it had in view. In thus pushing its tentacles as far out as possible, a political party
is only following the law of its being. The struggle,
which is perpetually going on under one form or another
in social life, is only more visible in great party contests
than in the private affairs of men.

As all government, in the last analysis, rests on a basis
of physical force, so in their degree do all political parties. The vote at the ballot-box is a display of forces.
The implication, which the defeated party accepts without further proof, is, that the dominant party is prepared

by force of arms to maintain its supremacy. Long experience teaches a self-governing people, as already suggested, that it is cheaper, more comfortable, hence, better,
in the long run, merely to show their forces in battle array, than to fight out political controversy to a bloody
issue. All the debate and uproar before the election is
to get recruits for the different sides from among the
wavering or indifferent. The best argument for frequent
elections in a republic is the training of the combative
energies, which is thus given in the direction of blood-
less strife, a result largely due to the knowledge that the
defeat of to-day may, in a very little time, be repaired by
the suffering party.

An inquiry very naturally suggests itself with reference
to the development of political parties during this century. Why is it that in the United States and Great
Britain we usually find only two great parties, while in
Continental countries those enjoying political rights are
split up into many factions? It will be found that where
the power of initiating legislation, and the power of
finally passing it are united in the same organ of government, as a parliament or congress, there the tendency is
toward two parties, and that where the proposing power
in legislation is vested in one organ of the government,
as an emperor, or king, or royal council, and only the
power to accept or reject is in the representative or parliamentary body, there the tendency is toward a number
of factions called parties.

A political party, at bottom, is not an association of
voters of like views merely to engage in friendly debate
with those entertaining different opinions. Persuasion,
it is true, is one, and perhaps the chief one, of its methods to achieve success. Its objective point must always
be the possession of the organ in the government which

expresses the will and uses the force of the state. If by a union of all those who desire to accomplish the same ends through the use of state power, this organ can be taken possession of and held, then the political party, as already suggested, has accomplished the end of its being. It is essential that it shall propose to do something with the instrumentalities of administration. The work of government is always to be done, and while, of course, it is not by any means necessary that governing depart- ments shall always be doing something new, still there must be somebody who can propose and decide what ought to be done when occasion arises.

Now, if a political party can acquire the control of the government, so as both to propose in legislation, and pass and make effective in laws, such lines of policy as it may adopt, it concentrates on its side all who are in favor of its measures, in addition to those who naturally go with the government, and it draws together all who are in opposition on the other side. But, perhaps, a stronger bias is given to the concentration of the voters in two camps, because naturally the party seeking control of the government must announce in advance what it proposes to do, and thus the simple alternative, affirmative or nega- tive, is presented to the voter. At almost all elections in- volving questions of policy, there is usually but one gen- eral proposition at stake, however many side-issues may be tacked to it, and the voters in substance say yes or no, upon some one point in controversy.

Whatever may be the occult reason, we see that in Great Britain and in the United States, where, for a long time, government has been by party, the voters range them- selves almost always on two sides only, and we also see the third parties, which from time to time do appear, are always squeezed out between the two greater organizations.

In those Continental countries where the monarch proposes the laws, and the parliamentary body merely accepts
or rejects them, there is no genuine party life. There
are groups, but not parties. The reason is, that no combination can have a constructive policy, with a chance of
success ; it must stand by and await the action of the
government, an attitude paralyzing to a political party,
because its vigor depends upon its having affirmative, not
mere negative power.

Bearing this distinction in mind, we can understand
the attitude of the Continental mind, which is often inex-
plicable to the American, the attitude in which the government is always looked upon as a party. There may be the
right, the left, and the centre, but there is always the government besides, and the position of these parties is determined by their support or opposition to the government.
In the Reichstag of the new German Empire, there were
said to have been, in 1880, nine groups called parties :
the Conservatives, Imperialists, National Liberals, Pro-
gressionists, Ultramontanes, Social Democrats, and others.
As we have seen, all legislation must be proposed by the
emperor through the Bundesrath, and as this power is un-
attainable by any combination of votes, all that any party
can do is to aid or resist the government. The necessary
result is, that the government is the principal factor, and
its efforts are to cajole and attach a sufficient number of
these minor groups to its policy for the moment, in order
to carry its measures. These groups shift about, change,
and amalgamate as the government shifts or changes.

During the time of Napoleon III., the French Constitution confided to the emperor the sole power of initiating the laws, and the same spectacle of many groups,
the right, the right centre, the centre, the left centre, the
left, the extreme left, and perhaps others, was presented.

All lacked the power of cohesion which springs from the possibility of capturing and entering the citadel which commands the sources of creative legislation.

And in confirmation of this view, we see that since the advent of the republic, and since the vesting of initiative power in the legislative body, the minor groups are absorbed into two great parties, one in possession of the government, and one in opposition, though it is true, the opposition is subdivided upon dynastic questions, but these base their foundations in causes which go to the very existence of the government itself, and are abnormal in their nature, because, as already suggested, the political system of a country cannot be said to be in a normal condition so long as any considerable party seeks to overthrow the government itself. In a country where it is always possible for a political party finally to control the state power there is always present the incentive for combination, argument, persuasion, and all the arts which train men in the practice of government, and also a stimulus, it is true, to aim at the possession of state instrumentalities for the mere profit that is in them.

But there is still a difference to be noted in the development of parties in the United States and Great Britain, and in the ways in which they act. A party in the latter consists of a leader or leaders, and a large indeterminate number of voters following them. The voters of the party elect members to parliament, and if these are in the majority in that body, they choose, or rather, by tacit consent, they permit the leaders to go into the cabinet, which, as has been well said, is a committee chosen from the majority in the House of Commons.

Theoretically, any member of parliament may, on leave being given, introduce a bill for the purpose of turning any measure he may choose into a law ; practically, however, no measure of any moment whatever, no measure which touches on party policy, can be introduced, except by the cabinet, or with its permission. In effect the party chooses its leaders, and turns over the initiative in legislation to them. Thus there is legislative absolutism based upon party. This absolutism is a necessity, because the dependence of the ministry upon the majority of the House for support requires that they should have all the power, as they have all the responsibility.

The tenure of office being so precarious, there is bred a quick sympathy with, and sensitiveness to, all changes of public opinion. The individual member of parliament, on account of the power of the leaders to dissolve the House, and send him back to all the expense and labor of a new election, has every inducement to stand by the ministry as long as he properly can ; while his dependence upon the good opinion of his constituency in case he should have to appear before them for re-election, an event which is always possible, induces him to keep as close to their views as he can. Consequently, the possession of power by a party is pretty closely dependent upon public opinion, as it exists at short intervals, or as it changes from one year to another. Another collateral result is that the press is influential in moulding and reflecting public opinion.

In the United States party conditions are quite different. The tenure of office of the President, the senators, and members of the House of Representatives, and of all members of the legislatures in all the states, is for fixed terms, and, therefore, public or party opinion can express itself only at definite intervals. Then, again, the President is in office for four years, the senators for six, and the members of the House for two, so that in national politics public opinion acts at irregular intervals, and, as

it were, in sections. Moreover, the variations in the fixed
tenures of State and municipal offices, still further cut up
party action. The consequence is, that a political party
may intrench itself in place, and retain the control of the
national government, in spite of frequent ebbs of popular
support. It takes a long time to bring public opinion
around to uniform and united action on public questions. This, in part, arises from the mere geographical extent of the country, and the absence of concentration of the
population, obstructive agents which are overcome, however, in large part, by the railroad, the telegraph, and
the newspaper. The larger cause in political matters lies
in the Federal system of parties derived from its proto-
type in the government. We have our national parties,
our State parties, even our city and our township parties,
and each has its separate organization, though, it is true,
connected by general ties with its corresponding national
party. The development has been toward the preponderance of national organizations, and the centralization
of party management, but this tendency has not produced
the same dependence of the dominant party upon the
support of a legislative majority as in England, because
the President, who possesses a large fraction of legislative
power through his qualified veto, is elected for a fixed
term, and he and his cabinet remain in office notwithstanding public opinion and a majority of both houses
of Congress may be against their policy. Even as early
as Washington's second term the opposition was in a majority in the lower House. Following the English custom, he and his cabinet would have resigned. Again, in
the twentieth Congress, during the presidency of John
Quincy Adams, the new democratic party, which had
emerged from the Monroe era of good feeling, in succession to the old republican party, obtained control of the

House of Representatives, and held it in opposition to the executive, and before the close of his term the Senate was also in opposition. Jackson was also met by an opposition which, in his first term, extended to both houses. Tyler was in the same predicament during most of his four years of office, and, without citing other instances, the administration of Johnson furnishes an example of how an absolute breach between the administration and the party which placed it in power may go on without affecting the stability of the latter.

The same hindrances which prevent the rapid centralization of power in the Federal government, and within that government in one of its branches, act in opposition to the centralization of power in national parties, but it may be safely asserted that the evolution is all toward centralization. Parties in the United States consist of oligarchies of managers of a hierarchy of organizations, national, state, county, city, and district, with an undeterminate following of voters in each. Two causes, aside from the general one that leadership is always developed among associated men, have produced this special product, which is sometimes styled the "American system." The one is universal manhood suffrage, and the other the multiplication of offices, and the election of their incumbents. Perhaps we should go further back and assert that the development of the equalizing spirit, which has been going on from early colonial days, has led to universal suffrage, and the election to all offices, executive as well as legislative, as its natural joint offspring. The accumulation of political labor imposed upon the citizen by the constant recurrence of national, state, municipal, county, and township elections, and the attendant claims upon his attention in choosing a multitude of officers, is so great, that the ordinary voter has not the physical energy, in addition to his bread-winning pursuit, to arrange and choose. Naturally, therefore, the universal law of the division of labor is applied to politics, and a certain number of men devote themselves especially to the management of party, so that it may be asserted that in proportion to the universality of the suffrage, and the number of offices to be filled, will be the tendency to absolutism in party management. The standard of those who are elected to office will be that of the greatest number of the voters, and the standard of those who manage parties will be the same. It does not follow, however, that universal suffrage alone is immediately productive of these results. A people may have the voting privilege, and yet be led gladly by those of superior education or social position. It is not merely the power, but the consciousness of the power, which must sink deep down into the people. As it does so sink, will the management of parties pass more and more into the forms of rigid organization, and into the hands of common men who make it their sole business. The equalizing spirit must have pervaded all of society before the full development of party absolutism is seen. The reason why in England the rapid extension of the voting suffrage has not been followed by the development of party oligarchies, as in this country, is because the whole social tone is opposed to equality. There is no person in the world who has so little real appreciation of the conjunction of equality and fraternity with liberty as the Englishman. It has been well said, that every Englishman looks up to, and down upon some other Englishman. Gladstone, a few years ago, said truthfully of his own people in one of his addresses : "There is no broad political idea, which has entered less into the formation of the political system of this country, than the love of equality . . . The love of freedom itself is hardly stronger in England than the love of aristocracy." *

On the contrary, in the United States the equalizing spirit appeared early in the social tone of the colonies, and has grown with especial rapidity since the Revolu-- tion. In our social and political systems equality is insisted upon. Twice in our history have the democratic masses asserted themselves in opposition to social and intellectual leadership ; first in 1801, in sweeping the Federal party out of office, and again in 1829, in electing Jackson. Each of these periods marks a rise in the democratic wave.

The inevitable tendency to the support of the leader, to oligarchy, to absolutism in party, fortunately finds its corrective among the adherents of party itself. These very vices tend constantly to drive off those whom the party tie does not bind very strongly, into opposition, or the formation of new parties, so that, as already suggested, political parties constantly tend to an equilibrium, and thus, in the free state, a continuous current of political activity is maintained, which, though accompanied with many disagreeable features, nourishes a vigorous life in the state.

* The growth of the English democracy in consciousness of power is illustrated in an article in *The Nation*, by A. V. Dicey, entitled, " Why do people hate Mr. Gladstone ? " No. 898, p. 218. Sept. 14, 1882.

CHAPTER XXI.

CONCLUSION.

In the foregoing pages we have sought to confine attention to an analysis of the nation or state, in order, if possible, to make clear to the mind the forces which determine its interior life. Starting with the nation as a social and political organic being, the line of examination has led us down through its interior constitution, bringing us finally to the political party, a purely voluntary combination of men within the nation, aiming to direct the national will and to wield the national force.

It may, perhaps, be thought that we should now take a further step and discuss the individual, the subject or citizen of the state, and more particularly the questions pertaining to his personal rights and obligations. But such an examination does not properly belong to analytical politics. Rights, whether those asserted to be inherent in every person, or those which are known as personal political rights, have no place in the discussion of analytical politics, because both can be recognized and protected under any form of government; they pertain to an inquiry into what a nation ought to do rather than into what it is.

We have seen that the idea of the sovereign state includes also the idea of despotic power lodged at some point in the state. Two questions of fact, then, necessarily arise : who possesses this power, and through what persons, as organs of the state, is it distributed ? If we examine an aristocracy we find the power lodged at one point, and distributed in one way ; if a democracy, at another point and in another way. Both may exist and flourish while recognizing and guarding the so-called inherent rights of men.

These inherent rights have been well formulated in our Declaration of Independence, as life, liberty, and the pursuit of happiness. Any and every form of government can foster these rights without affecting its form or internal action. To do so, must be accounted purely a matter of duty. And yet we know that when the supposed good of the State demands it our lives can be sacrificed in war, our liberty restrained by compulsory service in the army, and our pursuit of happiness subordinated to the needs of the community.

In the social state two kinds of rights are evolved : the rights which pertain to individuals because of their relations to each other, and the rights which arise in favor of the whole community as against the individual who is a member of it. Each has its attendant obligations.

The solution of the question, whether the individual has a divine or natural right to his life, is of no moment in a political point of view. We are concerned merely with his claim of right to life because of its interest to the political body. As between individuals, the right to life when looked at closely is found to be no more than an obligation or duty imposed on everybody not to kill his fellow. In the civilized state this duty is imposed by positive law. Why ? Not because it pertains to the inherent constitution of the state, but because the persons who make the law think it better, more expedient, to impose the duty than to allow private vengeance or passion full play. And so also with the enjoyment of liberty and the pursuit of happiness.

But on the other hand, it is supposable that the good of the state might be advanced if the state sacrificed the life of a particular individual ; this confers a right upon the state to take the life, and imposes an obligation upon the individual to surrender it. This is an extreme case, illustrating the double relations in which the members of society stand, first toward each other, and secondly toward the state. The first set of relations are regulated by private law, the second by public law. But both kinds of law, in fact all law, is simply the expression of will on the part of the state, and whether or not the laws shall be made or what shall be their tenor are purely considerations of expediency and morals. These considerations fall within the domain of practical politics, which should treat of what the state ought or ought not to do.

When we leave what are called inherent rights and come to political personal rights we perceive equally that they have no place in the discussions of analytical politics.

Important among these rights are : Freedom of worship, freedom of speech, freedom of the press, and freedom to assemble and to petition; that no soldier shall in time of peace be quartered on the citizen ; that the people shall be secure in their persons, houses, papers, and effects, against unreasonable searches ; that no one shall be held for capital or infamous crimes without presentment or indictment of a grand jury, or be twice put in jeopardy, or be compelled in a criminal case to be a witness against himself, or be deprived of life, liberty, or property without due process of law, or have his private property taken for public use without just compensation ; that an accused person shall have speedy public trial by an impartial jury, and be confronted by the witnesses against him ; that excessive bail shall not be demanded, nor cruel or unusual punishments inflicted ; that the

13

writ of *habeas corpus* shall be maintained ; that no *ex post facto* law shall be passed nor the obligation of a contract be impaired. These are all rights created and secured by positive law. They are not absolutely essential to the existence of a highly developed political organism. Whether they shall be recognized and acted upon depends altogether upon the determination of the person or persons controling the will and force of the state. We may assert that every state should have such a bill of rights. We know, however, that it is wanting in many highly civilized states ; but what is in point here is, that when we affirm that such a bill should be adopted, we are only affirming that the state should use its inherent power in a given way. Hamilton in the Federalist asserted that according to their primitive signification, as stipulations between kings and their subjects, abridging the prerogatives of the former, Bills of Right have no application to a constitution founded on the power of the people, and executed by their immediate representatives and servants.

The Declaration of the Rights of Man, adopted by the National Assembly of France in 1789, asserts that men are born and remain free and equal in law ; that the end of all political association is the preservation of natural rights ; that the principle of all sovereignty resides in the nation ; that liberty consists in the ability to do everything which shall not injure another, so that the exercise of the natural rights of each person is only limited by those which assure to other members of society the enjoyment of the same rights, and that these limits can only be determined by law ; and so on, with a minute declaration of general principles which are admirable, and could be applied under any form of government. But the members of this Assembly knew very well that this declaration of abstractions would be utterly valueless, unless they themselves had the supreme power of the nation at their command, and so, on the same day, they proceeded to enact in the new Constitution that the government was monarchical, but at the same time that the National Assembly should be permanent ; that all legislative power should reside in it, and that, though the king could refuse his assent to laws passed by the Assembly, yet that his veto had only a suspensive effect, and could be overruled by a succeeding Assembly. Thus actual sovereignty was lodged in the legislative body, and, as this body was the creator of the Constitution and could annul it, the Declaration of Rights imposed no limitation upon its power, and was in effect no more than a political homily addressed to the nation, pointing out certain things it should or should not do.

Rights, as the creation of public or private law, vary as the will of the nation varies, and their consideration falls, therefore, not in the realm of analytical politics, which deals with the nature and organization of the nation, but in the realm of practical politics, which deals with what the state wills and does, or should will and should do.

INDEX.

13*

Jamestown, settlement at, 91.
Jay's treaty, 180, 211.
Johnson, his controversy with congress, 216.
Judge-made law, 200.
Judiciary, in the Mass. Bay colony, 110 ; its position in the United
    States, 198, 216 ; checked by the legislature, 217 ; not a
    balance wheel between parties, 218.
Jury trial preserved in Virginia, 92.
Justices of the peace, 89, 90.

Kinship as the basis of political community, 30, 60.
Kleisthenes, 10.

Land in the New World, in theory owned by the king, 91.
Law, growth of, 3 ; as a command, 38, 52 ; constitutional, makers
    of, 142–154; Austin's view of, 154 ; administrative, Austin
    on, 154 ; makers of, 155–163 ; nature of, 155.
Law-making, organs of the sovereign in, 155 ; in the United States,
    156, 210 ; function of the courts in, 200.
Laws, why obeyed, 57 ; codification of in Virginia, 99 ; first, in
    New York, 117.
Leadership in the party, 271.
League, alternative tendencies in the, 139 ; in Greece, 139.
Legislation, in Mass. Bay colony, 108, 109 ; contrast as to details
    between English and French, 200 ; initiative in, 179–192.
Legislature, in the United States, 156 ; in the French Republic,
    158 ; in the German Empire, 159 ; of the Middle Ages, 166 ;
    nature of the, 176 ; tendency to extend its power, 218.
LeConte, on intelligence and instinct, 69.
Legitimists of France, 205.
Lieber, Francis, 13.
Literature, aids the growth of nationality in America, 131.
Leviathan, doctrine of, 43.
Local powers, 63–67, 119.
Locke, 121.
London, its government, 89.
Lords, House of, 171.
Louisiana, purchase of, by the United States, 276.
Lower house of legislature, 164, 173 ; in the Mass. Bay colony,
    109 ; in the United States, 178.

Rights of Man, Declaration of, 290.
Roads and bridges, 88, 89, 90.
Robinson and Brewster, 101.

Savigny, on the nation as the source of positive law, 26.
Scott, Dred, Case, 217.
Secession, doctrine of, the outcome of the "compact" theory, 238.
Self-government in England and the Colonies, 126–128.
Senate of the United States, 177, 178; function in diplomatic affairs, 180; appointing and impeaching power, 184; an oligarchy, 211.
Separation of powers, Montesquieu on, 195; thought to be complete in the British government, 213; significance of, 222.
Separatists and non-conformists, 114–115.
Servants in Virginia, 96.
Shaftesbury, 121.
Society, political, 33, 46.
Sovereign, the, 33–46; meaning of terms, 33–38; determination of, in any given state, 38; declares the will of the nation, 40; Hobbes on, 43; Pomeroy on, 46; organs of, 47–54; the person or body competent to amend the constitution, 144; makers of, 145–147, 153; in the United States, 151; in the German Empire, 152.
Sovereignty, divided between the states and the United States, 34; characteristic marks of, 37–38; our North American colonies, 36; discussed by Bodin, 41–43; by Hobbes, 43; attributes of, as stated by Bluntschli, 45; defined by Holland, 45, 46; itself indivisible, but the exercise of sovereign powers divisible, 233.
Spartan government, 208.
Spencer, his law of social evolution, 24; weakness of his political discussion, 80.
Sphere of the state, not dependent on its form of government, 3.
Staatenbund, 224.
Stamp Act, 133.
State, not synonymous with nation, 6; development of the idea of, 50.
State constitutions, specific restrictions of the later, 247.
State-rights, 229, 230; advocates of, 231; logical outcome of,

www.ingramcontent.com/pod-product-compliance
Lightning Source LLC
Chambersburg PA
CBHW031400270326
41929CB00010BA/1268